VISUAL QUICKSTART GUIDE

FreeHand 7

FOR MACINTOSH

D1314046

Sandee Cohen

Visual QuickStart Guide
FreeHand 7 for Macintosh
Sandee Cohen

Peachpit Press

2414 Sixth Street
Berkeley, CA 94710
510/548-4393
510/548-5991 (fax)
800/283-9444

Find us on the World Wide Web at:
http://www.peachpit.com
Peachpit Press is a division of Addison Wesley Longman

Cover design: The Visual Group
Production: Sandee Cohen and Janet Waggener
Original book design and concept: Elaine Weinmann
FreeHand 7 Visual QuickStart Guide design: Sandee Cohen
Index: Steve Rath
Testing: Terry DuPrât

This book was created using: QuarkXPress for layout, Macromedia FreeHand
for illustrations, Mainstay Captivate for screen shots, and Adobe Photoshop
for retouching on a Macintosh PowerMac 8500. The fonts used were Futura,
Times, and Zapf Dingbats from Adobe.

ISBN 0-201-68828-X

9 8 7 6 5 4 3 2 1

Printed and bound in the United States of America

Dedicated to

Nathan Cohen
who gives me total support.

Terry DuPrât
who taught me to have faith.

Bonnie and Jeffry
whose life together is better than any book.

Danny, Lizzie, and Sarah
who simply make me smile!

Thanks to

Nancy Ruenzel, Roslyn Bullas and the rest of the Peachpit gang.

Joel Dreskin, Pete Mason, Brian Schmidt, Doug Benson, John Dowdell, John Nosal, Rachel Schindler, Anna Sturvidant, David Mendels of Macromedia for their help, encouragement and technical advice. Also to Dave Gangwich for getting me in on the early beta testing.

Janet Waggener, who found and captured all the new dialog boxes, panels, Inspectors, and other screen shots.

Steve Rath, for his index—the most important part of any book.

Ted Alspach, who has been a terrific co-consultant to the AOL Illustrator SIG. And loves vectors just as much as I do.

Sharon Steuer, who has been not just a source of technical advice, but a wonderful friend—in person, on the phone, and in e-mail.

Olav Martin Kvern, who has written the best "advanced" book on FreeHand and gave me encouragement.

Mordy Golding, who explained all the "web stuff" to this print person.

Jen Alspach and the rest of my AOL vector friends, for all their support and advice.

Joyce Chen, and the staff of the New School for Social Research Computer Instruction Center. You've made it fun to come to work.

Pixel, who faithfully sat by my side and watched every page come out of the printer.

TABLE OF CONTENTS

Table of Contents

INTRODUCTION

Welcome to Macromedia FreeHand. If you're like most people who are just starting out with the program, you may find it a little overwhelming. For instance, there are 5 different Inspector palettes, FreeHand's main control devices. There are 11 other palettes or toolbars, each with its own variations. There are over 70 different menu commands spread out on seven different menus. Finally, there are 16 different tools, many of which have their own control settings. This *Visual QuickStart Guide* has been written to help you sort out the features.

The first few chapters are overviews of the program. You may find that you don't create any artwork in those chapters. Don't skip them. They contain information that will help you later.

The middle chapters of the book contain the most artistic

information. This is where you can see how easy it is to create sophisticated artwork using FreeHand.

The final chapters are about printing, preferences, and using your artwork with other applications. Some of this information refers to technical printing terms. If you are not familiar with these terms, speak to the print shop that will be printing your artwork.

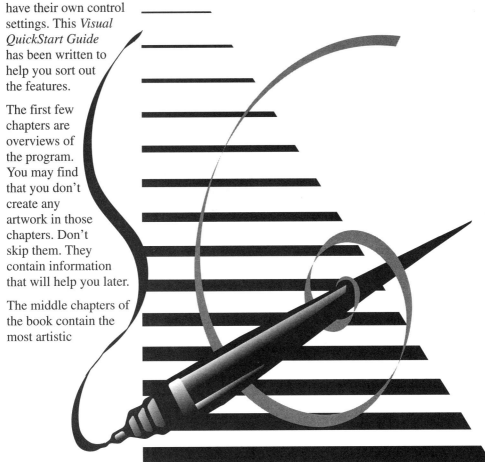

FreeHand is one of the most versatile programs for the Macintosh. At its simplest, FreeHand is a graphics, or drawing, program. It allows you to create artwork such as drawings, logos, and illustrations. But because FreeHand lets you bring in scanned artwork from programs such as Adobe Photoshop or Fractal Design Painter, it is also an excellent layout program. This allows you to create ads, book covers, posters, and so on. Finally, because FreeHand has a very sophisticated multiple-page feature, it is also a multipage document program. This allows you to create newsletters and flyers, as well as multipage presentations with differently sized pages.

FreeHand as a graphics program

There are two main types of computer graphics programs: bitmapped and object-oriented. FreeHand is an object-oriented, or vector-based, graphics program. Other object-oriented programs are Adobe Illustrator, CorelDraw, and part of Deneba Canvas. All of these programs, including FreeHand, create illustrations by combining many differently shaped objects. This is similar to cutting out different pieces of paper and layering them into position.

The other type of graphics program is the bitmapped, or pixel-based, drawing program. Pixel-based programs include Adobe Photoshop, Fractal Design Painter, and the grandparent of all Macintosh graphics programs, MacPaint. These programs create their illustrations by coloring hundreds of thousands of tiny squares. This is similar to the images created on television screens. If you get real close to the image, you can see the individual colored squares, or pixels. But if you stand back, the colors all merge together into one image.

Making changes in FreeHand

When you work in FreeHand, every object you create stays a distinct element that can be moved, reshaped, or recolored at any time while you are working on it. This means that if you have been working on an illustration and later decide you want to change a color or change the size of an object in that illustration, you can simply open up the file, select the object, and make the changes.

This is in distinct contrast to the bitmapped, or pixel-based, programs. When you're using those programs, you have to be very careful when you set the color or shape of an object. It is not so simple to go in later and make changes to your artwork.

Scaling artwork in FreeHand

When you work in FreeHand, artwork you create is called "resolution-independent." This is a technical term that means you don't have to worry about scaling the artwork to a new size. For instance, suppose you have created a logo 2″ by 2″ for a client. The client then decides they need to print that logo at 4″ by 4″. In an object-oriented program such as FreeHand there is practically no limit to how big or small you can scale the object. The edges of the artwork are actually mathematical formulas that can be scaled up or down at any time.

Things are not as simple in the bitmapped, or pixel-based, programs. Before you create your artwork or scan in the image, you have to be careful that your image is the right size for final output. This means that if you've been working on that 2″ by 2″ logo and you discover that you now need it at 4″ by 4″, you will need to rescan or redraw the logo to make it the correct size. If you scale up a pixel-based illustration, you run the risk of creating a rough or jagged edge (**Figure 1**).

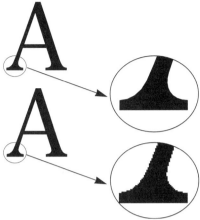

Figure 1. *The shape of an object drawn in FreeHand (top left) stays smooth no matter how much it is scaled up or down (top right). The shape of an object drawn in a bitmapped program (bottom left) can get rough or jagged when it is scaled (bottom right).*

File size in FreeHand

Another advantage of object-oriented programs is that the file sizes tend to be smaller than the equivalent bitmapped artwork. If you draw a 1″ square at a resolution of 300 pixels per inch using a bitmapped program, there are 90,000 pixels in that drawing. Each one of those pixels takes up disk space. And if the square is in color, there are actually four channels of 90,000 pixels each. This will mean a file of about 352K.

The same 1″ square in object-oriented programs is created by four anchor points. The set of instructions defining the type and position of these points is all that takes up disk space. In addition, the color is defined by a set of instructions, not by

four different layers. So a plain 1″ square created in FreeHand takes up only 8K— far less disk space than the square created in a pixel-based program.

FreeHand as a layout program

Some people use FreeHand to create artwork that they save in a certain format and then bring into layout programs such as Adobe PageMaker or QuarkXPress. However, FreeHand itself is quite capable of performing as a layout program. Instead of taking the artwork into another program with text and scanned pictures, you can use FreeHand as your final layout program. FreeHand lets you create artwork, add and style the text, and then place the photos on the page. The file is then ready for output as a finished layout. This makes FreeHand an excellent choice for working on projects in which you need to combine artwork with scanned photos, copy, display text, and so on.

FreeHand as a multipage program

Finally, FreeHand lets you work on multiple pages in one document. This means that if you are working on a three-fold brochure with information on the front and back covers, you can create individual pages and arrange them together as a front unit and a back unit.

Also, unlike other programs that must have to have their pages all the same size and shape, FreeHand lets you create multiple-page documents in which the pages are different sizes. This makes FreeHand an excellent choice for creating sophisticated presentations of differently sized pages such as letterheads, envelopes, and business cards. Using FreeHand's custom-size pages, each object will be on a page that is the correct size.

Objects in FreeHand

The objects you work with in FreeHand are all created using the same principles. Each object is really a path, or an outline. Along the path are elements called anchor points, or points which allow you to change the direction of a path. The different types of FreeHand anchor points are corner points, curve points, and connector points. If a path starts at one point and ends at another, it is considered to be an open path. This is similar to a piece of string. An open path can be arranged in any shape, but its ends are not connected. If a path starts and ends at the same point, it is considered to be a closed path. This is similar to a rubber band. A closed path can also be arranged in any shape, but it must be a shape that is self-contained with no open points.

Each of the tools in FreeHand is used to create different types of points or objects. FreeHand tools can be found in the toolbox as well as in the Xtra tools panel. The type and number of points in the object are determined by the tool used, by the settings in the dialog box for the tool, and by any modifier keys that may have been pressed.

The toolbox contains FreeHand's basic drawing tools. The Rectangle tool creates four-sided objects with corner points. The Oval tool creates four arcs that are joined with curve points. The Polygon tool creates multisided objects with as many sides as you select in its dialog box. The Line tool creates straight open paths. The FreeHand tool lets you create different types of paths that can look like lines, brush strokes, or the strokes of a calligraphic pen. The Tracing tool is used to create paths that trace artwork. The Pen and and the Bézigon tools let you draw paths with combinations of curve, corner, and connector points.

In addition to the toolbox, FreeHand has other tools located in the Xtra Tools panel that allow you to create other objects such as arcs and spirals.

Modifying the shape of objects

Any object in FreeHand can have its shape altered by manipulating the anchor points, changing the type of points, or manipulating its Bézier handles. Bézier handles are nonprinting lines that come out of the object's anchor points. Moving the Bézier handles will change the shape of the curve.

Filling and stroking objects

By stroking and filling an object, you create its look. The stroke of the object is applied along the path. Both open and closed paths can have visible strokes. The fill of the object is applied inside its path. Only closed paths can have fills. If a closed path has a fill of "None," then it will be an object that you can see through.

FreeHand offers a wide variety of strokes and fills. Some, such as basic colors, graduated fills, and radial fills, can be seen onscreen. Others, such as the custom or textured fills and strokes, can be seen only when the file is printed.

An object can have only one fill and only one stroke applied to it. If you wanted to have one path change from red to blue, you would actually need to have two separate paths: One path would be stroked red; the other blue.

Text in FreeHand

FreeHand gives you several options for working with text. You can have a single line of text, which is very useful for creating headlines or other short text. You can also have paragraphs of text that are contained inside a text block. This block governs the width of the paragraph. Changing the width of the block will cause the copy within the block to rewrap. You can also divide this text block into columns and rows, and the text will flow from one column to another. And text can be made to flow into irregularly shaped objects.

There are also several special text effects that are very useful. You can make text flow along a path, or you can convert text into paths. When text is converted into paths, it can then be reshaped and altered in different ways.

Transforming objects in FreeHand

Once you have created an object, it can be modified by using the transformation tools. The basic transformational tools are Rotating, Scaling, Reflecting, and Skewing. There are also tools in the Xtra Tools palette that let you creat special effects. These include 3D Rotation, Fisheye Lens, and Smudge.

In addition to changing the shape of objects, FreeHand lets you modify how two or more objects relate to each other. These are called path operations. Some of the more common path operations are to make one object punch a hole in another object, to join two separate objects together into one path, to simplify the number of anchor points in a path, and to remove the overlap between two objects.

FreeHand also has a sophisticated chart tool that lets you create various different type of charts and graphs. These graphs are linked to the data in spreadsheets so that if the data changes, the appearance of the graph will also change.

Web graphics in FreeHand

One of the most exciting areas of computer graphics is the World Wide Web. FreeHand offers a wide variety of special features for working on the web. You can create artwork that can be posted on the web with automatic links to other web pages. You can also save your vector-based artwork into special formats for the web.

Third-party Xtras

When you are working in FreeHand, you are not limited to just those features that are shipped with the program. FreeHand allows you to use the filters or plug-ins that are part of Adobe Illustrator. Recently, various third-party companies have created their own Xtras that can be used within FreeHand. These include KPT Vector Effects, Extensis DrawTools, Infinite FX, and Letraset Envelopes.

Working with colors

FreeHand offers a very extensive choice of color systems. If your artwork will be printed by a commercial printer, you will most likely want to use the process color CMYK mode or a spot color model such as Pantone or Toyo. If you are going to use your artwork for video or multimedia presentations, you may want to use the RGB (Red, Green, Blue) color system or the HLS (Hue, Lightness, Saturation) system. You can also pick colors using the traditional Apple color wheel. Finally, tints can be created from any color.

FreeHand utilities

Some of the FreeHand tools and commands are used not to create or modify objects, but to help you view or move around your artwork. The Zoom tool lets you magnify the image of your work to get a closer look at the details of your artwork. You can also zoom out to see more of your artwork in your monitor.

FreeHand also has another tool, called the Hand tool, or grabber, that doesn't appear in the toolbox. The Hand lets you move around your window without using the window scrollbars.

Working with other applications

FreeHand also lets you place pixel-based artwork that's been scanned in or created by programs such as Photoshop and Painter. In addition, FreeHand lets you modify those placed images, either by coloring them or by applying filters that are used with Photoshop. These may be the built-in filters that came with Photoshop or third-party filters such as Kai's Power Tools and Adobe Gallery Effects. FreeHand, however, is not a substitute for working with those programs—it is an auxiliary tool.

FreeHand also offers you several ways to convert your vector-based artwork into pixels. This lets you create images using FreeHand tools and then convert them so they can be manipulated by pixel filters while you are still in FreeHand.

Menus, submenus, and panels

FreeHand offers a wealth of panels and menus to control its commands and functions. Many times, these panels and menus perform the same functions; this way, FreeHand gives you a choice as to how you execute a command.

Outputting your work

Once you have created your FreeHand file, you will want to output it. FreeHand offers you several choices. You can print your file to a low-resolution printer or to a high-resolution imagesetter. You can also export your FreeHand file so it can be used in other programs.

Learning FreeHand

With a program as extensive as FreeHand, there will be many features that you never use. For instance, if you're an illustrator, you may never need any of FreeHand's text or layout features. Or you may never need to create charts or graphs. Don't worry. It's hard to believe but even the experts don't use all of FreeHand's features.

Find the areas you wish to master, then follow the exercises. If you are patient, you will find yourself creating your own work in no time.

And don't forget to have fun!

FILE PREPARATION

Y ou're now ready to actually start working. In this chapter, you will learn how to: launch FreeHand; start a new document or continue working in an old document; change the units of measurement for your document; change the size of your pages; change the orientation of your pages; add pages to your document; move pages together; change the page magnification; add a "bleed" area to your work page; save your work as a document or a template; close your document; and quit FreeHand.

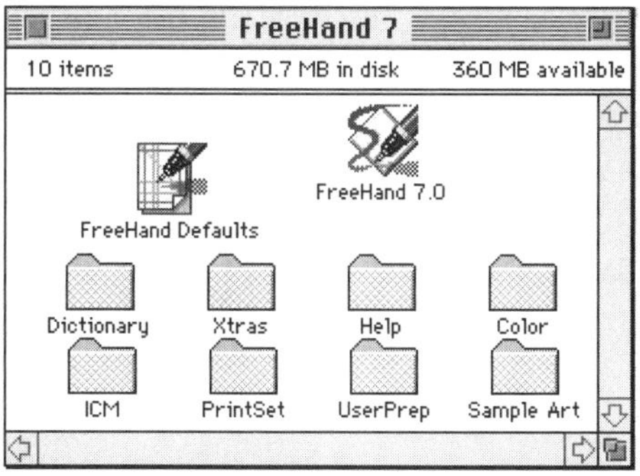

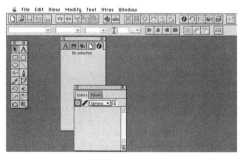

Figure 1. *Double-click on the FreeHand icon to launch the program.*

To launch FreeHand:

In the Macintosh Finder, open the folder that holds the FreeHand application. Double-click on the FreeHand application icon (**Figure 1**). This will launch FreeHand.

Tip

➡ If you have a previously saved FreeHand document, you can double-click on it. This will launch FreeHand and bring you directly to that document, where you can continue working.

If you double-clicked on the FreeHand icon, you will see the FreeHand menus and palettes on your screen, but you won't have an actual document open (**Figure 2**).

Figure 2. *Double-clicking on the FreeHand icon brings you into the **application**, but you will not have a document open.*

To create a new document:

To start working, you need to create a new document. To do so, choose New from the File menu (**Figure 3**). (*For a detailed listing of all the FreeHand menus, see Appendix A.*) This will create a window containing an untitled document.

Tips

➥ To tell whether FreeHand is the active application, look for the FreeHand application icon in the upper right corner of your screen.

➥ If you want to open a previously saved document, you can switch back to the Finder and double-click on the document, or you can choose Open from the File menu.

You now have an untitled document window on your screen. (*For a detailed listing of all the features in the document window, see Appendix A.*) Inside the document window is the rectangular work page. This is the actual area where you will be creating your work. Around the rectangular illustration page is a plain white area that is called the "pasteboard" (**Figure 4**). You can place objects in the pasteboard that you need to use, but don't want to print.

To change the units of measurement:

To change the units of measurement from points to inches, press on the pop-up menu at the bottom of the document window and choose inches (**Figure 5**).

Tip

➥ No matter which unit of measurement your document is in, you can still enter sizes in whatever units you want: For points, type "p" before the number. For picas, type "p" after the number. For inches, type "i" after the number. For millimeters, type "m" after the number.

Figure 3. *To create a new document, choose **New** from the **File** menu or press **Command-N.***

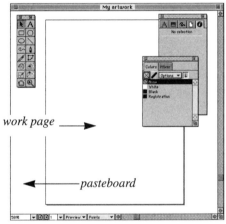

work page ⟶

◀———— *pasteboard*

Figure 4. *The **work page** sits inside the **pasteboard** area.*

Figure 5. *Press on the pop-up menu at the bottom of the document window to change the **units of measurement**.*

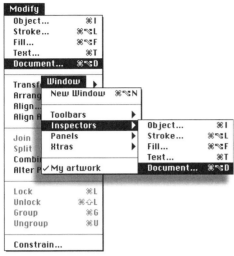

Figure 6. *To activate the* **Document Inspector** *palette, choose* **Document** *from the* **Modify** *menu or* **Document** *from the* **Inspectors** *submenu of the* **Window** *menu.*

Once you have a new document open, you may need to work with the Document Inspector.

To display the Document Inspector:

To see the Document Inspector, choose Document from the Modify menu, or Modify from the Inspectors submenu of the Window menu (**Figure 6**). (*For a detailed listing of all the Inspectors, see Appendix A.*)

To change the printer resolution:

1. Make sure the Document Inspector palette is open.

2. Drag across the field for the Printer resolution (**Figure 7**) and enter the amount of resolution for the type of printer you will be sending your document to.

Tip

➡ If you are unsure about the amount of printer resolution you will need for your final artwork, you can leave the setting low, and then change it later.

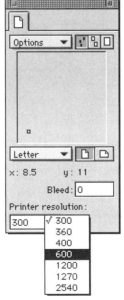

Figure 7. *In the Document Inspector, press on the pop-up menu to change the* **Printer Resolution** *for your document.*

Your work page may not necessarily be the same size as the paper you will be printing on. For instance, you may need to change your work page to a Tabloid or a Legal size.

To select a new work page size:

1. Make sure the Document Inspector is displayed.

2. To change the size of the work page to one of the preset page sizes, press on the page size pop-up menu (**Figure 8**) at the bottom of the palette.

If one of the preset sizes is not right for your job, you will need to create a work page with custom measurements. For instance, if you are creating business cards, you would want your work page to be the trim size of the card.

To create a custom-size work page:

1. Press on the page size pop-up menu of the Document Inspector and choose Custom.

2. Click in the area next to the x and type the horizontal measurement of your page.

3. Click in the area next to the y and type the vertical measurement of your page (**Figure 9**).

4. Press the Return key. Your page size will now be the custom size.

Tip

➥ If you are entering numbers in the same units of measurement as your document, you do not need to type "i" after the number for inches, "p" after the number for picas, etc.

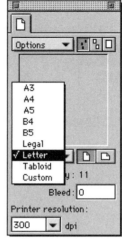

Figure 8. *There are eight different preset page sizes, plus* **Custom**, *which lets you enter the exact measurements for any work page size.*

Figure 9. *When you choose Custom from the* **Page Size** *pop-up menu, you can enter your exact measurements in the x (horizontal) and y (vertical) fields.*

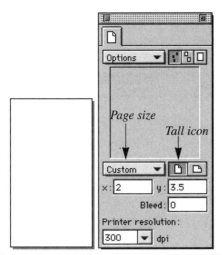

Figure 10a. *A Custom-size page with the **Tall** orientation selected.*

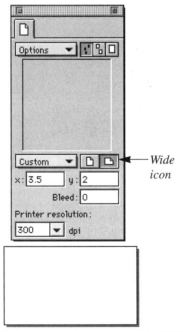

Figure 10b. *A Custom-size page with the **Wide** orientation selected.*

In the previous example, you may have created a custom-size page that is taller than it is wide. You may decide that you want to reverse the horizontal and vertical sizes of your document.

To change the orientation of a page:

1. Make sure the Document Inspector is displayed.

2. Click on the Wide icon next to the Page size. This will swap your horizontal and vertical measurements (**Figures 10a–b**).

Tip

- ◆ If you select the Tall icon and enter your measurements in the wrong order, FreeHand will automatically correct your mistake. Therefore, you can never have a work page that is wider than it is tall with the Tall icon selected. You can also never have a work page that is taller than it is wide with the Wide icon selected.

Change Orientation of a Page

Now that you've set your page size, you may need to create additional work pages. For instance, if you are creating a series of layouts for your client to choose from, you would need multiple work pages.

To create additional work pages:

1. Make sure the Document Inspector is displayed. Under the Options pop-up menu, choose Duplicate. This will create a new work page that is the exact size as your first page (**Figure 11a**).

   or

   Choose Add Pages from the Options menu. The Add Pages dialog box will appear. Type the number of pages you want. Use the pop-up menu to pick the page size. Click on the Tall or Wide icon for the proper orientation (**Figure 11b**).

2. Click on the OK button or press the Return key on the keyboard. Your pasteboard will then show the additional pages.

Figure 11a. *Choosing* **Duplicate** *from the* **Options** *pop-up menu of the* **Document Inspector** *will create a new work page the same size as the page selected.*

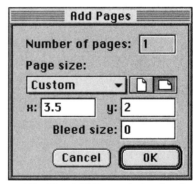

Figure 11b. *The* **Add Pages** *dialog box lets you specify how many pages you want to add, their size, their orientation, and the bleed size. This allows you to quickly create a FreeHand document with many work pages.*

Magnification icon

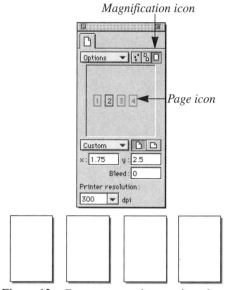

Page icon

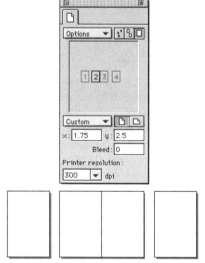

Figure 12a. *Four pages on the pasteboard next to each other. Notice that there are spaces between both the page thumbnails and the actual pages on the pasteboard.*

If you are working with multiple pages, you might want to move those pages around the pasteboard area. For instance, you might want two pages to touch each other so that you can bleed graphics from one page to another. This is extremely helpful if you are doing something like a three-page brochure. You might want each of the three pages to be next to each other so you can place artwork across the fold lines. In order to do this, you will need to use the Magnification icon in the Document Inspector.

To arrange pages next to each other:

1. Make sure you are working in a document that has at least two pages.

2. In the Document Inspector, click on the middle Magnification icon. Boxes should appear in the rectangular area of the Document Inspector. These are the page thumbnails in your document.

3. Drag one of the Page icons right next to the other Page icon. Look at the pasteboard area of your document. Notice how the pages now are right next to each other (**Figures 12a–b**).

Figure 12b. *Two of those four pages have been positioned so that they touch each other. This allows graphics to stretch from one page to another.*

Depending on the number and sizes of your work pages, you may find that the middle Magnification icon does not show you enough of your pages. In order to see more of the pages, you may need to change the page magnfication within the Document Inspector.

To change the page magnification:

1. Click on the first Magnification icon. This shrinks the size of the Page icons to the smallest size so that you can see more of them at once.

2. Click on the middle Magnification icon. This expands the size of the Page icons so that you can see them more clearly.

3. Click on the third Magnification icon. This expands the size of the Page icons to the largest size (**Figures 13a–c**).

Tips

⦿ If you are working on a single-page document, you will probably find the largest magnification setting the most useful.

⦿ If you are working on a two- or three-page document, you will probably find the middle magnification setting the most useful.

⦿ If you are working on a document with more than three pages, such as a newsletter, you will probably find the smallest magnification setting the most useful.

⦿ If you double-click on the Page icon in the Document Inspector, you will instantly go to that page and reduce the magnification out so that the whole page fits in the window.

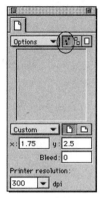

Figure 13a. *The **Magnification** icon (circled) for the **smallest size** setting.*

Figure 13b. *The Magnification icon (circled) for the **middle size** setting.*

Figure 13c. *The Magnification icon (circled) for the **largest size** setting.*

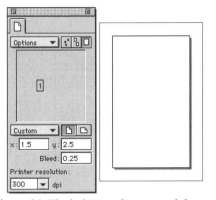

Figure 14. *The light gray line around the work page indicates the **bleed area**. Any artwork or graphics inside the bleed area will print on the final document.*

You may find that you need a "bleed" for your layout. A bleed is any artwork or graphic that extends off the edge of the work page. In order for you to have artwork bleed off the page, you will have to set a bleed size.

To set a bleed size:

1. Make sure the Document Inspector is displayed.

2. At the bottom of the Document Inspector, enter your desired bleed size. Press Return.

3. A light gray line will appear around your work page. This is the bleed area (**Figure 14**).

Tips

•➔ You can use the bleed area to hold fold marks or special instructions. These elements will print on your finished artwork but will not appear inside the live area of your artwork (**Figure 15**).

•➔ You do not have to manually create crop marks or registration marks inside the bleed area. FreeHand's print options let you create them automatically (*see page 250*).

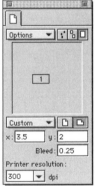

Figure 15. *The .25″ bleed area of this illustration contains notes about the layout (circled) and a "bleed" of the gray background. As long as these elements are in the bleed area, they will print on the final document.*

Now that you've created your pages in the correct size, you will want to save your work. This is not too different from the usual way of saving on the Macintosh. With FreeHand you do have a choice, however, of three options.

To save a document:

1. Choose Save from the File menu or type Command-S (**Figure 16**). The Save dialog box appears (**Figure 17**).

2. Press on the format pop-up menu and choose the file format you want. If you are just working on ordinary artwork, save it as a FreeHand document.

3. If you want to protect your document from inadvertent changes, save it as a FreeHand template.

4. If you want to bring your document into other applications such as Adobe PageMaker or QuarkXPress, save it as an editable EPS.

Tips

•• You can tell the difference between a FreeHand document, a FreeHand template, and an editable EPS by looking at their icons (**Figure 18**).

•• If you want to make changes to a template, open it and make the changes. Save the document with the same name as the original template. When the dialog box asks if you would like to replace the old template, click on the Replace button.

•• FreeHand uses the term template like most applications and the Macintosh Finder. This means a template in FreeHand is *not* a layer which lets you trace over a drawing. If you want to trace over artwork, you will need to create a non-printing layer (*see page 41*).

Figure 16. *Choose* **Save** *from the* **File** *menu to save your work.*

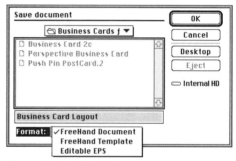

Figure 17. *The* **Save** *dialog box lets you choose between a* **FreeHand Document,** *a* **FreeHand Template,** *and an* **Editable EPS.**

Figure 18. *The difference between the icons for a FreeHand Document (top left), a FreeHand Template (top right), and an Editable EPS (bottom).*

File	
New	⌘N
Open...	⌘O
Close	**⌘W**
Save	⌘S
Save As...	⌘⇧S
Revert	
Import...	⌘⇧D
Export...	⌘E
Report...	
Page Setup...	
Print...	⌘P
Preferences...	⌘⌥U
Output Options...	
My artwork	
My artwork	
Quit	⌘Q

Figure 19. *To close a document, you can choose Close from the File menu or type Command-Option-W.*

To close a document:

Once you have saved your work, you can close the document by choosing Close from the File menu, clicking the Close Box or by typing Command-W (**Figure 19**). (*For a detailed listing of the menu commands, see Appendix B.*)

Tip

➥ If you try to close a document that has unsaved work in it, a dialog box will ask you if you want to save changes to the document (**Figure 20**). If you click on the Save button, your changes will be saved and the document will be closed. If you click on the Don't Save button, any changes since your last save will be discarded and the document will be closed. If you click on the Cancel button, your command to close the document will be canceled and you can continue working in the document.

⚠ Save changes to "My artwork"?

[Don't Save]   [Cancel]   [**Save**]

Figure 20. *The Save Changes dialog box alerts you that you are trying to close a document that has unsaved work in it.*

To revert to last saved version:

Choose Revert from the File menu (**Figure 21**). You will see a dialog box asking you if you want to revert changes to your document. Clicking on the Revert button will restore you to the last version you saved (**Figure 22**).

Tip

➡ You can also close the document without saving changes and then reopen it.

To quit FreeHand:

Choosing Quit from the File menu or type Command-Q. If you have more than one document open with unsaved work, a dialog box will tell you that there are documents with unsaved work and ask you if you would like to review them (**Figure 23**).

If you click on the Review button, you will then be shown each document along with the Save Changes dialog box. If you click on the Quit Anyway button, all documents will be closed and unsaved work will be lost. If you click on the Cancel button, you will cancel your command to quit FreeHand.

Tip

➡ By changing the Preferences settings, you can turn the Review feature on or off (*see page 269*).

Figure 21. *If you would like to go back to the last saved version of your document, choose* **Revert** *from the* **File** *menu.*

Figure 22. *Choosing Revert from the File menu opens to the* **Revert Changes** *dialog box. This allows you to restore your work to the last version you saved.*

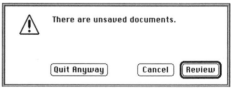

Figure 23. *Quitting FreeHand when you have unsaved work presents you with the* **Review** *dialog box. Click on the* **Review** *button to review each of the documents and save changes. Click on the* **Quit Anyway** *button to quit and discard unsaved work. Click on the* **Cancel** *button to cancel the command to quit FreeHand.*

VIEWS & PRECISION 2

There are many different features that affect what you see on the screen and how you work. While these features will not affect your final artwork, they are very important in how efficiently you work. In this chapter, you will learn about the features found in the View menu: the Preview and Keyline modes; the document window rulers; the guides; the grids; the "snap to" settings; using the Magnification menus; and the Hide Palettes feature. You will also learn about the Magnifying tool and the "zip" feature.

Once you have a document open, there are two different ways that your artwork can be displayed. The first is the Preview mode. In the Preview mode, you will see a very close likeness of your final artwork, including the fills, strokes, colors, patterns, placed art, etc.

The second is the Keyline mode. In the Keyline mode, all you see is the outline that defines the path; you do not see any of the fills, strokes, colors, patterns, placed art, etc. (**Figures 1a–b**).

100% ▼ ◀ ▶ 1 ▼ Preview ▼

Figure 1a. *When you view artwork in the Preview mode, you see the fills, strokes, and other elements that will print.*

100% ▼ ◀ ▶ 1 ▼ Keyline ▼

Figure 1b. *When you view artwork in the Keyline mode, all you see are the outline paths that define the shape of the objects. You do not see the actual fills, strokes, and other elements that will print.*

To view artwork in the Preview mode:

Choose Preview from the View menu
(**Figure 2**). If Preview is checked, you're
already in the Preview mode.

or

Press on the pop-up menu at the bottom
left of your document window. Choose
Preview from the choices (**Figure 3**). If
Preview is in the field or is checked,
you're already in the Preview mode.

Sometimes you may find it necessary to
view your artwork in the Keyline mode—
for example, so that you can see an object
that is sitting behind the one onscreen.

To view artwork in the Keyline mode:

If Preview is checked in the View menu,
choose it. This switches you out of
Preview and into Keyline.

or

Press on the pop-up menu at the bottom
left of your document window. Choose
Keyline. If the word Keyline is in the
field or is checked, you're already in the
Keyline mode.

Tips

• Pressing Command-K will toggle
 you in and out of the Preview and
 Keyline modes.

• You will find that it takes much less
 time for your screen to redraw when
 you're working in Keyline. This is
 especially true if you have artwork
 with complicated fills, such as
 gradients, or artwork that has been
 made into blends (*see Chapter 9,
 "Fills," and Chapter 11, "Blends"*).

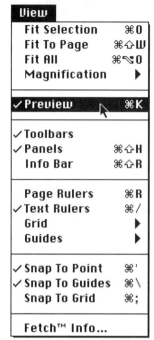

Figure 2. *Choosing **Preview** from the **File**
menu will switch you to the Preview mode. If
Preview is already checked, then choosing it
will switch you to the Keyline mode.*

Figure 3. *Choosing **Preview** from the pop-up
menu at the bottom left corner of the document
window will switch you to the Preview mode.
Choosing **Keyline** from the pop-up menu will
switch you to the Keyline mode.*

Preview and Keyline Modes

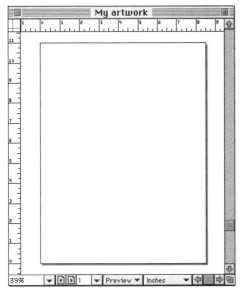

Figure 4. *The document window rulers run down the left and top sides of the document window.*

Once you're working in your document, you may find that you need to work more precisely. FreeHand offers several different features to let you work with very precise measurements. The first is the page rulers. These are two rulers that extend along the top and left sides of your document window (**Figure 4**).

To open the document window rulers:

Unless you have already changed your FreeHand settings, your document probably does not show the page rulers. To make the rulers visible, choose Page Rulers from the View menu (**Figure 5**). If Page Rulers is already checked, the rulers are visible. If you choose Page Rulers when it is checked, you will turn off the rulers.

Tip

➡ Pressing Command-R will toggle you in and out of viewing your page rulers.

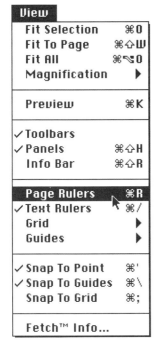

Figure 5. *To see the document window rulers, choose Rulers from the View menu.*

Once the rulers are visible, you can use them to create guides at specific places on your document.

To create Guides:

1. Press on the Guides submenu of the View menu to make sure that Show is checked. If Show is not checked, then choose it. This will allow you to see the guides you are creating (**Figure 6**).

2. Move your arrow so that it touches either the top (horizontal) ruler or the left (vertical) ruler.

3. For a horizontal guide, press and drag the arrow down into the page (**Figures 7a–b**). For a vertical guide, press and drag the arrow to the right into the page.

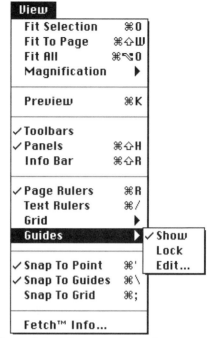

Figure 6. *In order to see the guides you create, make sure that **Show** is checked in the **Guides** submenu of the **View** menu.*

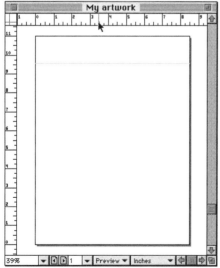

Figure 7a. *To drag a horizontal **Guide** from the **Rulers**, place your arrow on the top ruler and drag down into the page.*

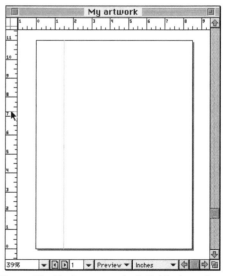

Figure 7b. *To drag a vertical **Guide** from the Rulers, place your arrow on the left ruler and drag to the right.*

Create Guides

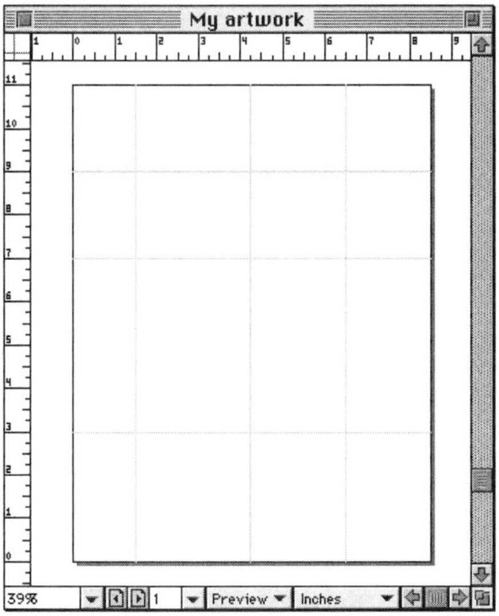

Figure 8a. *Guides in the **Preview** mode appear as colored lines.*

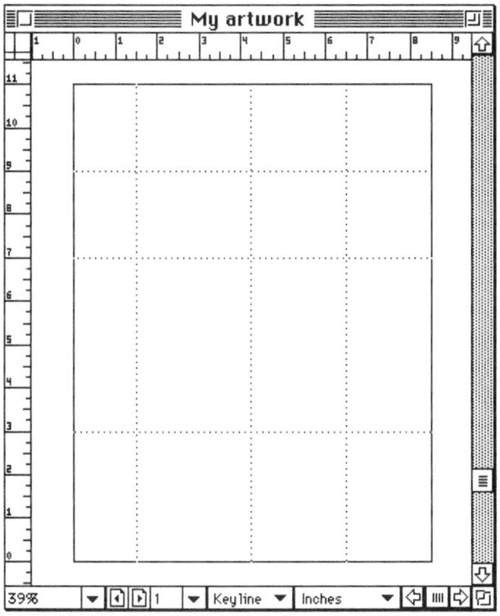

Figure 8b. *Guides in the **Keyline** mode appear as dotted lines.*

4. Let go. If you are in Preview, you will see a colored line on your page. If you are in Keyline, you will see a dotted line on your page (**Figures 8a–b**).

Tips

- If you are dragging a horizontal guide down from the top ruler, look at the vertical ruler on the left. A line will show you where your guide will be when you release the mouse.
- If you are dragging a vertical guide from the left ruler, look at the horizontal ruler at the top. A line will show you where your guide will be when you release the mouse.
- To move guides you have already positioned on the page, use the Selection tool in the toolbox. Press on the guide and drag it into position.
- To delete a single guide, use the Selection tool to drag the guide back into the ruler it came from. To delete many guides at once, see the section on the following page.
- You must drag your arrow from the ruler onto the page, not the pasteboard. If you drag it into the pasteboard, you will not create a guide.

You may want to delete a few guides at a time. Or you may find that you need to fill the page with many guides at exact intervals or that you need to position guides more precisely. While you could create or modify one guide at a time, it is easier to use the Edit Guides commands.

To delete guides:

1. Double-click on a guide or choose Edit from the Guides submenu of the View menu (**Figure 9**). You will see the Guides dialog box that lists the type of guides you have and their position on the page (**Figure 10**).

2. To delete a guide, click on the name of the guide in the dialog box. You should see the guide highlighted.

3. Click on the Delete key. This deletes the guide from the list. If you need to delete other guides, click on their names and then click the Delete key.

4. When you have finished deleting your guides, press the OK button.

Tips

◆◆ If you need to delete more than one guide at once, click on the name of the first guide you want deleted. Hold down the Shift key and then click on the name of the last guide you want deleted. The first and last guides and all the guides in-between will be selected. Press the Delete key and all the selected guides will be deleted.

◆◆ The Release button in the Guides dialog box will release the path from being a guide and turn it into a regular path that can be filled or stroked (*see Chapter 5, "Points and Paths;" Chapter 9, "Fills;" or Chapter 10, "Strokes"*).

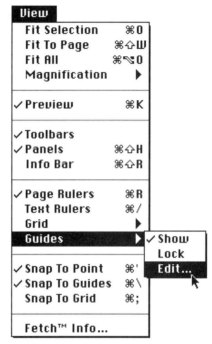

Figure 9. *To adjust more than one guide, choose **Edit Guides** from the **View** menu.*

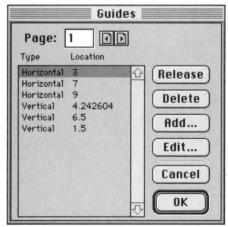

Figure 10. *The **Guides** dialog box gives you a list of all the guides on each of the pages as well as their positions.*

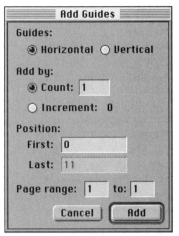

Figure 11. *The Add Guides dialog box allows you to create more than one guide at regular intervals down or across your work pages.*

To add guides numerically:

1. Choose Edit from the Guides submenu of the View menu. The Edit Guides dialog box will appear. Click on the Add button to open the Add Guides dialog box (**Figure 11**).

2. Choose either Horizontal or Vertical. (To make both horizontal and vertical guides, you need to make one type first, then the other.)

3. If you want a specific number of guides, click the Count button. Type the number you want.

4. If you want a specific distance between each guide, click the Increment button. Type the distance you want between the guides.

5. Click the Add button. This will bring you back to the Edit Guides dialog box. If you want another set of guides in the other direction, click the Add button and create the second set.

6. When you are finished, click the OK button in the Edit Guides dialog box. Your page will contain the new guides.

Tips

➡ If you want to create guides at regular intervals down or across your work pages, the First field under Position lets you specify the point on the page where you want your guides to start. The Last field lets you specify the point on the page where you want your guides to stop.

➡ Set the page range for the pages where you want to have guides.

➡ You can switch the page you are adding guides to by typing the page number at the top of the Guides dialog box or by clicking the small page icons to move from one page to another.

Add Guides

You may want to make sure your guides don't get moved inadvertently. To do so, you will need to lock them into position.

To lock guides:

Choose Lock from the Guides submenu of the View menu (**Figure 12**). If Lock is already checked, you will unlock the guides. You can also lock guides using the Layers palette (*see page 43*).

Tips

•• If you want the guides in front of the artwork, you will need to change the order of the Guides layer (*see page 39*).

•• If you want to turn any path into guides, you will need to place the path on the Guides layer (*see page 40*).

You may want all your objects to automatically align themselves or snap to the guide lines that you have created.

To turn on the Snap To Guides:

Choose Snap To Guides from the View menu. If it is checked, the Snap To Guides feature is already turned on. If you choose Snap To Guides when it is already checked, then you will be turning off the Snap To Guides feature.

Tips

•• When you move an object and it snaps to a guide, you will see the Snap To Guide indicator as part of the cursor (**Figure 13**).

•• By using the Preferences settings, you can change how close the object has to come to the guide before it will snap to (*see page 260*).

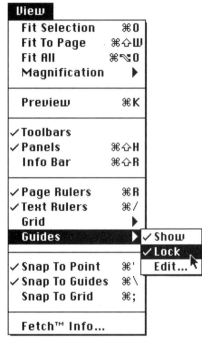

Figure 12. *Choosing Lock Guides from the View menu locks the guides so that they cannot be moved.*

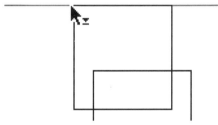

Figure 13. *The small triangle and line next to the arrow is the Snap To Guide cursor. This indicates that the object being moved will snap to a guide.*

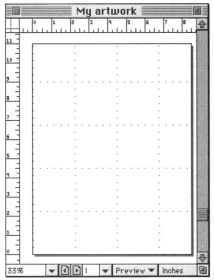

Figure 14. *The **visible grid** consists of dots evenly spaced into squares along your page. The **invisible grid** connects those dots.*

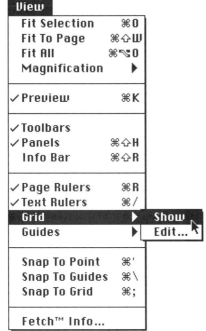

Figure 15. *Choosing **Grid** from the **View** menu allows you to see the visible part of the document grid.*

Another feature that helps you work precisely is the document grid. First, this is a visible grid of nonprinting dots spaced at regular intervals. Second, it is an invisible grid of lines connecting the visible dots. Objects, points, and text can snap to the invisible grid (**Figure 14**).

To view the document grid:

Choose Show from the Grid submenu of the View menu (**Figure 15**). If Show is already checked, then it is already visible. If you choose Show when it is checked, you will turn off the grid.

To change the document grid intervals:

1. Choose Edit from the Grid submenu of the View menu. The Edit Grid dialog box will appear.

2. In the Grid size field, type the distance you want between sections of your grid (**Figure 16**).

3. Click OK or press Return.

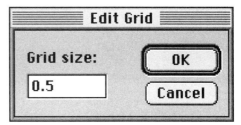

Figure 16. *The **Edit Grid** dialog box lets you change the increments of the invisible grid.*

View Grid; Change Grid

To Turn on Snap To Grid:

Choose Snap To Grid from the View menu (**Figure 17**). When Snap To Grid is checked, the Snap To Grid feature is on. If you choose Snap To Grid when it is checked, you will turn off Snap To Grid.

Tips

- If you turn on Snap To Grid in the middle of working, all previously drawn objects will remain where they were positioned. Only those objects that are newly drawn, moved, or resized will snap to the grid.

- If Snap To Grid is on, you may find it impossible to draw certain objects. For instance, if your grid is set in .5″ intervals and Snap To Grid is on, you will not be able to draw a rectangle that measures 2.25″ wide. Snap To Grid will force your rectangle to be 2″ or 2.5″ (**Figure 18**).

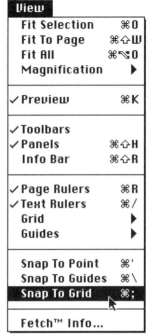

Figure 17. *Choose* Snap To Grid *from the* View *menu to turn on Snap To Grid.*

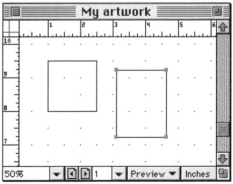

Figure 18. *When Snap To Grid is on, you cannot draw objects with dimensions between the grid intervals. The left rectangle was drawn with Snap To Grid on. Its sides are on the grid intervals. The right rectangle was drawn with Snap To Grid off. Its sides are between the intervals.*

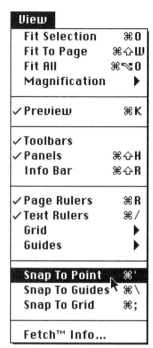

View

Fit Selection	⌘0
Fit To Page	⌘⇧W
Fit All	⌘⌥0
Magnification	▶
✓ Preview	⌘K
✓ Toolbars	
✓ Panels	⌘⇧H
Info Bar	⌘⇧R
✓ Page Rulers	⌘R
✓ Text Rulers	⌘/
Grid	▶
Guides	▶
Snap To Point	**⌘'**
Snap To Guides	⌘\
Snap To Grid	⌘;
Fetch™ Info...	

Figure 19. *To turn the Snap To Point feature on, choose* **Snap To Point** *from the* **View** *menu.*

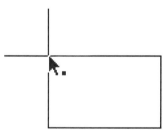

Figure 20. *The dot next to the arrow is the* **Snap To Point** *cursor. This indicates that the object being moved will snap to a point.*

FreeHand also lets you snap to points. This feature lets you move one object so that it aligns precisely on the point of another object.

To turn on Snap To Point:

Choose Snap To Point from the View menu (**Figure 19**). If Snap To Point is already checked, you will turn off the Snap To Point feature.

Tips

- When you move an object and it snaps to a point, the Snap To Point indicator will become part of the cursor (**Figure 20**).

- FreeHand also offers a series of audible snap to sounds that will play when the object snaps. These sounds are controlled in the Preferences settings (*see page 267*).

Turn on Snap To Point

When working in your document, you may find that you need to see different magnfications. There are several ways to zoom in and out of your document.

To zoom using the View menu:

1. To see all the pages in your document, choose Fit All.

2. To see the entire page you are working on, choose Fit to Page.

3. To zoom in on selected artwork, choose Fit Selection.

To zoom using the Magnifying tool:

1. Click on the Magnifying tool in the Toolbox.

2. Click the Magnifying tool on the object you wish to zoom in on. Keep clicking as many times as necessary to zoom in.

or

Drag the Magnifying tool around the area you wish to zoom in on. When you let go of your mouse, you will get the magnification necessary to see the area where you dragged the marquee (**Figures 21a–b**).

Tips

➡ Pressing the Command and Spacebar keys gives you the Magnifying tool without leaving the tool that is currently selected in the toolbox.

➡ Pressing the Option key while in the Magnifying tool turns the icon from a plus sign (+) to a minus sign (–). When you click with the minus sign Magnifying tool, you will zoom out (**Figure 22**).

Figure 21a. *Use the **Magnifying** tool to zoom in on a specific object by **dragging a marquee** around that object. The dashed line shows the area being marqueed.*

Figure 21b. *After dragging, the area that has been marqueed fills up the entire window.*

Figure 22. *Pressing the **Option** key while you are in the Magnifying tool will let you zoom out of an object.*

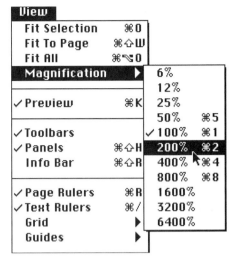

Figure 23a. *The **Magnification** submenu of the **View** menu allows you to choose one of 11 preset magnifications.*

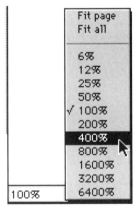

Figure 23b. *The **Magnification** pop-up menu allows you to choose one of the 11 preset magnifications.*

Figure 24. *Double-clicking or dragging across the number in the Magnification pop-up menu allows you to enter an exact magnification amount.*

To use the Magnification submenu or the Magnification pop-up menu:

1. From the View menu, choose one of the magnification amounts from the Magnification submenu (**Figure 23a**) or from the Magnification pop-up menu at the bottom of the document window (**Figure 23b**). Choosing a specific magnification will zoom you in or out to that exact magnification.

   or

   Type one of the following:
   Command-1 for 100%
   Command-2 for 200%
   Command-4 for 400%
   Command-8 for 800%
   Command-5 for 50%

2. Choosing Fit Page (Command-Shift-W) will zoom you in or out so that the page you are working on fits completely inside the document window.

3. Choosing Fit All (Command-Option-0) will zoom out to fit as many pages as is possible in the window.

Tip

⟿ When you choose one of the magnification settings from either the Magnification submenu or Magnification pop-up menu, FreeHand uses the center of your page as the center of the zoom.

To enter exact magnification amounts:

1. Double-click or drag across the number in the Magnification pop-up menu (**Figure 24**).

2. Type in the percentage at which you would like to view your page. (You do not need to type the "%" character.)

3. Press the Return or Enter key.

As you are working, you may want to hide onscreen elements such as the Toolbox.

To hide onscreen elements:

1. To hide Toolbars, choose Toolbars from the View menu.

2. To hide all the Inspectors and other panels, choose Panels from the View menu or press Command-Shift-H (**Figure 25**).

Tip

•❖ Choosing Panel will not hide the Toolbox. To hide the Toolbox, choose Toolbox from the Toolbar submenu of the Window menu or press Command-7.

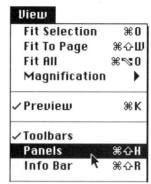

Figure 25. *Choosing* **Panels** *from the* **View** *menu allows you to show or hide any palettes that might be in the way of viewing your artwork.*

In addition to hiding panels, FreeHand lets you "zip," or close up, the panels.

To use the zip feature:

1. Click on the zip box in the upper-left-hand corner of the panel (**Figure 26a**). This will collapse the panel.

2. Click again on the zip box (**Figure 26b**), to expand the panel.

Tip

•❖ Docked panels (*see Appendix A*) will zip open and close together.

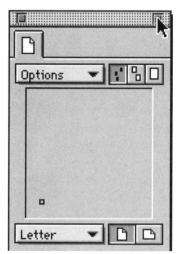

Figure 26a. *Clicking on the* **zip box** *will collapse a palette.*

Figure 26b. *Clicking on the zip box of a collapsed palette will expand that palette.*

Hide Panels; Zip Feature

LAYERS & LAYERING

As soon as you put more than one path on your page, you've already started working in layers. Since you can easily generate hundreds of paths in your document, you will very quickly need to manage the layers and the layering of your objects. In this chapter, you will learn: the difference between layering objects and the layers in the Layers panel; how to move objects within a layer and between layers; how to create, rename, remove, reorder, display, and lock layers; and how to lock objects. You will learn the difference between printing and nonprinting layers. You will also learn how to change the color assigned to the paths for each layer.

Figure 1a. *When two objects are side by side—although it may not be obvious—one object is layered in front of the other.*

Figure 1b. *When two objects overlap, it is obvious which object is in front of the other.*

Every object in FreeHand sits either above or below the other objects. The order in which the objects are layered follows the order in which they were created. If you create a red circle and then a blue square, the red circle will be behind the blue square. Though you may not see this when the two objects are sitting side by side, it is immediately apparent when one object overlaps the other (**Figures 1a–b**).

Once objects are in a certain order, you can move them to different positions on the layer.

To move objects to the front or back of a layer:

1. Click on an object in your artwork.

2. If you want the object to be moved to the very front of its layer, choose Bring To Front (Command-F) from the Arrange submenu of the Modify menu (**Figure 2**). Any objects in that layer that were in front of the object will now be behind the object (**Figures 3a–b**).

3. If you want the object to be moved to the very back of its layer, choose Send To Back (Command-B) from the Arrange submenu (**Figure 4**).

Sometimes you may want to move an object somewhere in the middle of a layer. To do this, you will need to use a different set of commands.

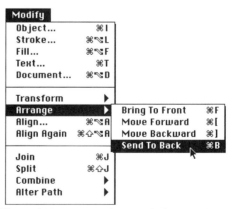

Figure 2. *To move an object to the front of the layer it is on, choose* **Bring To Front** *from the* **Arrange** *menu.*

Figure 3a. *The circle in this illustration was selected to be moved to the front.*

Figure 3b. *The same illustration after the circle was moved using the* **Bring To Front** *command.*

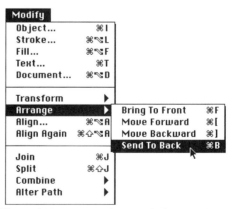

Figure 4. *To move an object to the back of the layer it is on, choose* **Send To Back** *from the* **Arrange** *menu.*

Move to Front or Back of a Layer

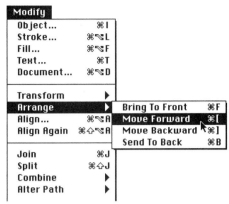

Figure 5. *To move an object in front of the first object it was behind, choose* **Bring Forward** *from the* **Arrange** *menu.*

Figure 6a. *In this illustration, the circle needs to be put in front of the triangle and square, but behind the oval and rectangle.*

Figure 6b. *The same illustration after the* **Bring Forward** *command was applied twice to the circle.*

To move objects within a layer:

1. Click on an object in your artwork.

2. To move an object forward in its layer, choose Move Forward (Command-[ ) from the Arrange submenu of the Modify menu (**Figure 5**). This will move the object in front of the first object it was behind.

3. To move the object farther up, choose Move Forward (Command-[ ) again. Repeat until the object is where you want it to be (**Figures 6a–b**).

4. To move an object backward, choose Move Backward (Command-]) from the Arrange submenu.

5. To move an object farther back, choose Move Backward (Command-]) again. Repeat until the object is where you want it to be.

Move Objects Within a Layer

It may not be feasible to choose Move Backward or Move Forward over and over. FreeHand offers you another way to move an object within its layer.

To move objects using Paste Behind:

1. Choose an object that you would like to move behind another object (**Figure 7a**).

2. Choose Cut from the Edit menu (**Figure 7b**).

3. Click on the object that you would like to be in front of the original object (**Figure 7c**).

4. Choose Paste Behind from the Edit menu. Your original object will be layered behind the object you chose (**Figure 7d**).

Tips

➡ If you choose Bring To Front or Send To Back on the single object of a group (*see Chapter 5, "Points and Paths," for working with groups*), the object will move to the front or back of the group.

➡ Locked objects cannot be moved within their layer.

➡ Other objects can, however, be sent to the front or back of locked objects.

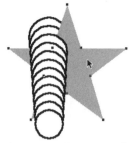

Figure 7a. *To move an object using **Paste Behind**, start by selecting the object you want to move. In this illustration, the star has been selected.*

Figure 7b. *Choose Cut (Command-X) from the **Edit** menu. In this illustration, the star has been cut.*

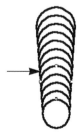

Figure 7c. *Select the object you want the original object to be behind. In this illustration, a circle farther up the row has been selected.*

Figure 7d. *Choose Paste Behind from the Edit menu. In this illustration, the star has been moved up within its layer.*

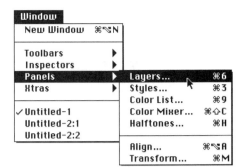

Figure 8. *To work with the Layers panel, choose **Layers** from **Panels** submenu of the **Window** menu.*

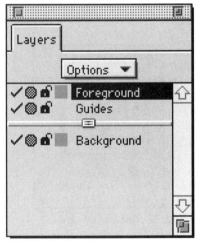

Figure 9. *The Layers panel with the three default layers: **Foreground**, **Guides**, and **Background**.*

Figure 10. *To rename a layer, double-click on the name to highlight it.*

Since FreeHand documents can easily contain hundreds, if not thousands, of objects, you may find that moving objects within their layers is not enough. In that case, you will need to use FreeHand's Layers panel.

To view the Layers panel:

1. If you do not see the Layers panel on your screen, choose Layers from the Panels submenu of the Window menu (**Figure 8**).

2. If you have not changed the default layers for your document, you should see three layers: Foreground, Guides, and Background (**Figure 9**).

Once you have created a layer, you may want to rename it so that it reflects the items on that layer. For instance, if you have an illustration of a farm scene, you may want to put the barn on a layer named "barn," the sky on a layer named "sky," and so on.

To rename a layer:

1. In the Layers panel, double-click on the name of the layer you wish to rename (**Figure 10**).

2. Type the new name of the layer.

3. Press Return or Enter, or click with the mouse anywhere on the Layers panel.

View Layers; Rename Layers

To duplicate a layer:

1. Click on the name of the layer you want to duplicate.

2. Press on the Options pop-up menu in the Layers panel.

3. Choose Duplicate (**Figure 11**). The layer and all of the objects on it will be duplicated.

Tip

•◆ The Guides layer cannot be renamed or duplicated.

Figure 11. *The Options pop-up menu lets you Duplicate a layer and the objects on that layer.*

To remove a layer:

1. Click on the name of the layer you wish to remove.

2. Press on the Options pop-up menu. Choose Remove (**Figure 12**). The layer and the objects on it will be removed.

Tips

•◆ You cannot delete the Guides layer or the very last drawing layer of a document.

•◆ An alert box will warn you if you try to remove a layer that has objects on it.

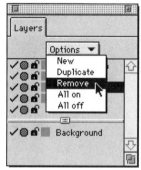

Figure 12. *The Options pop-up menu of the Layers panel lets you Remove a layer and the objects on that layer.*

Figure 13. *Dragging the name of a layer from one position to another will change the order in which the layers appear in the **Layers** panel.*

If a layer's name appears under another layer, then the objects on that layer will appear behind the objects on the other layer. But layers do not have to remain in the order in which you created them; you can reorder them.

To reorder layers:

1. Press on the name of the layer you want to reorder.

2. Drag the name of the layer to the spot where you would like it to be.

3. Let go. The name of the layer will disappear from where it was and reappear in its new position in the Layers panel (**Figure 13**). All objects on the layer will now be repositioned in the document (**Figures 14a–b**).

Tip

➡ If you want your guides to appear in front of your artwork, drag the Guides layer above the layer that contains the artwork.

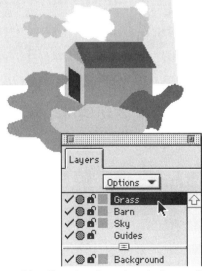

Figure 14a. *Changing the order of a layer will change how objects are displayed. In this illustration, the objects for the grass need to be positioned behind the barn and the sky.*

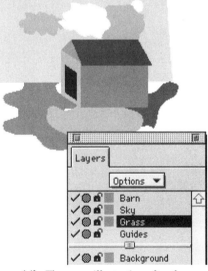

Figure 14b. *The same illustration after the grass layer has been dragged below the sky layer.*

When you are working, the objects you create will be placed on whichever layer is the active or highlighted layer. You may want to move artwork from one layer to another.

To move objects between layers:

1. Select the artwork you would like to move (**Figure 15a**).

2. Click on the name of the layer you want to move the artwork onto. The artwork will now be located on a new layer (**Figure 15b**).

Tip

➬ You cannot move artwork onto a locked layer.

There is a horizontal line that divides the Layers panel into two areas: top and bottom. Objects on layers above the line will appear normal and will print. Objects on layers below the line will appear dimmed and will not print (**Figure 16**). If you have done nothing to change the default settings, you will have one layer called "Background" below the line. As you work, you may find that you want to move layers between the two areas of the Layers panel.

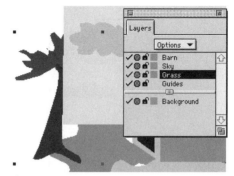

Figure 15a. *In this illustration, the tree needs to be moved from the grass layer. The tree has been selected.*

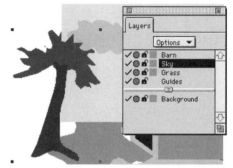

Figure 15b. *The same illustration after clicking on the name of the sky layer. The tree has been moved from the grass layer to the sky layer.*

Figure 16. *The default settings of the Layers panel. The **horizontal line** divides the layers into **printing** and **nonprinting** layers.*

Move Objects Between Layers

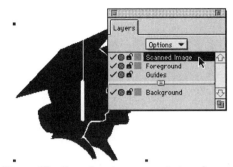

Figure 17a. *To make a layer nonprinting, drag the name of the layer below the horizontal line.*

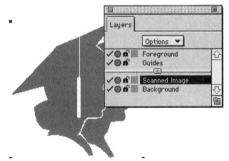

Figure 17b. *The results of dragging the name of the layer below the line.*

To create a nonprinting layer:

1. Press on the name of the layer you wish to make nonprinting (**Figure 17a**).

2. Drag the name of the layer below the dividing line in the Layers panel.

3. Release the mouse. The layer will now be positioned below the line, and any objects on the layer will be dimmed and will not print (**Figure 17b**).

To create a printing layer:

1. Press on the name of the layer you wish to make a printing layer.

2. Drag the name of the layer above the dividing line in the Layers panel.

3. Release the mouse. The layer will now be positioned above the dividing line, and any objects on the layer will print.

Tips

◆◆ Objects on the Guides layer will not print, regardless of where the Guides layer is, either above or below the line.

◆◆ Use nonprinting layers to hold images that have been placed for tracing (*see page 61*).

Nonprinting Layers; Printing Layers

You can also use the Layers panel to change how the objects on each layer are seen (**Figure 18**).

To change the display of a layer:

1. If there is a checkmark to the left of the layer name, click on the checkmark. This will delete the checkmark and make all the objects on the layer invisible.

2. If there is no checkmark to the left of the layer name, click on the blank space. This will bring back the checkmark and make all the objects on the layer visible.

3. If there is a solid gray dot to the left of the layer name, click on the dot. This will change the dot into a circle with an "X" in it and make any objects on the layer visible in the Keyline mode.

4. If there is a circle with an "X" to the left of the layer name, click on the circle. This will change the circle into a gray dot and make any objects on the layer visible in the Preview mode.

(*See pages 19–20 for more information about the difference between the Keyline and Preview modes.*)

Tips

•◆ If you have a layer that is invisible, any objects on that layer will still print. Before you send a file to be printed, check to make sure no layers are holding invisible objects.

•◆ If you hold the Option key as you click on the gray dot for any layer, you will make all the layers in your document appear in the Keyline mode.

The circle with the "X" indicates that this layer is in Keyline.

No checkmark indicates that this layer is invisible.

The solid gray dot indicates that this layer is in Preview.

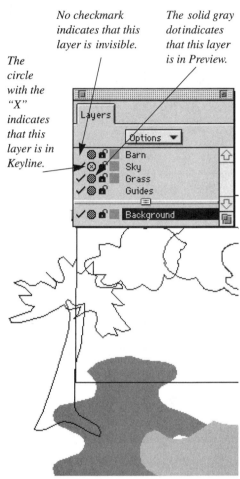

Figure 18. *The different ways layers can be set for display in the **Layers** panel.*

The closed padlock indicates that this is a locked layer.

Figure 19. *Clicking on the **padlock** will turn it to the **locked** or **closed** position. This will lock all objects on the layer, preventing them from being selected, resized, or transformed.*

Figure 20. *Choosing **Lock** from the **Arrange** menu will lock individual objects on a layer without locking the entire layer.*

There may be times when you want to see the objects on a layer, but you don't want to be able to select those objects. In this case, you need to lock the layer.

To lock a layer:

1. Look at the padlock to the left of the layer name. If the padlock is in the open position, it means the layer is unlocked.

2. Click on the padlock. This will cause the padlock to change to the closed position and will lock all objects on the layer (**Figure 19**).

3. If the padlock is already in the closed position, click on it. This will cause the padlock to change to the open position and will unlock all objects on the layer.

To lock an object on a layer:

1. Select the object or objects you wish to lock.

2. Choose Lock (Command-L) from the Modify menu (**Figure 20**).

To unlock an object on a layer:

1. Select the object or objects you wish to unlock.

2. Choose Unlock (Command-Shift-L) from the Modify menu.

Tips

•◆ Locked objects can be selected and their fills and strokes can be changed, but locked objects cannot be deleted.

•◆ Locked objects cannot be moved, resized, or transformed.

•◆ Locked text objects can have their text attributes changed or the text edited.

•◆ Locked objects can be copied, but they cannot be cut or deleted.

Lock Layers; Lock Objects; Unlock Objects

When you select an object, the path that defines that object will be displayed in a certain color (*see Chapter 5, "Points and Paths"*). You can change that display color by using the Layers panel.

To change the display color of a layer:

1. Drag a color from the Color List or Color Mixer (*see Chapter 8, "Working in Color"*). A small swatch of that color will appear.

2. Drag that swatch onto the name of the layer you want to change (**Figure 21**).

3. The colored square next to the name will change. All selected objects on that layer will then have their paths displayed in that color.

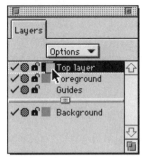

Figure 21. *To change the path display color of a layer, drag a color swatch onto the color box of that layer.*

CREATION TOOLS

Once you've got your document open, you will want to use FreeHand's creation tools to construct the different objects that will make up your artwork. In this chapter, you will learn how to create rectangles, squares, rounded-corner rectangles, ellipses and circles, polygons, stars, and lines. You will also learn how to use the Freehand, Variable stroke, and Calligraphic pen tools. You will learn the about the Pen and Bézigon tools and how these two tools let you draw more precisely. (Because these two tools are not as simple to use as the other creation tools, they are covered in detail in Chapter 6.) You will also learn how to use FreeHand's Spiral and Arc tools to easily make sophisticated spirals and arcs. Finally, you will learn how to use FreeHand's Trace tool to automatically trace scanned artwork.

One of the most basic objects to create is a rectangle. This includes regular rectangles, squares, and rounded-corner rectangles (**Figure 1**).

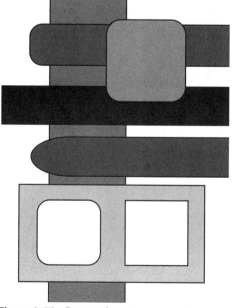

Figure 1. *The **Rectangle** tool creates rectangles, squares, and rounded-corner rectangles.*

To create a rectangle:

1. With a document open, click on the Rectangle tool in the toolbox (**Figure 2**).

2. Move your cursor into your work page area. You should see a plus sign (+) cursor (**Figure 3**).

3. Press and drag the plus sign (+) cursor along the diagonal line that would reach across your rectangle (**Figure 4**).

4. As you drag, you will see the four sides that define your rectangle. Let go of the mouse when you are satisfied with the size of the rectangle (**Figure 5**).

Tip

•➔ If you let go of the mouse too soon, you can change the dimensions of the rectangle (*see page 80*).

Figure 2. *When the **Rectangle** tool has been selected in the toolbox, the tool becomes shaded so that it looks recessed.*

Figure 3. *When the Rectangle tool is chosen, the cursor becomes a plus sign (+).*

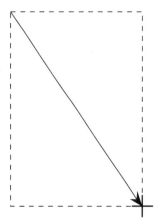

Figure 4. *When you draw a rectangle, your cursor should drag along the diagonal line that would run from the upper left corner to the lower right corner of the rectangle.*

Figure 5. *When you let go of the mouse after dragging with the rectangle tool, you will see the rectangle you have created.*

Rectangle

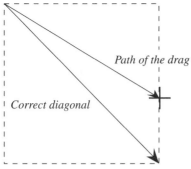

Figure 6. *Holding the Shift key constrains your rectangle into a square. Even if the path of your drag moves away from the correct diagonal, the object will still be a square.*

Figure 7. *When you let go of the mouse after dragging with the rectangle tool, you will see the square you have created.*

You may think of a square as different from a rectangle, but FreeHand doesn't make the distinction. You use the same tool to create both rectangles and square. You just hold the Shift key as you drag to make a square.

To create a square:

1. With a document open, click on the Rectangle tool in the toolbox.

2. Bring your cursor over your work page area. You should now see a plus sign (+) cursor.

3. With one finger pressing down on the Shift key, use the other hand to press and drag the plus sign (+) cursor along the diagonal line that would reach across your square. Notice that even if your hand is unsteady, your rectangle must be a square. This is because you are pressing the Shift key (**Figure 6**).

4. As you drag, you will see the line that defines your square. When you are satisfied with the size of the square, let go of the mouse first, then the Shift key. If you let go of the Shift key first, you may not draw a square (**Figure 7**).

Tip

➥ If you let go of the mouse too soon, you can always change the dimensions of the square (*see page 80*).

Square

Another type of rectangle has curved or rounded corners. The amount of the curve depends on the Corner radius (**Figure** 8).

To set the Corner radius for a rounded-corner rectangle:

1. Double-click on the Rectangle tool in the toolbox. The Rectangle Tool dialog box will appear (**Figure 9**).

2. In the Corner radius field, type the amount you want for the corner.

or

Press and drag on the slider to set the number you want for the Corner radius.

3. Once you have set the Corner radius, follow the steps for drawing a rectangle or a square.

Tip

➡ Once you draw an object, you can use the Object Inspector to change a rectangle's corner radius.

To create a rectangle from the center point outward:

1. Choose the Rectangle tool from the toolbox.

2. Press on the Option key and position your mouse where you would like the center point of the rectangle to be (**Figure 10**).

3. Press and drag with the mouse. As you drag, you will see the line that defines your rectangle. Let go of the mouse first, then the Option key, when you are satisfied with the size.

Tip

➡ If you press both the Option and the Shift keys as you drag, you will draw a square outward from the center point.

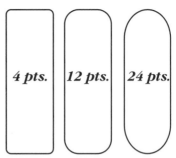

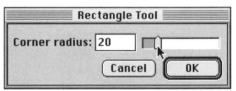

Figure 8. *Different **Corner radius** settings result in different looks for rounded-corner rectangles.*

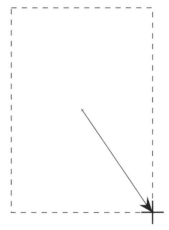

Figure 9. *Double-click on the Rectangle tool in the toolbox. The **Rectangle Tool** dialog box will appear and will let you set the amount of the Corner radius.*

Figure 10. *Pressing the **Option** key draws a rectangle from the center point outward.*

Figure 11. *The Ellipse tool when selected in the toolbox.*

Another type of object you can create is the ellipse. Since circles are perfect ellipses, the Ellipse tool will also create circles.

To create an ellipse or circle:

1. Click on the Ellipse tool in the toolbox (**Figure 11**).

2. Press and drag along the diagonal line that would reach across your ellipse.

3. If you want to make a circle, press the Shift key as you drag.

4. As you drag, you will see the line that defines the diameter of your ellipse. Let go of the mouse first, then the Shift key, when you are satisfied with the size of the object (**Figure 12**).

Tip

➡ Press the Option key to draw an ellipse from the center outward.

➡ Press the Option and Shift keys to draw a circle from the center outward.

➡ If you let go of the mouse too soon, you can change the dimensions of the object (*see page 80*).

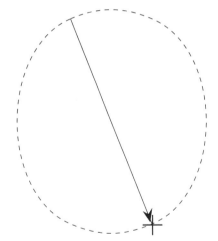

Figure 12. *When you let go of the mouse after dragging with the Ellipse tool, you will see the ellipse or circle you have created.*

Ellipse or Circle

While ellipses and rectangles are the basic objects of drawing, you will probably want to create other objects: triangles, stars, octagons, etc. (**Figure 13**). Fortunately, FreeHand has the Polygon tool.

To create a polygon:

1. Double-click on the Polygon tool in the toolbox (**Figure 14**).

2. You should now see the Polygon Tool dialog box (**Figure 15**).

3. Enter the number of sides for your polygon by typing the number in the field or by dragging the triangle slider.

4. Click OK, or press the Return or Enter key on your keyboard. This will return you to your work page.

5. Drag with the plus sign (+) cursor. You will be drawing your polygon from the center outward.

6. As you drag, you will see the shape that defines your polygon. Drag your mouse to rotate the polygon to the position you want. Let go of the mouse when you are satisfied with the size and position of the polygon (**Figure 16**).

Tips

•◆ If you let go of the mouse too soon, you can still change the dimensions of the polygon (*see page 80*).

•◆ If you do not like the orientation, you can use the Rotating tool to change it (*see page 94*).

•◆ Press the Shift key as you drag your polygon to constrain it to an upright position.

•◆ To draw a rectangle that can be rted as you draw it, set the polygon at 4 sides.

Figure 13. *Various objects that can be drawn using the* **Polygon** *tool.*

Figure 14. *Selecting the* **Polygon** *tool lets you draw different polygons and stars.*

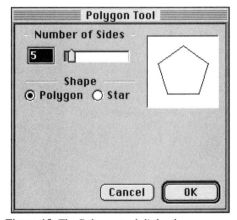

Figure 15. *The Polygon tool dialog box.*

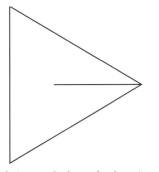

Figure 16. *A triangle drawn by dragging along the line indicated.*

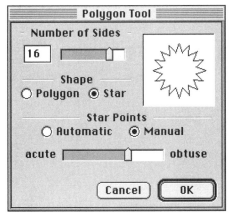

Figure 17. *Choosing the* **Star** *shape in the* **Polygon Tool** *dialog box gives you more choices about the type of* **Star Points** *you want.*

To create a star:

1. Double-click on the Polygon tool in the toolbox. Click on the radio button (*see Appendix A*) for the Star shape. You should now see the additional choices in the Polygon Tool dialog box (**Figure 17**).

2. Enter the number of points you want for your star in the number of sides fields. (This label is slightly incorrect, because a star with 5 points actually has 10 sides.)

3. If you want your star to have its segments automatically aligned, choose Automatic. If you want to shape the star yourself, choose Manual and then adjust the slider from acute to obtuse. The preview window will show what your changes will affect the star (**Figures 18a–c**).

Tip

➡ When you set the Polygon Tool dialog box to a certain setting, that setting will remain in effect until you reset the settings in the dialog box.

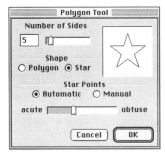

Figure 18a. *The Polygon Tool dialog box for an* **Automatic** *five-pointed star.*

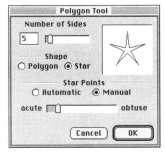

Figure 18b. *The Polygon Tool dialog box for a* **Manual** *five-pointed star at an* **acute** *setting.*

Figure 18c. *The Polygon Tool dialog box for a* **Manual** *five-pointed star at an* **obtuse** *setting.*

FreeHand is definitely the program for anyone who has said they can't even draw a straight line. With the Line tool, anyone can draw a straight line!

To create a straight line:

1. Click on the Line tool in the toolbox (**Figure 19**).

2. Press at the point where you would like your line to start.

3. Drag along the direction you would like your line to follow.

4. Move your mouse to change the length and direction of the line.

5. Let go of the mouse when you are satisfied (**Figure 20**).

Tip

➙ If you press on the Shift key as you use the Line tool, your lines will be constrained to 45° or 90° angles.

Figure 19. *Selecting the Line tool lets you draw straight lines.*

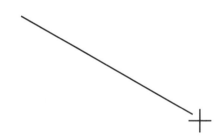

Figure 20. *A straight line drawn with the Line tool.*

Figure 21. *The Freehand tool settings:* **Freehand** *(top),* **Variable stroke** *(middle), and* **Calligraphic pen** *(bottom).*

The Freehand tool has three different tool operations: Freehand, Variable stroke, and Calligraphic pen. Each of these operations creates a different type of look (**Figure 21**).

The Freehand operation is useful for tracing over scanned images. The Variable stroke resembles a brushstroke. The Calligraphic pen resembles the stroke of a calligraphy pen. Both Variable stroke and Calligraphic pen are especially effective if you have a pressure-sensitive tablet that varies the width of the stroke, depending on how much or how little pressure you exert as you draw.

To choose the Freehand operation:

1. Double-click on the Freehand tool in the toolbox (**Figure 22**). This will bring you to the Freehand Tool dialog box (**Figure 23**).

2. To work with the Freehand tool, choose the Freehand button is chosen.

3. If you want your path to follow any minor variables as you drag, choose Tight fit.

4. If you want your path to smooth out any minor variables as you drag, make sure Tight fit is unchecked.

5. Click OK, which will return you to your work page.

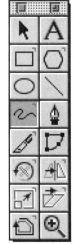

Figure 22. *The* **Freehand** *tool in the toolbox.*

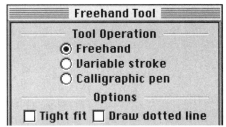

Figure 23. *Double-clicking on the* **Freehand** *tool opens the* **Freehand Tool** *dialog box.*

The Freehand Tool Settings

To draw with the Freehand tool:

1. Make sure the Freehand tool is selected.

2. Drag with the plus sign (+) cursor along the path you want to create.

3. Let go of the mouse when you have completed your path (**Figure 24**).

Tips

•➔ If your stroke doesn't keep up with your drag, open the Freehand Tool dialog box and check the box for Draw dotted line. This will create a dotted line that follows your path. FreeHand will then fill in that line with the actual path.

•➔ If you need to erase part of the path, press the Command key and drag backward over the part you want to erase.

•➔ If you want to close the path you are drawing, move the cursor near the start of the path. A small square will appear next to the plus sign (+) cursor, indicating that the path will close.

•➔ If you want part of the path you are drawing with the Freehand tool to be straight, press the Option key as you drag. Let go of the Option key (but not the mouse) to continue the freehand drag (**Figure 25**).

Figure 24. *Dragging with the **Freehand** tool will create a line that follows the path you dragged.*

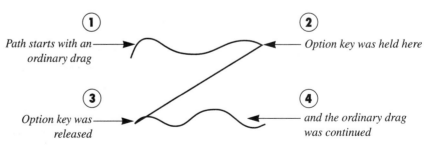

① Path starts with an ordinary drag

② Option key was held here

③ Option key was released

④ and the ordinary drag was continued

Figure 25. *Press the **Option** key as you drag with the **Freehand** tool to create straight lines.*

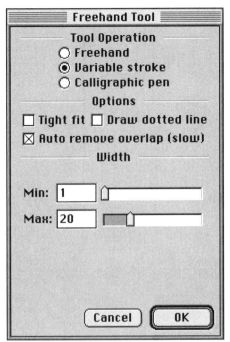

Figure 26. *Choosing* **Variable stroke** *gives you these options.*

To choose Variable stroke operation:

1. Double-click on the Freehand tool in the toolbox. The Freehand Tool dialog box will appear.

2. Choose Variable stroke (**Figure 26**).

3. In the Min field, enter the size for the thinnest part of your brush stroke (any point size from 1 to 72.)

4. In the Max field, enter the size for the thickest part of your brush stroke (any point size from 1 to 72.)

5. If you want to eliminate any parts of the path that cross over each other, choose Auto remove overlap (slow). This cleans up the path and makes it easier to reshape; it can also help you avoid printing problems later on. (You may notice a slight hesitation after you let go of your mouse as FreeHand performs the calculations necessary to remove any overlap.)

6. Click OK, which returns you to your work page.

To draw with the Variable stroke tool:

1. If you have chosen the Variable stroke tool in the dialog box, you should see the Variable stroke icon in the toolbox (**Figure 27**).

2. Drag with the plus sign (+) cursor to create the path.

3. If you have a pressure-sensitive tablet, any changes in the pressure you exert on the tablet will change the thickness of your stroke (**Figure 28**).

Tips

➻ The object created by the Variable stroke tool is a closed path. This means that to change the color of the object you change the Fill, not the Stroke.

➻ If you do not have a tablet, you can still vary the thickness of your stroke by pressing the following modifier keys:

To increase the thickness, press the right arrow, the right bracket ( ]), or the number 2 key

To decrease the thickness, press the left arrow, the left bracket ([ ), or the number 1 key.

➻ If you draw with a mouse without using modifier keys, FreeHand will use the Min field setting as the width of your stroke.

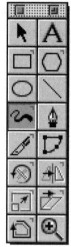

Figure 27. *When you choose the the **Variable stroke** tool, its icon appears in the toolbox.*

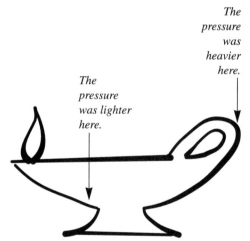

The pressure was heavier here.

The pressure was lighter here.

Figure 28. *Changing the pressure while drawing with the Variable stroke tool will change the thickness of the lines created.*

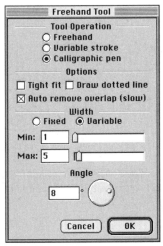

Figure 29. *Clicking on the radio button for* **Calligraphic pen** *gives you these options.*

Figure 30. *The* **Bézigon** *tool in the toolbox.*

Figure 31. *The* **Pen** *tool in the toolbox.*

Figure 32. *The differences (circled) between drawing with with the* **Freehand** *tool (top) and the* **Pen** *tool (bottom).*

To choose Calligraphic pen operation:

1. Double-click on the Freehand tool in the toolbox. The Freehand Tool dialog box will appear.

2. Choose Calligraphic pen (**Figure 29**).

3. If you are using a pressure-sensitive talbet, click on the Variable button under the Width option if you want the thickness of the lines to change as you vary the pressure.

4. Under the Angle options, type in the degree of the angle or rotate the wheel to set the angle your stroke uses for its calligraphic lines.

5. Click OK, which returns you to your work page.

The other two creation tools in the toolbox are the Bézigon (**Figure 30**) and the Pen (**Figure 31**) tools. Both of these tools allow you much greater control over the shape of the path that you are drawing. This is especially true when they are compared to the Freehand tool (**Figure 32**).

Both the Pen and the Bézigon tools create much more precise, uniform, and exact paths. This makes either tool extremely useful for working on precision drawings such as architectural illustrations, logos, technical illustrations, etc. Because these two tools are not as simple to use as the other creation tools, they are covered separately in Chapter 6.

Calligraphic Pen Settings; Pen and Bézigon Tools

Finally, FreeHand provides you with two more creation tools that are not in the toolbox: the Spiral tool and the Arc tool. With these two tools, it is very easy to draw a wide variety of paths (**Figure 33**).

To choose settings for the Spiral tool:

1. To open the Xtra Tools toolbox, choose Xtra Tools from the Xtras submenu of the Window menu or press Command-Shift-K (**Figure 34**).

2. Double-click on the Spiral tool in the Xtra Tools toolbox (**Figure 35**).

3. You should now see the Spiral dialog box (**Figure 36**).

4. Choose between the nonexpanding and expanding Spiral type. Expanding creates a spiral in which the space between the rotations increases as the spiral rotates from the center. Nonexpanding creates a spiral where the space remains constant between the rotations.

5. If you have chosen an expanding spiral, you will see an Expansion field (**Figure 36**). This controls how fast your spiral expands (**Figure 37**). The higher the number, the greater the expansion rate. Enter this amount by typing in the field or by dragging the triangle slider.

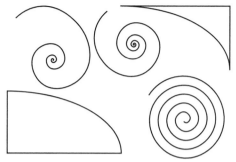

Figure 33. *The Spiral and Arc tools let you create different types of spiral and arc paths.*

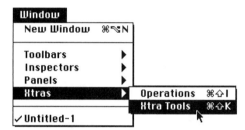

Figure 34. *Choose Xtra Tools from the Xtras submenu of the Window menu to open the Xtra Tools toolbox.*

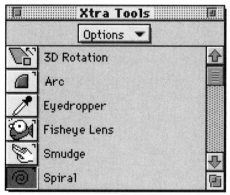

Figure 35. *The Xtra Tools toolbox with the Spiral tool selected.*

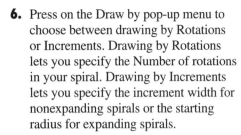

Figure 36. *The **Spiral** dialog box allows you to choose the type of spiral, the rate of expansion, the width increments, the number of rotations, the direction from which to draw the spiral, and the direction of the spiral.*

6. Press on the Draw by pop-up menu to choose between drawing by Rotations or Increments. Drawing by Rotations lets you specify the Number of rotations in your spiral. Drawing by Increments lets you specify the increment width for nonexpanding spirals or the starting radius for expanding spirals.

7. Press on the Draw from pop-up menu to choose between drawing from the Center, the Edge, or the Corner of the location of the Spiral tool (**Figure 38**).

8. Click on one of the Direction icons to choose either a counterclockwise or a clockwise spiral. Click OK to implement all your settings.

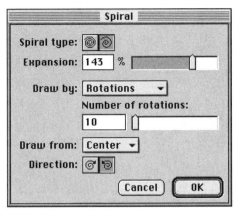

Figure 37. *A comparison between a spiral drawn with an **Expansion** rate of 50% (left) and one drawn with a rate of 100% (right).*

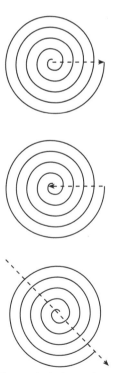

Figure 38. *Three spirals drawn from the **Center** (top), the **Edge** (middle), and the **Corner** (bottom). The dashed lines show the length and direction of the drags.*

To choose settings for the Arc tool:

1. Open the Xtra Tools toolbox. (Choose Xtra Tools from the Xtras submenu of the Window menu or press Command-Shift-K.)

2. Double-click on the Arc tool in the Xtra Tools toolbox (**Figure 39**).

3. You should now see the Arc dialog box (**Figure 40**).

4. Choose Create open arc if you want your arc to remain open. Deselect this option if you want your arc to be closed (**Figure 41**).

5. Choose Create flipped arc to flip your arc from one direction to another (**Figure 42**).

6. Choose Create concave arc to create an arc that sits concave inside a corner (**Figure 43**).

Tips

- Pressing the Option key after you start the drag with the Arc tool will create a flipped arc.

- Pressing the Command key after you start the drag with the Arc tool will create a closed arc.

- Pressing the Control key after you start the drag with the Arc tool will create a concave arc.

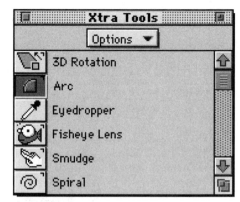

Figure 39. *The Arc tool selected in the Xtra Tools toolbox.*

Figure 40. *The Arc dialog box allows you to choose the type of arc: open, flipped, or concave.*

Figure 41. *The difference between an open arc (left) and a closed arc (right).*

Figure 42. *An open arc (left) and the same arc set to be flipped (right).*

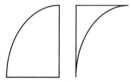

Figure 43. *A closed arc (left) and the same arc set to be concave (right).*

Arc Tool Settings

Figure 44a. *To trace an image, choose* **Import** *from the* **File** *menu.*

Figure 44b. *Any* **PICT, TIFF,** *or* **EPS** *file may be selected in the* **Import document** *dialog box.*

Figure 44c. *A imported image with its* **four** *anchor points.*

There may be times when you have a piece of scanned artwork that you want to convert into FreeHand paths. You may want to be able to scale that piece of artwork up or down without worrying about resolution, to apply spot colors to certain parts of the it, or to make a rough sketch more precise. In these situations, you can use FreeHand's Trace tool.

To import artwork for tracing:

1. With your document open, choose Import from the File menu or press Command-Shift-D (**Figure 44a**).

2. Use the navigational tools to find the PICT, TIFF, or EPS file that you would like to trace. Click the Open button (**Figure 44b**).

3. After you choose the file you want to import, you will see your cursor change to a corner symbol.

4. Click with the corner symbol. The image will be placed with four anchor points surrounding it (**Figure 44c**).

Tips

•➔ Though you can trace art on any layer, most people put imported images on layers below the horizontal line of the Layers panel so that the imported images do not print (*see page 41*).

•➔ Once you have imported the image on a layer, lock that layer so that you do not inadvertently select the imported image. You can then select a printing layer to be the layer for the traced artwork.

•➔ For best results using the Trace tool, turn on the High-Resolution TIFF display (*see page 265*).

Place Artwork for Tracing

To trace an image:

1. Double-click on the Trace tool in the toolbox (**Figure 45a**).

2. The Trace Tool dialog box will open (**Figure 45b**).

3. Press on the pop-up menus to choose the number of colors, the resolution, what layers will be traced, the type of tracing you want, and how detailed your tracing will be. Click OK to apply those settings.

4. Drag a marquee with the Trace tool around the part of the image you want to trace (**Figure 45c**).

5. Release the mouse. Your artwork will be traced.

Tip

•◆ When tracing photographic images, you will create many objects after your trace. Group the objects created by the trace (Command-G).

Figure 45a. *Double-click on the **Trace** tool to open the **Trace Tool** dialog box.*

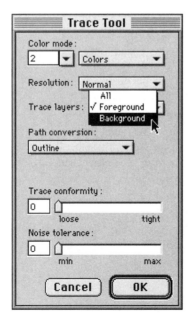

Figure 45b. *The **Trace Tool** dialog box.*

Figure 45c. *Drag a marquee with the Tracing tool to trace your image.*

POINTS & PATHS 5

E very object in FreeHand is really an arrangement of points connected along a path. In this chapter, you will learn how to select single points, multiple points, an entire object, or multiple objects. You will learn how paths can be grouped or ungrouped. You will learn how to follow the rules for effective placement of points. You will learn the difference between the types of points: corner, curve, and connector. You will also learn how to convert points from one type to another. You will learn how to add and delete points on a path. You will learn the difference between open and closed paths and how to convert one to the other. And you will learn how to change the positions and dimensions of objects.

Figure 1. *When you stop drawing a path, the path is displayed with its **anchor points** (black squares) selected.*

Figure 2. *The **Selection** tool in the toolbox.*

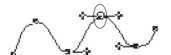

Figure 3. *When you select a point on a path, it is displayed as a **hollow dot** (circled).*

Select Points by Clicking

To select points by clicking:

1. Draw a wavy line with the Freehand tool (*see page 53*). As soon as you let go of the mouse, you will see your path. There will be black squares along the path. These are the anchor points that define the path (**Figure 1**).

2. Click on the Selection tool in the toolbox or press the number 0 key (**Figure 2**). This will switch you to the Selection tool.

3. Select the point by placing the tip of the arrow on one of the points. Click. The point will turn into a hollow dot with two levers (**Figure 3**). If your levers look different from the ones shown, you can change them with the Preferences settings (*see page 260*).

(Continued on the following page.)

4. To change the shape of the path, move, or drag, the point you have selected (**Figure 4**).

5. To select additional points, press the Shift key and click on those points.

Tips

•◆ Press the Command key to temporarily go to the Selection tool.

•◆ You can deselect points by clicking anywhere off the object.

•◆ If you wish to deselect a point, press the Shift key and click on the point you want deselected.

Figure 4. *One way to change the shape of a path is to drag a point on that path.*

Another way to select points is by dragging with the Selection tool. This will create a selection marquee.

To select points or objects with a selection marquee:

1. With the Selection tool chosen, place the arrow cursor outside the point or points you want to select.

2. Press and drag to create a rectangle surrounds the points you want selected (**Figure 5a**).

3. Let go of the mouse. Any points that were inside the rectanglular marquee will be selected (**Figure 5b**).

Tip

•◆ To select points in more than one area, create your first selection marquee as usual. Then press the Shift key and create your next selection marquee.

Figure 5a. *Dragging a* **marquee** *with the Selection tool.*

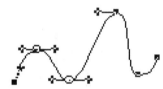

Figure 5b. *The* **points** *that were within the rectangle created by the marquee will be selected.*

Figure 6a. *A line dragged with a **preview**.*

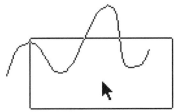

Figure 6b. *A line dragged with a **bounding box**.*

To select and move an entire object:

1. Use the Selection tool to press on a line segment of an object. Your object is now selected with its anchor points as black dots.

2. If you hold for a moment, you will see a four-headed cross. If you drag with that cross, you will see a preview as you drag your object (**Figure 6a**).

3. If you start your drag quickly, you will see a box and a single arrow as you drag. This is the bounding box that contains the object you are dragging. Position the box where you want your object and release the mouse. You will now see your object (**Figure 6b**).

Tips

➡ If you want to select more than one object, press the Shift key and click on any additional objects.

➡ If you have selected multiple objects and wish to deselect one of them without losing your other selections, press the Shift key and click on the object you wish to deselect.

➡ If you drag multiple objects, you may not see the preview drag. Change the Preferences setting for Redraw to see multiple objects when you drag (*see page 265*).

➡ If you have your Preferences set so that you do not see a preview of the objects, tap the Option key after you start your drag to see a preview.

Select and Move Objects

As you have seen, dragging a point will change the shape of an object. In order to protect the shape of your object, or to make it easier to select multiple objects, you can group the points on the path or the multiple objects.

Figure 7. A grouped object displays four group anchor points.

To group paths:

1. Select the path or objects you want to group.

2. Choose Group from the Modify menu or press Command-G. Instead of the individual points selected, there will be four group anchor points arranged in a rectangle around the path or paths (**Figure 7**).

Figure 8a. Drag on one of the group anchor points to resize a grouped object.

To work with grouped objects:

1. To select a grouped object, click with the Selection tool on the object.

2. To reshape a grouped object, drag on one of the four group anchor points that surround the object (**Figure 8a**).

3. To resize the object without distorting its shape, press the Shift key as you drag on one of the group anchor points (**Figure 8b**).

*Figure 8b. Press the **Shift** key while dragging to resize without distorting the shape of the object.*

Figure 9a. *When a group is selected, you cannot see its individual anchor points.*

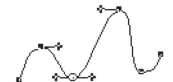

Figure 9b. *Pressing the* **Option** *key allows you to select the individual points of a grouped object.*

Once you have grouped an object, you may want to select and reshape an individual point on that object. Because the object is grouped, you will need to follow some special steps (**Figure 9a**).

To select individual points within a group:

1. With the object selected, press the Option key and click with the Selection tool on the object. You should then see the individual points of the grouped object (**Figure 9b**).

2. Still pressing the Option key, click on the point you wish to select.

3. If you wish to select additional points, press the Shift key and click on those points.

Tips

➡ Rectangles and ellipses are grouped when you draw them.

➡ To select the individual points of a rectangle or ellipse, choose Reverse Direction from the Alter Path submenu of the Modify menu. This will both ungroup the object and change how it is drawn. Group the object. You will then be able to select individual points using the Option key.

When you are working with grouped objects, you may want to create levels of groups to make it easier to select certain objects. This is called "nesting."

To nest objects:

1. Select and group the first object (**Figure 10a**). After the object is grouped, deselect it.

2. Select the next object and group it (**Figure 10b**). After that object is grouped, deselect it. If you have additional objects that you want to nest, repeat this step.

3. Select all the groups and group them (**Figure 10c**).

Tips

•➤ There is a limit of 8 levels for nested objects.

•➤ Numerous nesting levels can cause problems when it comes to printing your file.

Figure 10a. *To nest objects, select and group the first object.*

Figure 10b. *Continue to select and group each object. Each grouped object will display its own* **group anchor points.**

Figure 10c. *Select all the individual groups and group them. There will now be another set of group anchor points for the larger group.*

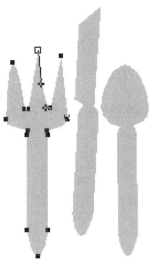

Figure 11a. *To select an individual object or point in a nested group, press the **Option** key as you click on the group. You will then see the individual anchor points of the object.*

To work with nested groups:

1. Press the Option key to select an individual object or point in a nested group (**Figure 11a**).

2. Press the Tilde (~) key to select the next level of the nest (**Figure 11b**).

3. Continue to press the Tilde key until you have all the levels you want selected (**Figure 11c**).

To ungroup an object:

1. Select the grouped object.

2. Choose Ungroup from the Modify menu or press Command-U. Your object will be ungrouped and its individual anchor points will be visible.

Tip

➥ If you have nested objects in a group, you will have to ungroup them for each level of the nest.

Figure 11b. *To select the next level of the nest, press the **Tilde** key.*

Figure 11c. *Continue to press the Tilde key until you see the **group anchor points** for the final level of the nest.*

Work with Nested Groups; Ungroup Objects

The basics of points

Once you start working with points, you will discover that there are levers, or handles, which extend out of points. These are called point handles or Bézier (pronounced Bay-zee-ay) handles, named after the French mathematician Pierre Bézier. Point handles are nonprinting lines that control the direction along which any path curves. Changing the direction of the point handles will change the shape of the path (**Figures 12a–b**).

Tip

➡ FreeHand provides two types of handles on the levers that come out of the points. The illustrations in this book show the larger handles. You can work with the smaller handles by switching the Preferences settings (*see page 260*).

There are three different types of points that make up FreeHand objects: Corner points, curve points, and connector points. In order to have a complete understanding of FreeHand, it is vital to understand how these points work.

Corner points

Corner points are anchor points that allow paths to have an abrupt change in direction. Depending on how they were created, there are three different types of corner points: points with no handles, points with two handles, and points with one handle (**Figure 13**).

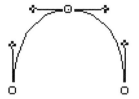

Figure 12a. *An object with its* **point handles** *visible.*

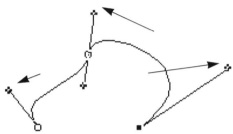

Figure 12b. *The same object with the point handles manipulated in the directions indicated.*

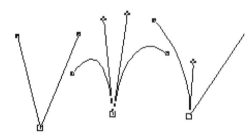

Figure 13. *The three different types of* **corner points** *with their point handles visible: a corner point with no handles (left), a corner point with two handles (middle), and a corner point with one handle (right).*

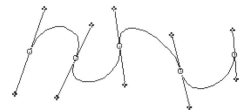

Figure 14. *Different **curve points** with their point handles visible. The length of the point handle governs the shape of the curve.*

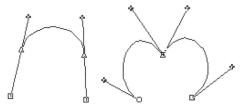

Figure 15. *Two types of **connector points** with their point handles visible: connector points between a straight line and a curved segment (left) and connector points between two curved segments (right).*

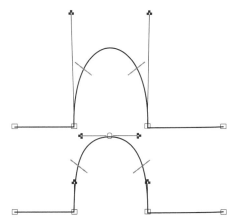

Figure 16. *You are breaking the **one-third rule** if the point handles for any segment extend more than one-third of the length (gray lines) of that segment (top). Add another point to reduce the length of the handles (bottom).*

Curve points

Curve points are anchor points that make a smooth, curved transition along the direction of the path. The length of the point handles governs the shape of the curve (**Figure 14**).

Connector points

The purpose of connector points is to constrain the transition between segments so that they cannot be moved out of a special alignment. There are two types of connector points: those that control the transition between a straight-line segment and a curved segment, and those that control the transition between two curved segments.

When there is a connector point between a straight-line segment and a curved segment, there is only one point handle which runs along the same direction as the straight line. When a connector point is between two curved segments, there are two point handles which are constrained by the position of the points on either side of the connector point (**Figure 15**).

The one-third rule

In general, you need only two curve points to create a curve on a path. If your curve is too steep, however, you will find that the point handles start to break the one-third rule. This rule states that the point handles for any segment should not extend more than one-third of the length of that segment (**Figure 16**).

What happens if you break the one-third rule? Well, no one will come to arrest you, but you will find it difficult to edit your curves with huge point handles that pivot all over the place.

The best way to learn about points is to convert them from one type to another. Fortunately, FreeHand provides a very simple way of doing this.

To manipulate and convert points using the Object Inspector:

1. Use the Freehand tool to create a wavy line with at least three anchor points.

2. Use the Selection tool to select one of the anchor points on the inside of the path. Notice that if you rotate the point handle on one side of the point, the other handle on the opposite side also moves. It is this "lever" action that makes the curve transition smooth (**Figure 17**).

3. Open the Object Inspector (Command-I) or choose Object from the Inspector submenu of the Window menu. Under Point type, you will see the Curve Point icon selected (**Figure 18**).

Figure 17. *A curve point with its point handles selected. Rotating one handle will also move the handle on the other side.*

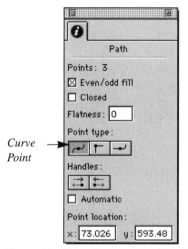

Curve Point →

Figure 18. *Object Inspector and the Curve Point icon selected as the Point type.*

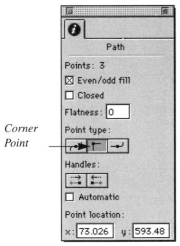

Corner
Point

Figure 19. *To change a point to a corner point, click on the **Corner Point** icon.*

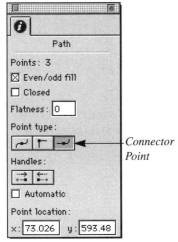

Figure 20. *Pressing and dragging the **point handles** of a **corner point** will change its shape.*

Connector
Point

Figure 21. *To change a point to a connector point, click on the **Connector Point** icon.*

4. Under Point type, click on the Corner Point icon (**Figure 19**). The point and the handles will not change shape, but the anchor point will change from a white circle to a white square. Use the Selection tool to drag one of the handles that extends from this point. You will see that you can create different shapes depending on how you move the handles (**Figure 20**).

5. To convert this point to a connector point, click on the Connector Point icon in the Object Inspector (**Figure 21**). You will notice that the white square has changed to a triangle (**Figure 22**). The two point handles that extend from the connector point cannot be moved from side to side but they can be lengthened.

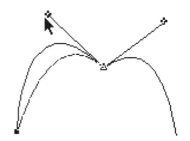

Figure 22. *A **connector point** is displayed as a white triangle.*

Manipulate and Convert Points

When you convert a curve point to a corner point, the corner point still has two point handles extending from it. To create a corner point with straight lines extending from it, you will need to retract both of the handles into the point.

To retract corner point handles using the Object Inspector:

1. Select a corner point with two point handles that extend out from it.

2. Click on one of the Handles icons in the Object Inspector (**Figure 23**). One of the point handles on the corner point will retract (**Figure 24**).

3. Click on the other Handles icon to retract the other handle.

4. If the points on either side are curve points, your line segment will not be straight. To make it straight, you need to retract the point handles for those curve points.

Once you've retracted the point handles, you can use the Object Inspector to extend those handles from the point.

To extend handles using the Object Inspector:

1. Click on the point from which you want to extend the point handles.

2. If it is a corner point, use the Point Type icons to convert it to either a curve point or a connector point.

3. Click on the Automatic checkbox under the Handles icons (**Figure 25**). If the point is a curve point, there will be two handles. If the point is a connector point, there will be one or two handles, depending on the shape of the path.

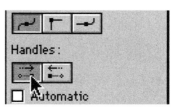

Figure 23. *To retract point handles, click on the* **Handles** *icons.*

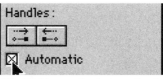

Figure 24. *When you click on the Handles icons in the Object Inspector, the point handles will retract into the point.*

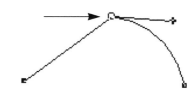

Figure 25. *Clicking on the* **Automatic** *checkbox will restore point handles to a curve or connector point.*

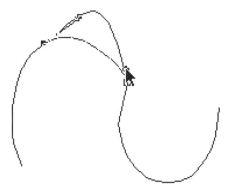

Figure 26. *You can manually drag a point handle back into its anchor point.*

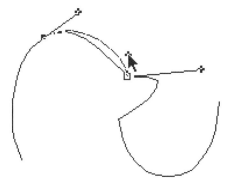

Figure 27. *Press the Option key and then dragging from a point allows you to manually extend point handles from that point.*

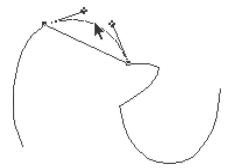

Figure 28. *Pressing the Option key and then dragging on a line segment allows you to manually extend point handles from both ends of the segment.*

You can also use the Selection tool to retract or extend handles from a point.

To retract handles manually:

1. Make a wavy line and select a point so that its handles are visible.

2. Place your Selection tool on the four dots at the end of the handle.

3. Drag the handle back into the anchor point (**Figure 26**).

To extend handles manually:

1. Click with the Selection tool to select the point from which you want to extend the handles.

2. Press the Option key, then drag out from the point. You should see the handle extending from the point (**Figure 27**).

3. If you press the Option key and then drag along the line segment, you will extend the point handles from both points on the segment (**Figure 28**).

Once you create an object's points or paths, you may find that you want to eliminate them. Though the procedure is the same for deleting both points and paths, the results are different.

To delete an object:

1. Choose the object so that all its anchor points are visible or its four group anchor points are visible.

2. Press the Delete key or choose Clear from the Edit menu. The object will be deleted.

To delete a point from a path:

1. Choose the point you want to delete so that the selected point is white and the other points are black.

2. Press the Delete key. (Do not choose Clear from the Edit menu or you will eliminate the entire object.) The point will be deleted and the path will be reshaped (**Figures 29a–b**).

To join points:

1. Choose two open paths.

2. Choose Join from the Modify menu. FreeHand will create a path between the two closest endpoints of the paths (**Figure 30**). If the two points are on top of each other, FreeHand will merge them into one point.

To split a point:

1. Choose a single point on a path.

2. Choose Split from the Modify menu. FreeHand will split the point into two points. These points will be on top of each other (**Figure 31**).

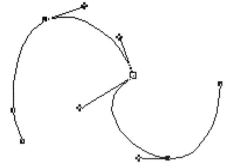

Figure 29a. *To delete a point from a path, select the point.*

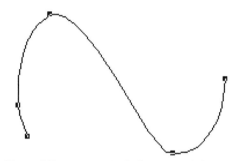

Figure 29b. *Pressing the **Delete** key will delete the selected point and reshape the path.*

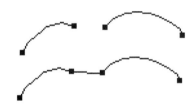

Figure 30. *The top path was selected and the **Join** command was applied connecting the points and creating the bottom path.*

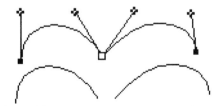

Figure 31. *The top path was selected and the **Split** command was applied, separating the paths (bottom).*

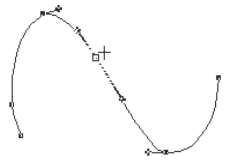

Figure 32. *To **add** a point, click with the **Pen** or the **Bézigon** tool on the path. A new point will appear at the spot where you clicked.*

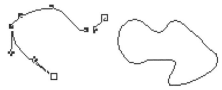

Figure 33. *An **open path** (left) has endpoints. A **closed path** (right) has no endpoints.*

Figure 34. *To close a path as you are drawing, simply bring your cursor over the first point you drew. The path will be closed.*

Adding a point to a path is a little more sophisticated. You will need to use either the Pen or the Bézigon tool.

To add a point to a path:

1. With the path selected, click on either the Pen or the Bézigon tool in the toolbox. (*For an explanation of the differences between these two tools, see Chapter 6, "Pen and Bézigon."*)

2. Move the plus sign (+) cursor close to the path. The small square next to the plus sign will turn into a small V. This indicates that the point will be placed on the path.

3. Click. A point will appear at the spot where you clicked (**Figure 32**).

4. You may now move or manipulate the point as you wish.

Tip

◆ If you click too far away from the path, you will create a new point that is not part of the path.

There are two types of paths you can create: open and closed. Open paths start at one point and end on another. Closed paths go round and round with no start or end. A piece of string is an example of an open path. A rubber band is an example of a closed path (**Figure 33**).

To close a path as you are drawing:

If you are drawing with the Freehand, the Pen, or the Bézigon tool, you can close a path by placing a point over the first point you drew (**Figure 34**).

Tip

◆ A small square will appear next to the cursor when you are about to close a path.

To close a path previously drawn:

If you have already created an open path and decide you want to close it, drag one of the endpoints onto the other. As soon as the points touch, FreeHand will close the path (**Figure 35**).

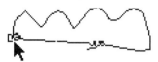

Figure 35. *To close a previously drawn path, drag one of the **endpoints** over the other.*

Tip

➡️ If Snap to Point is turned on, you will see a small square next to the cursor when you are precisely over the point to close the path.

To determine if a path is open or closed:

If you have selected a path, you can determine if it is open or closed by looking at the Object Inspector. Closed objects have the Closed checkbox filled. Open objects do not (**Figure 36**).

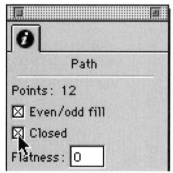

Figure 36. *A checkmark next to **Closed** in the **Object Inspector** indicates an open path. No checkmark indicates an open path.*

To open or close a path using the Object Inspector:

1. Click on the object you wish to change.

2. Choose the Object Inspector panel.

3. If you want to close the path, click on the blank Closed checkbox. (An "X" will appear, indicating that the path is closed.) The path will automatically be closed with a line that extends between the two endpoints (**Figure 37**).

4. If you want to open the path, click on the "X" in the Closed checkbox. The path will automatically be opened by deleting the segment between the two endpoints.

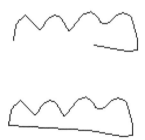

Figure 37. *Closing an open path (top) will automatically draw a line between the two endpoints (bottom).*

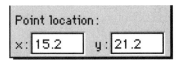

Figure 38. *If you select a single point, its x and y coordinates are listed at the bottom of the Object Inspector.*

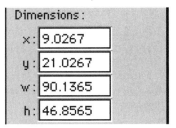

Figure 39. *If you have selected a grouped object, the x and y coordinates of the lower-left anchor points of the grouped object are listed in the Document Inspector.*

Once you have created an object, you may wish to reposition it or resize it. Though it is rather easy to just drag with the Selection tool to manually move a point or reshape an object, there may come a time when you will want to move or resize numerically.

To move a point or a grouped object numerically:

1. Click on the point or grouped object.

2. Choose the Object Inspector.

3. If you have chosen a point, you will see the information for that point on the path. At the bottom of the palette, you will see the x and y coordinates for your Point location (**Figure 38**).

4. If you have chosen a grouped object, you will see the dimensions for the group. At the top of these dimensions, you will see the x and y coordinates for the lower-left group anchor point (**Figure 39**).

5. Double-click on the x and y fields and enter the coordinates of the position where you would like your point or grouped object to be moved. Unless you have changed your zero point, the x coordinates start in the lower left of the page and increase as you move horizontally to the right. The y coordinates start in the lower left of the page and increase as you move up.

6. Press the Return or Enter key to set the new coordinates.

Tip

➭ If you wish to move an object numerically without grouping it, you can use the Move distance settings in the Transform palette (*see page 100*).

Move Points or Objects Numerically

To change the size of a grouped object numerically:

1. Select the grouped object.

2. Choose the Object Inspector.

3. In the middle of the palette you will see the width (w) and height (h) listed under the Dimensions. (**Figure 40**).

4. Double-click on the fields and enter the dimensions you would like the grouped object to be.

5. Press the Return or Enter key to set the new coordinates.

Tips

➡ All rectangles and ellipses are automatically grouped. However, they do not show the label Group in the Object Inspector.

➡ The dimensions for the x and y coordinates and the object's width and height are listed in the same unit of measurement as the document. (*To change the unit of measurement for your document, see page 8.*)

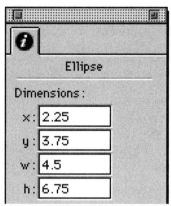

Figure 40. *The width (w) and height (h) dimensions of a grouped object are listed in the Object Inspector.*

PEN AND BÉZIGON

A s mentioned in Chapters 4 and 5, the Pen and the Bézigon tools allow you to draw much more precisely. In this chapter, you will learn the differences between the Pen and the Bézigon. You will learn how to make the different types of points with each tool. You will also learn the most efficient way to place points on different types of paths.

Figure 1. *The Pen tool in the toolbox.*

Figure 2. *The Bézigon tool in the toolbox.*

The difference between the Pen and the Bézigon tools

As you saw in Chapter 4, both the Pen (**Figure 1**) and the Bézigon (**Figure 2**) allow you to draw much more precisely than the Freehand tool. But the question is, What is the difference between the two tools? At first glance, there is very little difference. In fact, once a path has been created, there is no way to tell which tool created it. The main difference is that the Pen tool allows you to place points and manipulate their point handles at the same time. The Bézigon tool allows you to quickly click to place points, but all the points created with the Bézigon tool have their point handles set at the automatic settings. After you place points with the Bézigon tool, you must then go back to adjust their point handles.

Because so many beginners to FreeHand find the Pen tool daunting, the Bézigon is an excellent way to learn how to create precise paths. But if you wish to truly master FreeHand, you will need to become proficient with the Pen.

The exercises in this chapter are listed first for the Bézigon and then for the Pen. If there is no difference between the steps for both tools, then the exercise is listed only once.

To create an object with straight sides:

1. Choose either the Pen or the Bézigon from the toolbox.

2. Position the plus sign (+) cursor where you would like the object path to start. Click. You will see a corner point that appears as a white square (**Figure 3a**).

3. Position the plus sign (+) cursor where you would like the next point of the object to be. Click. You will see a line extending from the first point to the second corner point you have just created.

4. Continue clicking until you have created all the sides of your object (**Figure 3b**).

5. If you want to create a closed path, click again on the first point you created. FreeHand will close your path.

Tips

➻ If you have created an open path and wish to start a second path, you will need to deselect the first path. Press the Tab key. This will deselect your path and allow you to continue drawing.

➻ Press the Shift key while clicking to constrain your lines to a vertical or horizontal axis, or to a specific constrain angle. The default constrain angle is set in the Document Inspector as 0°. If you change the constrain setting, pressing the Shift key will constrain your artwork to the new angle (**Figure 4**).

Figure 3a. *Clicking with either the **Pen** or the **Bézigon** tool creates a **corner point** shown here as a hollow square.*

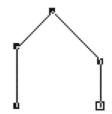

Figure 3b. *As you create more corner points, straight lines extend between them.*

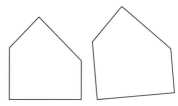

Figure 4. *An object drawn with a **constrain angle of 0°** (left) and the same object drawn with a **constrain angle of 15°** (right).*

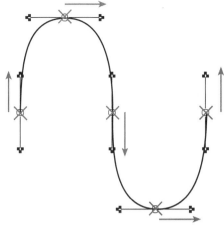

Figure 5. *A smooth curved path with its point handles visible. The point handles control how the curve is shaped. The gray arrows show how the path is dragged with the* **Pen**. *The "X's" show where the* **Bézigon** *is clicked while the* **Option** *key is being pressed.*

One of the benefits of drawing with the Pen and Bézigon tools is that you can draw perfectly smooth curves. A smooth curve is one where the transition from one direction to another is smooth, with no abrupt changes. Think of a smooth curve as the type of curve created by a rollercoaster. There are no abrupt changes as the track moves up and down. Though the process to create the points differs between the Pen and the Bézigon, both tools position their points at the same spots to create a smooth curved path (**Figure 5**).

To create a smooth curved path using the Bézigon tool:

1. Choose the Bézigon and press the Option key until you have finished drawing the path.

2. Start with the left point and click on each spot where the anchor points need to be (**Figure 5**).

3. Continue clicking until you have completed laying down the points.

4. Adjust the point handles so that the curve is the proper shape (**Figure 6**).

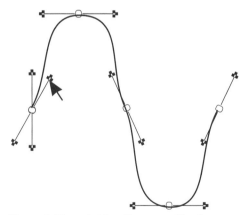

Figure 6. *The* **point handles** *created by the* **Bézigon** *tool need to be manually adjusted after they are formed.*

To create a smooth curved path using the Pen tool:

1. Choose the Pen.

2. Start with the left point and drag up (do not click) until you have created a point handle that extends about a third of the way up the curve you want to create (**Figure 7a**).

3. Continue dragging until you have completed laying down the points (**Figure 7b**). If you want to start a new path, press the Tab key to deselect the first path.

Tip

→ Start your drag and then press the Shift key to constrain your point handles to horizontal or vertical lines.

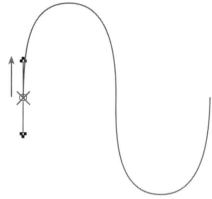

Figure 7a. *To draw a smooth curved path with the Pen tool, drag up until you have created a point handle that extends a third of the way up the curve you want to create. (In the rest of this chapter, the light gray line indicates the intended paths.)*

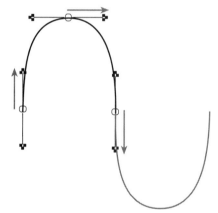

Figure 7b. *The point handles created by the Pen tool can be positioned correctly by dragging in the proper direction (indicated by gray arrows).*

Smooth Curved Path with Pen

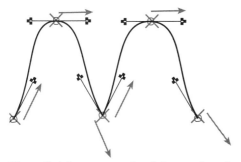

Figure 8. *A bumpy curved path is one where the curve abruptly changes direction.*

Life is not all smooth and neither are most curved paths. So, there will be times you will need to create a bumpy curved path. Think of a bumpy curve as the path a bouncing ball would take. The abrupt change is where the ball hits the ground and then bounces back up (**Figure 8**).

To draw a bumpy curved path with the Bézigon tool:

1. The first point is a corner point, so click with the Bézigon tool (**Figure 9a**).

2. The next point is a curve point, so press the Option key as you click (**Figure 9b**).

3. The third point is a corner point, so click (**Figure 9c**). Notice that there are point handles from the corner points. This is because FreeHand automatically extends handles out from corner points that are connected to curve points.

4. The fourth point is a curve point, so press the Option key as you click.

5. The last point is a corner point, so click with the Bézigon tool.

6. Manually adjust the point handles until the curved path is the shape you want.

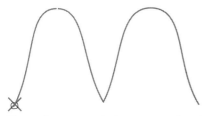

Figure 9a. *To start the bumpy curved path, click with the Bézigon tool. This creates a **corner point**.*

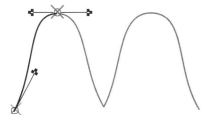

Figure 9b. *To continue the bumpy curved path, **Option-click** with the Bézigon tool. This creates a **curve point**.*

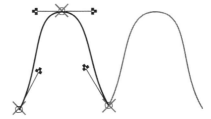

Figure 9c. *To continue the bumpy curved path, click with the Bézigon tool. This creates a **corner point**. Notice that FreeHand automatically fills in handles when a corner point is connected to a curve point.*

To draw a bumpy curved path with the Pen tool:

1. Press the Option key as you drag with the Pen to create the first corner point with a handle (**Figure 10a**).

2. Drag to create the second point, a curve point (**Figure 10b**).

3. Drag down at the third point. You will see the point handle extend from the point. Do not let go of the mouse.

4. When this point handle has extended backward enough, press the Option key. Rotate the front point handle so that it is aligned in the proper direction (**Figure 10c**).

5. Drag to create the fourth point, a curve point.

6. Drag to create the final point. You will see the point handle extend from the point. Do not let go of the mouse.

7. When this point handle has been extended backward enough, release the mouse.

8. Press the Option key and click on the final point. This will retract the point handle extending from it.

Figure 10a. *To start the bumpy curved path, press the **Option** key and drag with the **Pen** tool. This creates a **corner point** with a handle extending up.*

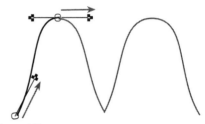

Figure 10b. *To continue the bumpy curved path, drag with the Pen tool at the top of the bump. This creates a **curve point**.*

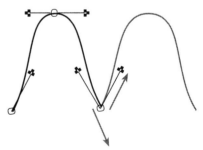

Figure 10c. *To continue the bumpy curved path, drag with the Pen tool. When the handle extends backward enough, press the Option key and then drag in the direction of the second arrow pointing to the upper right. This creates a corner point with two handles.*

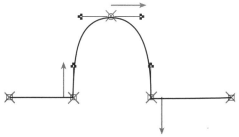

Figure 11. *A straight-to-bumpy path with its point handles visible. The arrows indicate the direction of the drags with the* **Pen**. *The "X's" indicate where the* **Bézigon** *is clicked.*

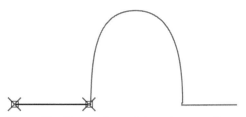

Figure 12a. *To start the straight-to-bumpy path, click with the Bézigon tool at the first two positions. This creates two corner points.*

Imagine you are riding in a car, and there is suddenly a bump in the road. Then the road continued smoothly. That's the shape of a straight-to-bumpy path (**Figure 11**).

To draw a straight-to-bumpy path with the Bézigon tool:

1. The first point is a corner point, so click with the Bézigon tool where the first point should be.

2. The next point is a corner point, so click with the Bézigon tool. To constrain the line as you click, press the Shift key (**Figure 12a**).

3. The third point is a curve point, so Option-click with the Bézigon tool where you want the top of the bump to be (**Figure 12b**).

4. The fourth point is a corner point, so click with the Bézigon tool.

5. The last point is a corner point, so click with the Bézigon tool (**Figure 12c**).

6. Manually adjust the point handles to the shape you want. Notice that point handles were automatically added to the points created in Steps 2 and 4.

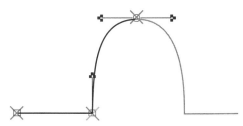

Figure 12b. *To continue the straight-to-bumpy path, press the Option key as you click with the Bézigon tool. This creates a* **curve point** *at the top of the curve.*

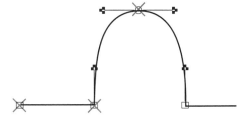

Figure 12c. *To continue the straight-to-bumpy path, click with the* **Bézigon** *tool at the last two positions. This creates two* **corner points**.

To draw a straight-to-bumpy path with the Pen tool:

1. The first point is a corner point, so click with the Pen tool where the first point should be (**Figure 13a**).

2. The next point is a corner point with one handle extending from it, so press the Option key first, then drag with the Pen tool (**Figure 13b**).

3. The third point is a curve point, so drag with the Pen tool where you want the top of the bump to be.

4. The next point has a handle extending up, so drag with the Pen tool to create a curve point with two handles. Release your mouse when you are satisfied with the length of the handle extending into the curve.

5. You need to convert the curve point you just created into a corner point with one handle. Press the Option key and click on the point you created in Step 4. This will convert the point into a corner point and retract the second handle coming out of the point (**Figure 13c**).

6. The last point is a corner point, so click where you want that point located.

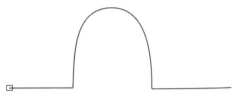

Figure 13a. *To start the straight-to-bumpy path, click with the **Pen** tool at the first position. This creates a **corner point**.*

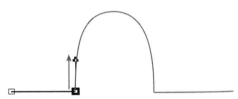

Figure 13b. *To make a **corner point with only one handle** with the Pen tool, press the Option key and then start your drag on the point indicated (bold outlined dot).*

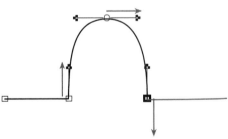

Figure 13c. *To convert a curve point into a corner point with only one handle, press the **Option** key and click again on the point indicated (bold outlined dot). This will retract the forward handle coming out of the point, leaving just the one shown.*

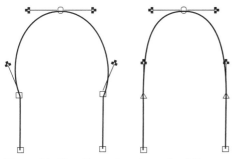

Figure 14. *This illustration shows the difference between using **corner points** as the transition between segments (left) and using **connector points** (right).*

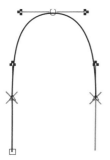

Figure 15. *To create connector points with the **Bézigon** tool, press the **Control** key as you click. (The connector points are indicated by "X's.")*

In FreeHand, connector points are used to create a smooth transition between a straight-line segment and a curved segment. Connector points are indicated by a triangle (**Figure 14**).

To create connector points using the Bézigon or the Pen tools:

1. With the Bézigon tool, press the Control key and click. This will create a connector point. The handle will be automatically created and aligned when you create the segment that follows (**Figure 15**).

2. With the Pen tool, press the Control key and drag to create a connector point with a handle that extends out from the point. The handle will automatically be aligned with the straight-line segment that precedes it.

3. With the Pen tool, hold the Control key and click to create a connector point with a handle that extends backward from the point. The handle will automatically align when you create the straight-line segment that follows it (**Figure 16**).

Figure 16. *To create connector points with the **Pen** tool, press the Control key as you drag to create handles that extend out from the point (indicated by a gray arrow). Press the Control key as you click to create handles that extend backward from the point (indicated by "X").*

You may finish creating a path and later realize you want to add more segments to it. You will need to add points to the end of the path. (This only works with open paths. Closed paths have no endpoints.)

To add points to the end of a path:

1. Select the path you want to add to.

2. Select one of the path's endpoints so that it is white.

3. Click or drag with the Pen or the Bézigon tool at the spot where you want the next point to occur (**Figure 17**). FreeHand will fill in the line segment. You can then continue adding segments as needed.

Tip

●◆ Other path operations, such as joining two open paths together, splitting paths, and cutting paths, are covered in Chapter 16, "Path Operations."

Figure 17. *To continue a path, select one of the endpoints. Then click or drag with the* **Pen** *or* **Bézigon** *tool where you would like the next point to be (indicated by "X").*

MOVE & TRANSFORM

Just because you've created an object doesn't mean you can't change it. In fact, by moving and transforming your objects you can create very sophisticated effects. In this chapter, you will learn: how to move objects; how to copy as you move; and how to move, scale, rotate, skew, and reflect objects both by eye and numerically. We will cover what the settings on the Info Bar mean. You will learn how to cut, copy and paste objects and the difference between the Cut, Copy, and Paste commands and the Clone and Duplicate commands. Finally, you will also explore the technique called "Power Duplicating."

As discussed on page 65, you can move an object by simply selecting it and dragging it anywhere on your page. If you would like to know the distance and the position of the object you are dragging, you can see that information in the Info Bar at the top of your document window.

To read the Info Bar:

1. Choose Info Bar from the View menu or press Command-Shift-R to show the Info Bar (**Figure 1a**).

(Continued on the following page)

Info Bar

Figure 1a. *The Info Bar is shown at the top of the document window.*

2. The Info Bar readings change depending on the position of your cursor, the tool chosen, or the action taken (**Figure 1b**). The following are explanations of the various categories on the Info Bar.

padlock: indicates the selected object or objects are locked.

units: indicates the current unit of measurement

x: position of cursor along the horizontal axis

y: position of cursor along the vertical axis

dx: horizontal distance you have moved an object

dy: vertical distance you have moved an object

dist: total distance along any angle you have moved an object

angle: angle along which any object is being moved, created, or transformed

cx: horizontal location of the center point around which any object is being created or transformed

cy: vertical location of the center point that any object is being created or transformed around.

sx: horizontal scale or skew of an object expressed as a ratio to object's original size (e.g., 1.00 = 100%)

sy: vertical scale or skew of an object expressed as a ratio to object's original size (e.g., 1.00 = 100%)

width: width of rectangle or ellipse.

height: height of rectangle or ellipse

radius: size of radius of polygon

sides: number of sides of polygon

Note: The Info Bar does not allow you to enter numbers directly into it.

🔒 units: inches

x:5.699732 y:7.111112

dx:1.843908 dy:4.555556

dist:0.58195 angle:83

cx:4.010576 cy:8.621686

sx:0.33 sy:0.46

width:2.13360 height:3.42195

radius:1.343478 sides:5

Figure 1b. *Other displays which are seen on the Info Bar.*

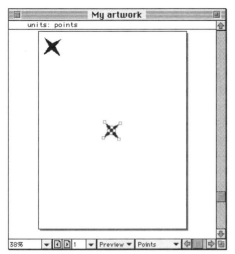

Figure 2. *An object that is cut or copied from one position (upper left) will be pasted in the **center of the window**.*

Figure 3a. *To make an Option-copy of an object, hold the **Option** key as you move the object. You will see an **arrow with a plus sign (+) cursor** as you drag.*

To cut, copy, or paste objects:

Once you have selected an object, you can choose Cut (Command-X) or Copy (Command-C) from the File menu. You can then choose Paste (Command-V) from the File menu to paste the object onto the same page, a different page, or a different document. The object will be pasted in the center of the window (**Figure 2**).

To move and copy an object:

1. Select the object you want to copy.

2. Start dragging the object. Press the Option key as you drag. You will see an arrow with a plus sign (+) cursor (**Figure 3a**). This indicates that you are creating a copy of the object.

3. When the object is in the position you want, release the mouse first, then the Option key. The original object will be in its position and a copy will be at the point where you stopped dragging (**Figure 3b**).

4. If you choose Duplicate from the Edit menu or press Command-D, you will continue to make copies of the original object, each positioned the same distance away from the previous copy (**Figure 3c**).

Figure 3c. *If you choose **Duplicate** from the **Edit** menu or press **Command-D** after you have made an Option-copy of an object, you will continue to create additional copies of the object.*

Figure 3b. *When you let go of the Option key after you move an object, you will have an exact duplicate of the object.*

Cut, Copy, or Paste; Move and Copy

The transformation tools allow you to modify simple objects into more sophisticated shapes. Rotation allows you to change the orientation of an object.

To rotate an object by eye:

1. Select the object you want to rotate and click the Rotating tool in the toolbox (**Figure 4a**).

2. Move your cursor over to the work page. Your cursor will turn into a star.

3. Position the star on the spot around which you would like the object to rotate. This is considered the transformation point. For instance, if you want to rotate an object around its lower-left corner, place the star on the lower-left corner of the object (**Figure 4b**).

4. Press down on the point you have chosen. Do not let go of the mouse. You will see a line extend out from the transformation point. This is the rotation axis (**Figure 4c**).

5. Still pressing down, drag your cursor away from the transformation point. Then move the rotation axis. You will see your object rotate as you change the rotation axis (**Figure 4d**).

6. Hold down the Shift key to constrain your rotation to 45° increments.

7. Release the mouse when you are satisfied with the position of the rotated object. Your object will now be rotated into position (**Figure 4e**).

Figure 4a. *To rotate an object by eye, click on the Rotating tool in the toolbox.*

Figure 4b. *When you choose the Rotating tool, your cursor turns into a star. Position the star on the point you want the object to rotate around.*

Figure 4c. *Pressing down with the Rotating tool shows the rotation axis, the line that the object will be rotated around.*

Figure 4d. *As you drag the object to be rotated, the rotation axis and the preview shows the position to which the object will be rotated.*

Figure 4e. *The original object rotated by eye.*

Rotate by Eye

Figure 5. *When you perform a rotation or a reflection, move your cursor along the line to a point away from the transformation point (circled). This will make it easier to control the transformation.*

Figure 6a. *To scale an object by eye, click on the **Scaling** tool in the toolbox.*

Figure 6b. *When you choose the Scaling tool, your cursor turns into a **star**. Position the star on the point from which you want the object to scale.*

Figure 6c. *As you press down with the Scaling tool and then drag, you will see an **outline** of the object that indicates the scaling of the object.*

Figure 6d. *The original object scaled by eye.*

Tip

➡️ The farther you drag your cursor away from the transformation point during rotation or reflection, the easier it will be to control its transformation (**Figure 5**).

Scaling allows you to change the size and proporations of an object.

To scale an object by eye:

1. Choose the object you want to scale and click on the Scaling tool in the toolbox (**Figure 6a**).

2. Move your cursor over to the work page. Your cursor will turn into a star (**Figure 6b**).

3. Position the star on the spot from which you would like the object to scale. This is considered the transformation point. For instance, if you want to have an object grow from the bottom up, you would place the star on the bottom edge of the object.

4. Press down on the point you have chosen. Do not let go of the mouse.

5. Still pressing down, drag your cursor away from the transformation point. You will see an outline of your object change its size as you move the cursor (**Figure 6c**).

6. Hold down the Shift key to constrain the scale to a proportional change.

7. Release the mouse when you are satisfied with the size of the scaled object. Your object will now be scaled into position (**Figure 6d**).

Scale by Eye

Reflection allows you to create a mirror image of an object. This is very helpful when making shadows.

To reflect an object by eye:

1. Choose the object you want to reflect and click on the Reflecting tool in the toolbox (**Figure 7a**).

2. Move your cursor over to the work page. Your cursor will turn into a star.

3. Position the star on the point around which you want the object to reflect (**Figure 7b**). This is considered the transformation point. For instance, if you want to reflect an object around a spot to the right of the object, place the star on that spot.

4. Press down on the point you have chosen. Do not let go of the mouse. You will see a line extend out from the star. This line is the reflection axis (**Figure 7c**). Think of the reflection axis as the mirror in which your object is being reflected.

5. Still pressing down, drag your cursor away from the transformation point. You will see an outline of your object change its position and shape as you move the cursor (**Figure 7d**).

6. Hold down the Shift key to constrain your reflection to 45° increments.

7. Release the mouse when you are satisfied with the position of the reflected object. Your object will now be reflected into position (**Figure 7e**).

Figure 7a. *To reflect an object by eye, click on the **Reflecting** tool in the toolbox.*

Figure 7b. *When you choose the Reflecting tool, your cursor turns into a **star**. Position the star on the point you want the object to reflect around.*

Figure 7c. *Pressing down with the Reflecting tool shows the **reflection axis**. The reflection axis is the line around which the object will be reflected around.*

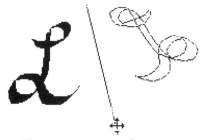

Figure 7d. *As you drag, the **reflection axis** and **preview** show the position to which the object will be reflected.*

Figure 7e. *Releasing the mouse will reflect the object to the new position.*

Reflect by Eye

Figure 8a. *To skew an object by eye, click on the Skewing tool in the toolbox.*

Figure 8b. *When you choose the Skewing tool, your cursor turns into a **star**. Position the star on the point from which you want the object to skew.*

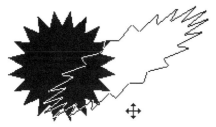

Figure 8c. *As you press down with the Skewing tool and then drag, you will see an **outline** of the object, which indicates the skewing of the object.*

Figure 8d. *The original object skewed by eye.*

Skewing (sometimes called shearing) is a way of altering an object along an axis. This is type of distortion is very common when making shadows.

To skew an object by eye:

1. Choose the object you want to skew and click on the Skewing tool in the toolbox (**Figure 8a**).

2. Move your cursor over to the work page. Your cursor will turn into a star.

3. Position the star on the spot from which you would like the object to skew (**Figure 8b**). This is considered the transformation point. For instance, if you want to skew an object around its lower-left corner, you would place the star on the lower-left corner of the object.

4. Press down on the point you have chosen. Do not let go of the mouse.

5. Still pressing down, drag your cursor away from the transformation point. You will see an outline of your object change its shape as you move the cursor (**Figure 8c**).

6. Hold the Shift key to constrain the skew. If you drag in a general horizontal direction, the skew will be constrained exactly horizontal. If you drag in a general vertical direction, the skew will be constrained exactly vertical.

7. Release the mouse when you are satisfied with the position of the skewed object. Your object will now be skewed into position (**Figure 8d**).

Skew by Eye

To copy as you transform an object:

Start dragging the object you want to copy as you make the transformation. You will see a plus sign (+) next to the star cursor. Let go of the mouse first, then the Option key, to create a copy of the original object transformed to the position you chose (**Figure 9a**). If you do not see the plus sign (+), check the Preferences settings for Object Editing (*see page 261*). Choose Duplicate from the Edit menu or press Command-D (**Figure 9b**) to create additional transformed copies.

Figure 9a. *If you hold down the **Option** key while performing any of the transformations, you will see a **plus sign** (+) next to your cursor. When you let go of the mouse, you will have a copy of the original object transformed into position.*

Figure 9b. *Once you have made a copy by holding down the Option key, choosing **Duplicate** from the **Edit** menu or pressing **Command-D** will create additional transformed copies of the object.*

Copy as You Transform

Figure 10a. *To do a **Power Duplication**, you need to clone your object. Choose **Clone** from the **Edit** menu or press **Command-=**.*

Figure 10b. *Perform the **first transformation** on the clone. In this case, the object was rotated.*

Figure 10c. *Perform any **additional transformations** to the clone. In this case, the object was scaled.*

Figure 10d. *Choose **Duplicate** from the **Edit** menu or press **Command-D**. You will create new copies, each one with all transformations applied. In this case, the two transformations have created new objects that move in a circle and grow bigger.*

FreeHand offers a sophisticated technique called "Power Duplicating." This allows you to "store" up to five transformations: move, rotate, scale, reflect and skew. You can then apply all the transformations together as you make copies.

To use the transformation tools for Power Duplicating:

1. Choose the object you want to transform.

2. Choose Clone from the Edit menu or press Command-=. You have just created a clone (copy) of your object that is on top of the original (**Figure 10a**).

3. Move this clone with your arrow, or use any of the transformation tools to modify the clone (**Figure 10b**).

4. If you wish, you can apply any of the other transformations (**Figure 10c**). You cannot apply a transformation function more than once.

5. Each of the transformations you have performed is now stored. There is a limit of five transformations that can be stored.

6. Choose Duplicate from the Edit menu or press Command-D. The object you created will be copied according to the transformations you stored.

7. Choose Duplicate again and again. Each command will create a new object transformed according to the stored transformation settings (**Figure 10d**).

8. If you deselect the object before choosing Duplicate, you will not be able to make the Power Duplication.

So far, we've done our transformations by eye. If you've got a steady hand and a keen eye on the Info Bar, you can be pretty precise. To easily work even more precisely though, you need to use the Transform panel.

To view the Transform panel:

Choose Transform panel submenu of the the Window menu, press Command-M, or double click on any of the transformation tools in the toolbox. The Transform panel will appear.

To move an object using the Transform panel:

1. Choose the object you want to move. Click on the Move icon in the Transform panel (**Figure 11**).

2. Enter the distance amounts you want to move the object in the x and y fields.

3. Check either the Contents or the Fills settings to have any contents or fills moved along with the path (*see Chapter 9, "Fills" or Chapter 16, "Path Operations"*).

4. Click on the Apply button, or press the Return or the Enter key to apply the move.

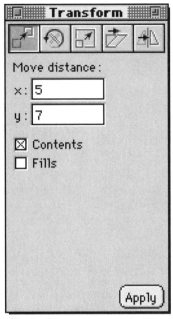

Figure 11. *The Move settings in the Transform panel let you move objects numerically. Click on the Move icon in the Transform panel to see the Move distance settings.*

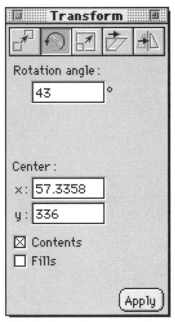

Figure 12a. *The Rotation settings of the* *Transform panel.*

To rotate an object using the Transform panel:

1. Choose the object you want to rotate. Click on the Rotation icon in the Transform panel (**Figure 12a**).

2. Enter the angle amount you want to rotate the object in the Rotation angle field.

3. To change the point of transformation from the center, enter the coordinates you want in the x and y fields. (If you need to know the coordinates for a certain point, position your cursor over that point and look at the x and y listings in the Info Bar.)

4. Check either the Contents or the Fills settings to have any contents or fills rotated along with the path (**Figure 12b**).

5. Click the Apply button, or press the Return or Enter key to apply the rotation.

Figure 12b. *The top whale was rotated to the* *bottom two positions. The left position had the* **Contents box checked** *so the pasted-in lines* *rotated with the object. The right position had* *the* **Contents box unchecked** *so the pasted-in* *lines did not rotate with the object.*

Rotate Using Transform Panel

To scale an object using the Transform panel:

1. Choose the object you want to scale. Click on the Scale icon in the Transform panel (**Figure 13a**).

2. Enter the scale amount you want to change the object. For a proportional scale, keep the Uniform box checked. To scale the object nonproportionally, deselect the Uniform box and fill in the settings for the x (horizontal) and y (vertical) fields.

3. To change the point of transformation from the center, enter the coordinates in the x and y fields.

4. Check the Contents, the Fills, or the Lines settings to have any contents, fills, or strokes scaled along with the path (**Figure 13b**).

5. Click the Apply button, or press the Return or Enter key to apply the scale.

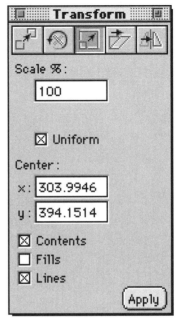

Figure 13a. *The Scale settings of the Transform panel.*

Figure 13b. *The top cookie jar was scaled to the bottom three jars. The left jar had the **Fills box checked** so the pattern tile scaled with the object. The middle jar had the **Fills box unchecked** so the pattern tile did not scale with the object. The right jar was scaled with the **Uniform setting unchecked**.*

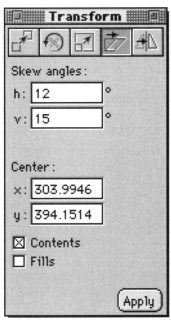

Figure 14. *The Skew settings of the **Transform** panel.*

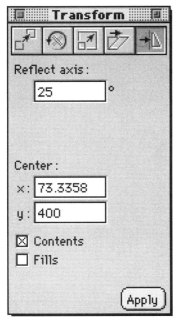

Figure 15. *The Reflection settings of the* **Transform** *panel.*

To skew an object using the Transform panel:

1. Choose the object you want to skew. Click on the Skew icon in the Transform panel (**Figure 14**).

2. Enter the horizontal angle amount of the skew in the h field. Enter the vertical amount of the skew in the the v field.

3. To change the point of transformation from the center, enter the coordinates you want in the x and y fields.

4. Check either the Contents or the Fills settings to have any contents or fills skewed along with the path .

5. Click the Apply button, or press the Return or Enter key to apply the skew.

To reflect an object using the Transform panel:

1. Choose the object you want to reflect. Click on the Reflection icon in the Transform panel (**Figure 15**).

2. Enter the angle amount that you want the object to reflect around in the Reflect axis field.

3. To change the point of transformation from the center, enter the coordinates you want in the x and y fields.

4. Check the Contents or Fills settings to have them reflected along with the path.

5. Click the Apply button, or press the Return or Enter key to apply the reflection.

Skew Using Transform Panel;
Reflect Using Transform Panel

As you draw, move, or transform objects, FreeHand positions the objects along an invisible axis called the Constrain axis. The default setting of this axis is 0°. This means that your objects line up in an oridinary horizontal fashion. However, by changing the Constrain axis, you can make all your objects automatically align along any angle you choose.

To change the Constrain axis:

1. Choose Constrain from the Modify menu. The Constrain dialog box will appear (**Figure 16**).

2. Enter the angle you want for the Constrain axis by typing the amount in the Angle field or by rotating the wheel. Click OK. All your objects will be drawn along the angle you have just set (**Figure 17**).

Tip

•◦ Changing the Constrain axis will only affect those objects created from that point on. It will not affect any previously created objects.

Figure 16. *Use the* **Constrain** *dialog box to change the horizontal axis along which objects are drawn.*

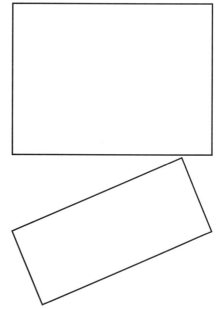

Figure 17. *The top rectangle was drawn with a* **Constrain axis** *of 0°. The bottom rectangle had a Constrain axis of 23°.*

WORKING IN COLOR

One of the most versatile parts of FreeHand is the way it works with color. In this chapter, you will learn how to define colors in the Color Mixer using FreeHand's color systems: CMYK, RGB, HLS, Tint, and the Macintosh color settings and wheel. You will also learn how to use FreeHand's Color List to add a color; rename a color; convert process and spot colors; move, duplicate, or remove colors; make a tint; and add multiple colors. Finally, this chapter will cover how to work with color-matching libraries and how to create a custom color library.

There are two different panels that control most of the color functions in FreeHand: (1) The Color List panel is where all the colors in your FreeHand document are stored. (2) The Color Mixer panel is where you can define new colors. We'll start with the various ways to define colors using the Color Mixer and then describe how to add them to the Color List.

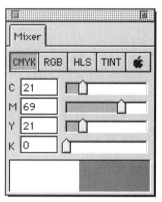

Figure 1. *The Color Mixer in the CMYK mode.*

Five ways to define colors in the Color Mixer:

1. **CMYK**: Defines the color according to the four process colors used by most commercial printers—Cyan, Magenta, Yellow, and Black. This is the most common and best-known color system used by graphic artists (**Figure 1**).

2. **RGB**: Defines the color according to Red, Green, and Blue components. This is primarily a video color system; many people who design for multimedia and the World Wide Web use RGB to define colors (**Figure 2**).

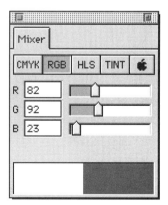

Figure 2. *The Color Mixer in the RGB mode.*

3. HLS: Defines the color according to Hue, Lightness, and Saturation components (**Figure 3**). This system lets you pick different colors with similar values. Pastel colors are examples of colors with similar lightness and saturation but different hues.

4. Tint: Takes a previously defined color and displays the different tints available for that color (**Figure 4**).

5. : Shows the Macintosh color settings and wheel (**Figure 5**).

Which color system to use:

If you are defining a color for use in a four-color printing process, you will most likely want to use the CMYK color system to define your colors. But if you are trying to match colors that are defined by applications that use other systems, you should use those systems when defining your colors.

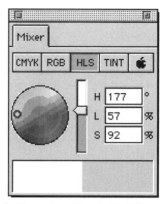

Figure 3. *The Color Mixer in the HLS mode.*

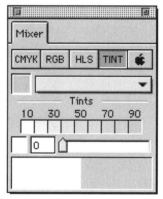

Figure 4. *The Color Mixer in the Tint mode.*

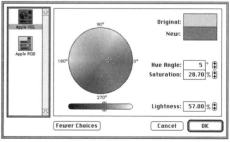

Figure 5. *The Macintosh color settings and wheel, shown when the is chosen.*

(side margin) Define Colors in Color Mixer; Color Systems

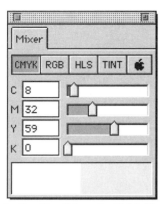

Figure 6a. *Double-click on the C, M, Y, and K fields to enter exact values for your color.*

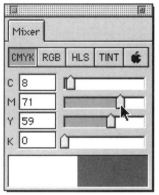

Figure 6b. *Use the **sliders** to change the CMYK values of your color.*

Figure 6c. *In HLS, click on the **color wheel** to define the hue and saturation. Use the slider to adjust the lightness.*

To define a color:

1. Choose Color Mixer from the Panel submenu of the Window menu or press Command-Shift-C.

2. Click on the mode you want to use.

3. In the CMYK mode, double-click in the C, M, Y, and K fields to enter the color values (**Figure 6a**). Once a field is highlighted, use the Tab key to move from one field to another.

or

In the CMYK mode, drag the sliders to change the values of the colors (**Figure 6b**).

or

In the HLS mode, click on the desired portion of the color wheel (**Figure 6c**).

Tips

➥ If the Mixer is not displayed, double-click on any color swatch in the Colors panel (*see page 108*) to display the Mixer.

➥ If the Mixer is displayed, double-click on any color swatch in the Colors panel to hide the Mixer.

Define a Color

Once you've defined a color, you will want to store that color in your document. To do this, you need to use the Colors panel.

To add a color to the Colors panel:

1. Choose Colors (Command-9) from the Panel submenu of the Window menu.

or

Double-click on the bottom color area of the Color Mixer to open the Colors panel.

2. Place your arrow on the color square created in the Mixer. Drag that color off the Mixer (**Figure 7**).

3. Once you have dragged the color off the Mixer, you can drop it onto the Colors drop box (**Figure 8a**).

or

Choose New from the Options pop-up menu (**Figure 8b**). The color defined in the Color Mixer will be added to the Colors panel.

or

Drop the color into the Colors panel (**Figure 8c**). This allows you to position new colors where you would like them.

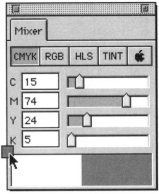

Figure 7. *To store a color, drag the color off the Color Well, which is in the bottom area of the Color Mixer panel.*

Figure 8a. *To add colors to the Colors panel, you can drop them into the color drop box.*

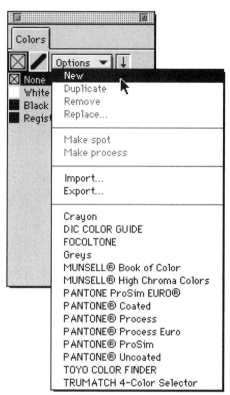

Tip

↬ Once you have added a new color to the Colors panel, you will see that the color is named according to its CMYK values. Even if you define the color using one of the other modes, such as RGB, the color will be displayed in the Colors panel according to the CMYK values.

Figure 8b. *To add colors to the Colors panel, you can choose* **New** *from the Colors* **Options** *pop-up menu.*

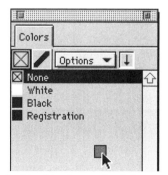

Figure 8c. *To add colors to the Colors panel, you can drop the color swatch onto the* **Color List** *in the spot you would like the color to appear.*

To rename a color:

1. Double-click on the name of the color in the Colors panel. The name will appear highlighted, indicating that it is selected (**Figure 9a**).

2. Type the new name for the color (**Figure 9b**).

3. Press Return, or click on another color in the Colors panel. The color will now be renamed (**Figure 9c**).

Figure 9a. *To rename a color in the Color List, double-click on the name of the color that is to be renamed. This will highlight the name.*

Figure 9b. *Type the new name for the color.*

Figure 9c. *Press **Return** or click on another color.*

Figure 10a. *Process colors are listed in an **italic** typeface in the Color List. **Spot** colors are listed in a **roman** typeface.*

All colors you define in the Mixer come as process colors, which means they will be broken down into CMYK color plates during the separation process. If you want, you can change colors from process to spot. Spot colors will not be broken down into their CMYK values; they will be separated onto their own plates.

To convert process and spot colors:

1. Click on the name of the color in the Colors panel. Process colors are written in italic type; spot colors are written in roman type (**Figure 10a**).

2. If the color is a process color, choose Make spot from the Options pop-up menu (**Figure 10b**).

3. If the color is a spot color, choose Make process from the Options pop-up menu (**Figure 10c**).

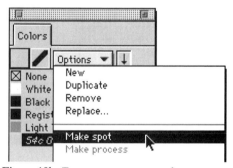

Figure 10b. *To convert a process color to spot, choose **Make spot** from the **Options** pop-up menu.*

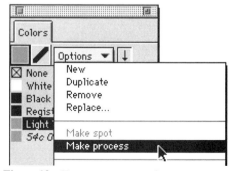

Figure 10c. *To convert a spot color to process, choose **Make process** from the **Options** pop-up menu.*

Convert Process and Spot Colors

If you're working with a lot of colors, you'll likely want to list your favorite colors at the top of the Colors panel. Or, you may want to group certain colors together. To do so, you can move the colors around in the Color panel.

To move colors in the Colors panel:

1. Press on the name of the color you want to move.

2. Drag it to the new position and then release the mouse (**Figure 11**).

To duplicate a color:

1. Click on the name of the color you wish to duplicate.

2. Choose Duplicate from the Options pop-up menu (**Figure 12**). The color will be duplicated with the name as "Copy of [Color Name]."

To remove a color:

1. Click on the name of the color you wish to remove. The name will be highlighted.

2. If you want to remove a group of colors listed together, click on the top name, hold down the Shift key, and click on the bottom name. All the names will be highlighted.

3. Choose Remove from the Options pop-up menu (**Figure 13**). All the highlighted colors will be removed.

Figure 11. *To move a color to a new position in the Colors panel, drag the color and then release the mouse.*

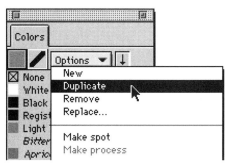

Figure 12. *Choose **Duplicate** from the **Options** pop-up menu to make a copy of the selected color.*

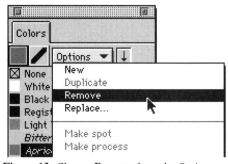

Figure 13. *Choose **Remove** from the Options pop-up menu to remove all selected colors from the Color List.*

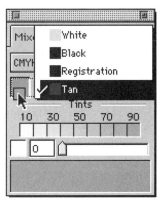

Figure 14a. *To create a tint of a base color, drag the swatch of that color from the* **Colors** *panel into the* **Tint** *drop box of the* **Color Mixer** *or press on the pop-up menu to choose the color*

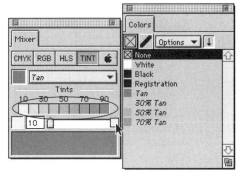

Figure 14b. *To store a tint in the Color List, drag one of the tint swatch boxes (circled) from the Color Mixer.*

Figure 14c. *To put a tint swatch in the Colors panel, drop the swatch on the Colors drop box or on the list itself.*

If you have defined a color, you can use that color as the basis for a tint. This is useful if you are working with spot colors and wish to apply tints of those colors.

To make a tint of a color:

1. Make sure both the Colors panel and the Tint mode of the Color Mixer are displayed.

2. Place your arrow on the color swatch—not on the name—of the color you want to create a tint of. Drag the color swatch from the Colors panel and put it onto the drop box at the top left of the Mixer Tint area or press on the pop-up menu to choose the color (**Figure 14a**).

3. Drag one of the tint swatch boxes from the Mixer back into to the Colors panel (**Figure 14b**).

4. Drop the tint swatch onto the Colors panel drop box or onto the list itself (**Figure 14c**).

5. The tint will be listed as a percentage of the color's name.

Tip

•◆ If you change a base color from process to spot (and vice versa), any tints defined from that base color will change from process to spot.

So far you have been adding colors to the Colors panel one at a time. Though this is fine for one or two colors, it could be laborious if you need to add many colors. FreeHand has other ways of adding colors to the Color List.

To add colors from copied objects:

If you have created an object with a named color in one FreeHand file, and you copy and paste that object into another file, the color will be added to the Colors panel.

To add colors from imported EPS files:

If you import an EPS file that uses named colors, those named colors will be added to the Colors panel (*for more information about importing images, see pages 227–230*).

Color-matching system libraries

FreeHand supplies you with various pre-made color libraries (**Figure 15a**) that are used by many commercial printers, artists, and designers. These color libraries may be either process or spot. They are customarily used with printed swatches that allow you to pick a color from the library and compare it to a specific color.

Some of the color-matching systems that ship with FreeHand include Pantone (both process and spot), Trumatch (process), and Toyo (process).

In addition, FreeHand supplies a Library of colors called Crayon. FreeHand also supplies a Library of colors called "Greys," which are both spot and process gray colors separated into 1% increments. Neither the Crayon nor the Greys Library is part of any color-matching system. If you need more information on which color-matching system to use, consult with the print shop that will be printing your work.

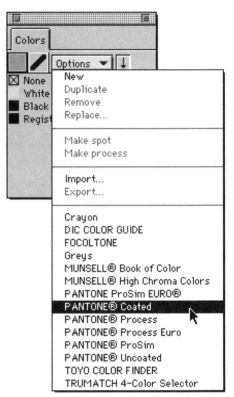

Figure 15a. *Under the **Options** pop-up menu of the **Colors** panel, choose the name of the color-matching system from which you want to add colors.*

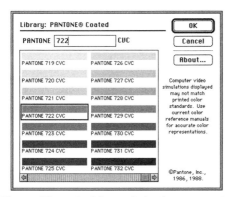

Figure 15b. *In the* **Library** *dialog box, type in the name or code number of the color or click on the color you want to add to your Colors panel.*

To add colors from color-matching system libraries:

1. Choose the name of the color-matching system from the Options pop-up menu (**Figure 15a**).

2. In the Library dialog box, type in the name or code number of the color or click on the color you want to add to your Colors panel (**Figure 15b**).

3. Click OK to add the color to your Colors panel.

4. If you want to add more than one color, hold down the Shift key and click on any additional colors. Click OK when you have selected all the colors you want.

Once you have created your own list of Colors, you can export those colors as your own custom color library.

To export your own custom color library:

1. Choose Export from the Options pop-up menu (**Figure 16a**).

2. The Export Colors dialog box will appear. Hold down the Shift key to select as many colors as you want from the Colors panel (**Figure 16b**). Click OK.

3. In the Create color library dialog box, enter the Library name and the File name (**Figure 16c**). The Colors per column and Colors per row fields control how the library will be displayed.

4. Choose Save to place your custom color library in the Color folder located in the FreeHand application folder. Choose Save as to specify a different folder or disk.

Tips

•➤ To delete custom color libraries from the Options pop-up menu, delete them from the Color folder in the FreeHand application folder.

•➤ To have a list of colors always appear in new documents, you need to add colors to the FreeHand Defaults file. (*To create a new defaults file, see page 272.*)

•➤ The FreeHand Xtras commands let you name all colors; adjust the values of colors; and saturate, desaturate, lighten, and darken the colors in objects. (*For more information on changing colors using the Xtras commands, see Chapter 17, "Xtras."*)

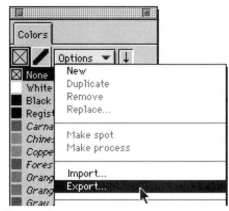

Figure 16a. *To create your own custom color library, choose* **Export** *from the* **Options** *pop-up menu.*

Figure 16b. *In the* **Export Colors** *dialog box, use the* **Shift** *key to select as many colors as you want from the Color List.*

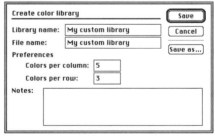

Figure 16c. *In the* **Create color library** *dialog box, the* **Library name** *is how the library will be listed in the Colors List. The* **File name** *is how the file will be named. The* **Colors per column** *and* **Colors per row** *fields govern how the colors are arranged.*

Once you have an object on your page, you will want to fill it in various ways. In this chapter, you will learn which objects can be filled. You will learn the different types of fills: Basic, Gradient, Tiled, Custom, Textured, Pattern, PostScript, and Multi-Colored. You will also discover how to apply the different types of fills to objects, as well as special techniques for making the fills look their best. We will cover the use of None as a fill. Finally, you will learn the basics of the Overprint option.

You can apply a fill to any object, but only closed paths will display the fill you apply. If you close an open path that has a fill applied to it, you will see the fill. To see if an object is open or closed, choose the Object icon of the Inspector palette and see if the Closed box is checked or unchecked. (*For more information on open and closed paths, see page 78.*)

To see the Fill Inspector:

1. Choose Fill from the Inspector submenu of the Window menu or press Command-Option-F.

2. The Fill Inspector will appear (**Figure 1**).

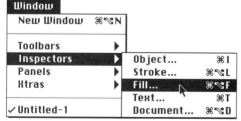

Figure 1. *To see the* **Fill Inspector***, choose* **Fill** *from the* **Inspectors** *submenu of the Window menu.*

To apply a Basic fill using the Fill Inspector:

1. Select the object to which you wish to apply the fill.

2. With the Fill Inspector displayed, choose Basic from the pop-up menu (**Figure 2**).

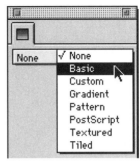

Once you apply a Basic fill, there are many ways to change the fill color. Choose whichever method is most convenient for you.

Figure 2. *To see the various fill choices, press on the **Fill** icon **pop-up** menu of the **Inspector** palette.*

To change the color of a Basic fill:

With the object selected, click on the name of the color in the Colors panel (**Figure 3a**). Notice that the Fill drop box in the upper left has a black line around it (**Figure 3b**). This indicates that the color clicked will become the color of the fill. The box next to the Fill drop box controls the color of the stroke (*see Chapter 10, "Strokes"*).

or

Drag a color swatch from the Color Mixer or the Color List onto the drop box in the Inspector palette or press on the pop-up menu (**Figure 4**).

or

Drag a color swatch from the Color Mixer onto the Fill drop box in the Color List (**Figure 5**).

or

Drag a color swatch from the Color Mixer or the Color List onto the middle of the object (**Figure 6**).

or

Press on the Colors pop-up menu in the Fill Inspector. Choose from the list of colors from the Colors panel (**Figure 7**).

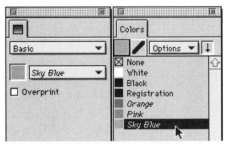

Figure 3a. *Clicking on the **name** of the color in the **Color List** or choosing it from the pop-up menu will apply that color to whichever object is selected.*

Figure 3b. *If the **Fill drop box** has a black line around it, clicking on a color will apply that color to the fill of the object.*

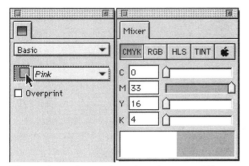

Figure 4. *To change the color of a Basic fill, drag a swatch from the **Color Mixer** or **Color List** onto the **drop box** of the **Inspector** palette or press on the pop-up menu.*

•• If you have not selected an object, any changes you make to the Fill icon of the Inspector palette or the Fill drop box of the Color List will be applied to the next object created.

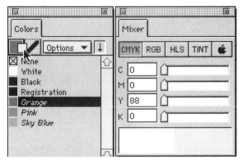

Figure 5. *To change the color of a Basic fill, drag a swatch from the **Color Mixer** onto the **Fill drop box** in the **Color List.***

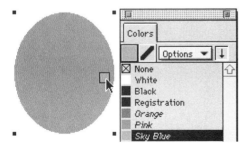

Figure 6. *To change the color of a Basic fill, drag a swatch from the **Color Mixer** or the **Color List** onto the **middle of the object.***

Figure 7. *To change the color of a Basic fill, press on the **Colors pop-up menu** in the Fill Inspector.*

FreeHand lets you create Gradient fills that start with one color and change into another. There are two types of Gradient fills: Linear and Radial. In a Linear fill, the colors change along a line that can be angled in any direction. In a Radial fill, the color starts at a center point and moves outward in a circle to the other color. A Radial fill is like a sun radiating colors outward.

To create a two-color Linear fill:

1. With the object selected, choose Gradient from the pop-up menu in the Fill Inspector. The settings for the Gradient fills will appear (**Figure 8**).

2. Press on one of the pop-up menus to choose the color you want to have start the Linear fill. (You can also drag colors from the Colors panel into the drop box.)

3. Press on the other pop-up menu to choose which color you want to end the Linear fill.

4. Click on the Linear icon in the Fill Inspector.

5. Choose Linear or Logarithmic from the Taper pop-up menu. A Linear taper changes in uniform increments from one color to another. A Logarithmic taper changes in increasing increments from one color to another (**Figure 9**).

6. Use the Angle field or rotate the wheel to enter the angle along which you want the fill to change.

Figure 8. *The Gradient fill settings in the Inspector palette.*

Figure 9. *The difference between a Linear fill (left) and a Logarithmic fill (right).*

Figure 10a. *To start a 3-D button, fill the circle with a **Gradient** fill.*

Figure 10b. *To finish the button, create a smaller circle with another **Gradient** fill.*

You can use Linear fills to create various effects.

To create a 3-D button using Linear fills:

1. Create a circle. Fill it with a Linear Gradient fill that changes from black to white along a 180° angle and has a Linear taper (**Figure 10a**).

2. Create a smaller circle and place it inside the larger one. Fill the smaller circle with a Linear Gradient fill that changes from black to white along a 0° angle and has a Logarithmic taper (**Figure 10b**).

To apply a Linear fill by dragging a color:

1. Select an object.

2. Drag a color swatch onto the object while holding down the Control key (**Figure 11a**). The object will take on a Linear fill with the color you dragged as the second color. The angle of the fill is determined by the spot where you dropped the swatch (**Figure 11b**).

Figure 11a. *If you hold down the **Control** key as you drag a color swatch onto an object...*

Figure 11b. *...you will apply a **Linear Gradient** fill to that object.*

To create a two-color Radial fill:

1. With the object selected, choose Gradient from the pop-up menu in the Fill Inspector. The settings for the Gradient fills will appear (**Figure 12**).

2. Choose the color you want on the outside of the Radial fill by changing the top color.

3. Choose the color you want on the inside of the Radial fill by changing the bottom color.

4. Click on the Radial icon in the Fill Inspector.

5. Move the center point in the Locate center box to change the position of the Inside color (**Figures 13a–b**).

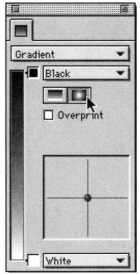

Figure 12. *The **Radial** fill settings in the **Inspector** palette.*

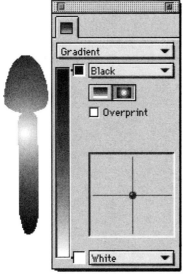

Figure 13a. *A **Radial** fill with the **center location** in the center of the object.*

Figure 13b. *The same **Radial** fill with the **center location moved** by dragging the **Locate** center point in the **Radial** fill settings of the **Inspector** palette.*

Figure 14a. *To **start** a spherical 3-D button, fill the circle with a **Radial** fill.*

Figure 14b. *To **finish** the button, create a smaller circle and fill it with a **Radial** fill. Change the center to the upper-left quadrant of the circle.*

Like the Linear fill, the Radial fill can be used to create 3-D effects.

To create a spherical 3-D button using Radial fills:

1. Create a circle. Fill it with a Radial fill that goes from black outside to white inside with the center left in the middle of the object (**Figure 14a**).

2. Create a smaller circle and place it inside the larger one. Fill this circle with a Radial fill that goes from black to white, but position the center of the fill in the upper-left quadrant of the object. The button will take on a 3-D appearance (**Figure 14b**).

To apply a Radial fill by dragging a color:

1. Select an object.

2. Drag a color swatch onto the object while holding the down Option key. The object will take on a Radial fill with the color that you dragged as the Inside color.

3. The center of the fill will be positioned on the spot where you dropped the color swatch.

Tips

- ↦ Once you have applied a Radial fill to an object, you can change the Inside and Outside colors by dragging color swatches directly onto the object. Where you drop the swatch sets the angle of the color change.

Using Radial Fills; Apply Radial Fills by Dragging

Gradient fills can contain more than one color. This allows you to create mettalic effects.

To add colors to Gradient fills:

1. To add a color to a gradient fill, drag a color swatch from the Colors panel or the Mixer onto the gray area next to the Gradient ramp between the top and the bottom colors. This will create a new color box (**Figure 15**).

2. You can continue to add more colors in this fashion.

3. To copy colors, drag the color swatch from the top or bottom of the Fill Inspector onto the gray area. This will create a new color box.

4. To delete a color from a Gradient fill, drag the color box off of the gray area. (You cannot delete the top or bottom color boxes of the Gradient fill.)

Tip

➡ You can alter the spacing between the colors for more dramatic effects.

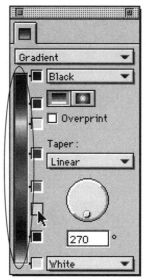

Figure 15. *To add colors to a gradient fill, drag a color swatch onto the gray area next to the* **Gradient ramp** *(circled).*

Figure 16a. *To create a **Tiled** fill, start by creating the artwork that you would like to repeat. Copy it.*

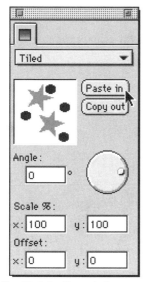

Figure 16b. *Click the **Paste in** button to paste the copied artwork into the **Tiled** fill settings box.*

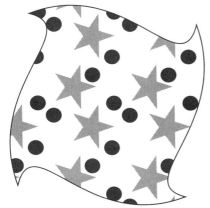

Figure 16c. *The object selected will have that **Tiled** fill applied to it.*

You have to create the next kind of fill—called a Tiled fill—by yourself. A more common term for a Tiled fill is pattern.

To create and apply a Tiled fill:

1. Create the artwork you would like to repeat and copy it (**Figure 16a**). Deselect your artwork.

2. Select the object you would like to be filled with the Tiled fill.

3. Choose Tiled from the Fill Inspector pop-up menu.

4. Click the Paste in button. The artwork you copied will appear in the Tiled preview box (**Figure 16b**). Your object will be filled with the Tiled fill (**Figure 16c**).

Tips

➡ If you want your Tiled fill to have a white or colored background, place your artwork on a rectangle filled with white or the color. Select both the artwork and the rectangle to copy and paste into the Tiled fill box.

➡ If you want your Tiled fill to be transparent, leave your artwork on an empty area or on a rectangle with no fill.

➡ The more complex the artwork, the longer it takes for your screen to redraw and for the artwork to print.

➡ Any object that can be copied can be used as a Tiled fill except EPS and bitmapped graphics, and objects that already have Tiled fills applied to them.

To adjust a Tiled fill:

1. With the Fill Inspector displayed, select the Tiled fill object.

2. To change the size of the Tiled fill, use the Scale % x and y fields (**Figure 17**). To scale the fill uniformly, use the same amounts for both the x and y fields.

3. To move a Tiled fill within the object, enter positive or negative values in the Offset x and y fields (**Figure 18**).

4. To angle a Tiled fill within the object, move the angle wheel or enter the exact angle in the Angle field (**Figure 19**).

Tips

➡ Positive x values in the Offset field move the fill to the right.

➡ Positive y values in the Offset field move the fill up.

➡ Negative x values in the Offset field move the fill to the left.

➡ Negative y values in the Offset field move the fill down.

Figure 17. *A Tiled fill object with **no scaling** applied (left) and with a **75% scaling** applied (right).*

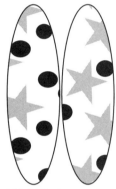

Figure 18. *A Tiled fill object with **no offset** applied (left) and with a **half-inch offset** applied (right).*

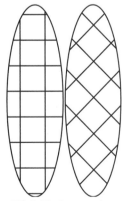

Figure 19. *A Tiled fill object with **no angle** applied (left) and with a **45° angle** applied (right).*

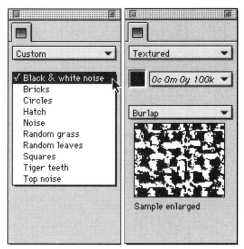

*Figure 20. The settings for the **Custom** and **Textured** fills.*

Custom and Textured fills are pre-made patterns that simulate the look of various textures. After you choose a Custom or Textured fill, you can still make changes to the texture.

To apply a Custom or Textured fill:

1. Select the object and choose Custom or Textured from the pop-up menu in the Fill Inspector.

2. Choose one of the Custom or Textured fills from the second pop-up menu that appears (**Figure 20**).

3. If applicable, change the color and make whichever other changes you want to the settings of the fill.

4. Instead of seeing a preview of the fill in the object, you will see a series of "C's" that fill the object (**Figure 21a**). You will only be able to see the fill by printing your object (**Figure 21b**).

Tips

➥ To see all the Custom and Textured fills, refer to Appendix C.

➥ Custom and Textured fills cannot be scaled with an object and do not print to non-PostScript printers.

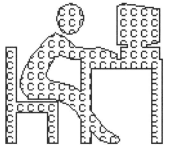

*Figure 21a. How an object filled with a **Custom** or **Textured** fill appears **onscreen**.*

*Figure 21b. How an object filled with a **Custom** or **Textured** fill **prints**.*

Pattern fills are bitmapped patterns that can be edited pixel by pixel. They are familiar to anyone who has used programs such as MacPaint.

To apply a Pattern fill:

1. Select an object and choose Pattern from the Fill icon pop-up menu in the Inspector palette.

2. Use the slider bar at the bottom of the Inspector palette to choose one of the Pattern fills from the series of small boxes (**Figure 22**).

3. Use the large preview box on the left to edit the pattern by clicking on each of the pixels. The large preview box on the right shows what your pattern will look like when applied to the object.

4. Use the Clear button to clear all the pixels from the large preview boxes so that you can start on a fresh edit.

5. Use the Invert button to change the black pixels into white and vice versa.

6. Use the color drop box to apply any color to the dark pixels of a pattern. (*See the Tips on the next page for important information on how colored Pattern fills will print.*)

7. The Pattern fills appear the same way onscreen as they will print (**Figure 23**).

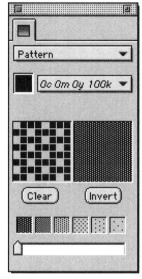

Figure 22. *The Pattern fill settings in the Inspector palette.*

Figure 23. *An object filled with a Pattern fill displays and prints that pattern.*

Pattern Fills

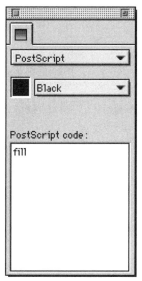

Figure 24. *The PostScript fill settings in the Inspector palette.*

Tips

•◆ To see all the Pattern fills, refer to Appendix C.

•◆ All of the Pattern fills have opaque backgrounds. Any objects behind these fills will not be visible through the empty spaces of the fills.

•◆ Pattern fills cannot be transformed with an object.

•◆ Pattern fills are designed for use on low-resolution printers (including non-PostScript devices), not high-resolution imagesetters and film recorders.

•◆ All of the Pattern fills let you apply any color to the fill. This color will be applied to the solid-color portion of the fill. Any white area of the Pattern fill will remain white.

•◆ On PostScript Level 1 printers, Pattern fills print correctly only if the spot colors are not tints and the process colors use inks at 100%.

•◆ On PostScript Level 2 printers, Pattern fills will print correctly using any spot or process colors.

To apply a PostScript fill:

When you choose a PostScript fill from the Fill icon pop-up menu, you will see a large box with the word "fill" in it (**Figure 24**). The purpose of this box is to allow you to type in specific PostScript code that will create a pattern. Learning and working with PostScript code is much too advanced to cover here. If you are interested in working with PostScript in FreeHand, consult *Real World FreeHand* by Olav Martin Kvern (Peachpit Press).

Pattern Fills; PostScript Fills

When you apply a None fill, your object becomes see-through (**Figure** 25). If you apply a None fill , you will probably want to add a stroke so that you can see the edges (*see Chapter 10, "Strokes"*).

To apply a None fill:

1. Choose the object you wish to fill with "None."

2. Make sure the Fill drop box is selected in the Colors panel.

3. Click on the None name. An "X" will appear in the Fill drop box, indicating that None has been applied as a fill (**Figure 26**).

To use the Overprint feature:

If you set an object to Overprint (**Figure 27**), that object will not knock out any colors below it, but will mix the colors. You cannot see overprinting on your screen. Any objects that have an overprint applied will be displayed with a pattern of white "O's" on top (**Figure 28**). You will not see overprinting in the output of most color printers. You need to make separations of your colors to see where the colors will overprint.

You can simulate the effect of overprinting by applying the Transparency command (*see page 201*).

Tips

•• If you do not want to see the "O's" in an overprinting object, you can change the Preferences settings (*see page 265*).

•• If you do not understand overprinting, talk to the print shop that will be printing your artwork.

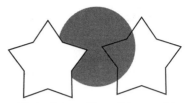

Figure 25. *Applying a **None** fill to an object lets you see through that object.*

Figure 26. *The **Fill drop box** with a **None** fill applied.*

Figure 27. *Setting a Basic fill to **Overprint**.*

Figure 28. *How an overprinting object appears onscreen.*

I f fills are what fill up the inside of objects, strokes are what surround the outside of objects. While there aren't as many choices for strokes as there are for fills, there are still quite a few types of effects you can create using strokes. In this chapter, you will learn how to set the attributes of a Basic stroke: Color, Width, Cap, Join, Miter limit, Dash, and Arrowheads. You will learn how to create your own Dash patterns using the Dash Editor and how to create your own arrowheads using the Arrowhead Editor. You will learn how to create special stroke effects such as multi-colored dashes and a "string of pearls." You will also learn about the three other stroke settings: Custom, Pattern, and PostScript.

Unlike fills, strokes can be applied to both open and closed paths. All the strokes in FreeHand are chosen through the Stroke Inspector. Once you have chosen the Stroke Inspector, you can access the different types of strokes through the pop-up menu.

To apply a Basic stroke:

1. Select the object to which you want to apply the stroke.

2. Choose Stroke from the Inspector submenu of the Window menu or press Command-Option-L.

3. Choose **Basic** from the pop-up menu (**Figure 1**).

Figure 1. *The Basic choices of the Stroke Inspector.*

Basic Stroke

Once you have applied a Basic stroke, there are more choices that you must make for your stroke. The first is color. Like the choices for fills, there are many different ways to change the color of a stroke.

To change the color of a stroke:

With the object selected, click on the name of the color in the Colors panel. If the Stroke drop box has a black line around it, then that color will be applied to the stroke of the object (**Figure 2**).

or

Drag a color swatch from the Mixer or the Colors panel onto the Stroke color drop box.

or

Drag a color swatch from the Mixer onto the drop box in the Colors panel.

or

Hold down the Command key and drag a color swatch from the Mixer or the Colors panel onto the object (**Figure 3**).

or

Press on the Colors pop-up menu in the Stroke Inspector. Choose from the list of colors (**Figure 4**).

Tip

➠ If you have not selected an object, any changes you make to the Stroke Inspector or the Stroke drop box of the Colors panel will be applied to the next object created.

Stroke drop box

Figure 2. *The black line around the Stroke drop box indicates that the box is selected. Any changes to the color selected in the Color List will apply to the stroke.*

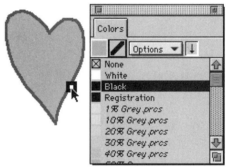

Figure 3. *Holding down the Command key while dragging a color swatch onto an object will change its stroke color.*

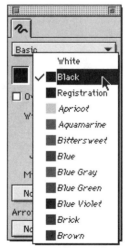

Figure 4. *Press on the Colors pop-up menu in the Stroke Inspector to choose a stroke color.*

Color of a Stroke

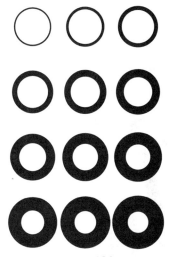

Figure 5. *Changing the* **Width** *amount changes the thickness of the stroke. These circles were drawn to the same size but have different stroke widths.*

To change the width of a stroke:

1. Select the object you want to change. There should be a Basic stroke applied to it.

2. In the Width field box, type the amount of the thickness for your stroke.

3. Press the Return key on your keyboard or click anywhere on the Stroke Inspector. The width of the stroke will change (**Figure 5**).

Tips

➙ Even if your document is in inches, you can enter the width of your stroke in points by typing "p" and then the number.

➙ The width of a stroke is applied to both the inside and outside of the path.

The next choice you have is how the ends of the stroke will be treated. This is called the "Cap" of the stroke. Changing the Cap of a stroked object only affects open paths, since they are the only ones with end points.

Figure 6. *The three different* **Cap** *choices:* **Butt** *(top),* **Round** *(middle), and* **Square** *(bottom). The difference between the Butt and Square is that the Square extends out beyond the anchor points.*

To apply a cap to a stroke:

1. Select an open path. In order to see the effects of changing the Cap, choose a rather thick width such as 24 points (**Figure 6**).

2. The default Cap is the Butt cap. This cap means that the stroke stops exactly on the endpoint of the path.

3. Click on the Round cap icon. This choice means that the stroke extends past the endpoints in a curved shape.

4. Click on the Square cap icon. This choice means that the stroke extends past the endpoints in a square shape.

Width of a Stroke; Cap of a Stroke

The next choice you have is how the joints of the stroke will be treated. This is called the "join" of the stroke. Any path that has a corner or connector point inside the path will be affected by changing the join.

To change the join of a stroke:

1. Select a path. In order to see the effects of changing the join, choose a rather thick width such as 24 points. Make sure at least one point inside the path is a corner point or a connector point (**Figure 7**).

2. Click on the Miter join icon. Choosing this join means that the stroke of the path extends out into a "V" where the two line segments change directions. The sharper the angle between the two segments, the longer the extension of the stroke.

3. Click on the Round join icon. Choosing this join means that the stroke of the path makes a curve between the two line segments.

4. Click on the Bevel join icon. Choosing this join prevents the "V" extension between the two line segments and cuts the stroke in a straight line between the two segments.

Tip

➡ Use the Round join together with the Round cap for a look similar to that of the soft tip of a marker pen.

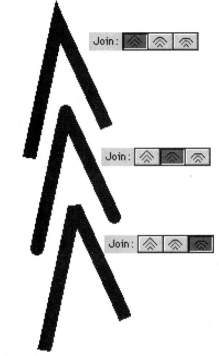

Figure 7. *The three Join choices: Miter (top), Round (middle), and Bevel (bottom).*

Figure 8. *A higher* **Miter limit** *(left) will allow a spike between line segments. A lower Miter limit (right) cuts the spike off into a Bevel join.*

The next choice you have is the Miter limit. Changing the Miter limit of a stroked object prevents joins with very steep angles from becoming too spikey.

To change the Miter limit:

1. Select a path with a Miter join. In order to see the effects of changing the Miter limit, choose a rather thick width such as 24 points and create two line segments with a very acute angle between them. This should look like a spike (**Figure 8**).

2. Lower the Miter limit to 1 or 2 and notice how you have eliminated the spike between the two segments (**Figure 8**).

The next choice you have is the dash pattern of the stroke. Both open and closed paths, with any kinds of points, can have dash patterns applied to them.

To apply a dash pattern:

1. Select a path. In order to see the effects of changing the dash, choose a rather thick width such as 24 points. Choose a Butt cap.

2. Press on the Dash pop-up menu and choose from the default list of pre-made dash patterns. Each of these choices will create a new dash pattern for your stroke (**Figure 9**).

Tip

•❖ The spaces between the dashes of a stroke are transparent, not white. If you lay your dashed stroke over another object, you will see through the spaces to that other object.

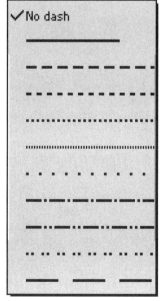

Figure 9. *The default pop-up list of* **Dash** *patterns.*

You may find that you want to create your own dash patterns for strokes. That is done by using the Dash Editor dialog box.

To edit a dash pattern:

1. With the Stroke Inspector displayed, hold down the Option key as you select one of the dash patterns from the Basic stroke settings. The Dash Editor dialog box will appear (**Figure 10**).

2. The length of the visible portion of the dash is set by entering a number in the On field.

3. The length of the space between the dashes is set by entering a number in the Off field.

4. Up to four different sets of On and Off values can be entered.

5. When you have finished entering the pattern, click OK. The dash pattern you created will be displayed at the bottom of the dash list. You will not have eliminated the original pattern.

With just a little experience you can create very sophisticated effects using dashes.

To create a multi-colored dash:

1. Create a line with the Basic stroke you want. Use a fairly thick stroke, such as 12 points, with no dash.

2. Choose Clone (Command-=) from the Edit menu. You now have a copy of that line sitting on top of your original line.

3. Choose a smaller width and add a contrasting color for the clone. Choose a dash pattern that creates large spaces in the cloned line. You will now have a dashed line with two colors (**Figure 11**).

Figure 10. *The Dash Editor dialog box lets you enter your own dash patterns. Choose up to four sets of On and Off patterns.*

Figure 11. *To create multi-colored dashed lines, use two or more stacked lines. This effect uses a bottom, solid black line and a top dashed line stroked with a lighter color and with a smaller stroke width.*

Edit a Dash Pattern; Multi-Colored Dash

Figure 12a. *The stroke settings for creating the "string of pearls."*

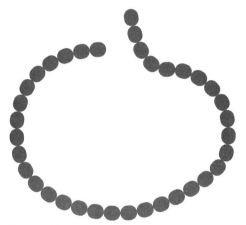

Figure 12b. *The finished string of pearls.*

You can also use dash patterns and cap shapes to make a dotted line.

To use dash patterns and cap shapes:

1. Use one of the tools to draw an open path.

2. Set the Width to 24 points.

3. Set the Cap to Round. (This makes the dashes a round shape.)

4. Hold down the Option key and choose any of the dash patterns. (This gives you the Dash Editor dialog box.)

5. Set your dash pattern to On 1, Off 24. Click OK.

6. Your path will now be a dotted line (**Figures 12a–b**).

Tip

➥ If you have two or more objects on top of each other, hold down the Control key as you click on the top object. This will allow you to select objects beneath the top object.

Dash Patterns and Cap Shapes

The last choice for Basic strokes is arrowheads. You can only see arrowheads on open paths.

To apply arrowheads:

1. Select a path. In order to see the different arrowheads, choose a rather thick stroke such as 24 points.

2. Make sure that the Stroke Inspector is displayed.

3. To add an arrowhead to the start of your path, press on the left Arrowheads pop-up menu and choose from the default list of pre-made Arrowheads.

4. To add an Arrowhead to the end of your path, press on the right Arrowheads pop-up menu and choose from the default list of pre-made Arrowheads (**Figure 13**).

Tips

➽ The arrowheads take their size from the point size of the stroke.

➽ Even if your path started on the right, the left pop-up menu controls the arrowheads at the start of the path.

➽ Even if your path ends on the left, the right pop-up menu controls the arrowheads at the end of the path.

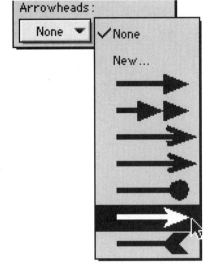

Figure 13. *The Arrowheads pop-up menu lets you add arrowheads to open paths with Basic strokes.*

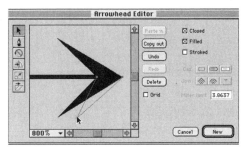

Figure 14. *The Arrowhead Editor dialog box lets you modify the pre-made arrowheads or create your own custom arrowheads.*

FreeHand gives you the Arrowhead Editor dialog box where you can create your own arrowheads.

To edit the pre-made arrowheads:

1. Hold down the Option key as you select one of the arrowheads from either the left or right Arrowheads pop-up menu of the Basic stroke Inspector palette. The Arrowhead Editor dialog box will appear with the arrowhead that you chose in the window (**Figure 14**).

2. Use any of the Arrowhead Editor tools to modify the arrowhead in the Arrowhead Editor window.

3. When you are satisfied with the results of your work, click on the New button. The arrowhead you modified will appear at the end of the left and right lists of arrowheads. The original arrowhead will be unchanged in the arrowhead lists.

To create custom arrowheads:

1. Press on either the left or right Arrowheads pop-up menu and choose New. You will now see the Arrowhead Editor dialog box.

2. Use any of the Arrowhead Editor tools to create an arrowhead.

3. When you are satisfied with the results of your work, click on the New button. The arrowhead you created will appear at the end of the left and right lists of the arrowheads.

Tip

➡ Use the Paste in and Copy out buttons to transfer arrowheads between the Arrowhead Editor and the work page. This allows you to use all the FreeHand tools to create arrowheads.

Edit Arrowheads; Custom Arrowheads

Just as there are Custom fills, FreeHand provides you with Custom stroke patterns.

To apply a Custom stroke pattern:

1. Choose Custom from the Stroke pop-up menu of the Inspector palette (**Figure 15**).

2. Choose the color you want for your stroke.

3. Choose the width for the stroke.

4. Choose the Custom stroke Effect from the pop-up menu. Use the Sample enlarged window to judge the look of the Custom stroke.

5. Set the Length field to control the size of the repeating element in the stroke.

6. Set the Spacing field to control the space between each repeating element in the stroke (**Figure 16**).

Tips

➥ To see all the default Custom strokes, see Appendix C.

➥ Custom stroke patterns appear solid on the screen.

➥ White areas of the Custom stroke patterns (except Arrow, Braid, and Neon) are transparent when printed. This means that any objects behind a stroked object will show through the spaces of the Custom stroke.

➥ The Custom stroke patterns do not transform with the object.

➥ The Custom stroke patterns print to any PostScript device.

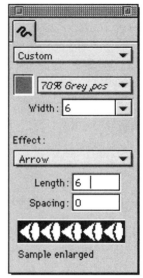

Figure 15. *Choose **Custom** from the **Stroke** icon section of the **Inspector** palette to see the settings for the Custom strokes.*

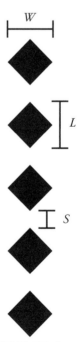

Figure 16. *The **Width**(W), **Length**(L), and **Spacing** (S) settings control the look of a **Custom** stroke.*

Custom Stroke Pattern

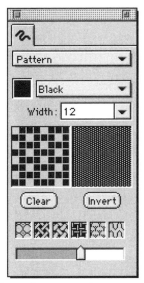

Figure 17. *The **Pattern** stroke settings in the Inspector palette.*

Figure 18. *An object with a **Pattern** stroke displays and prints that pattern.*

The next set of strokes are the Pattern strokes. Like the Pattern fills, these are bitmapped patterns that can be edited pixel by pixel.

To apply a Pattern stroke:

1. Select the object and choose Pattern from the Stroke Inspector.

2. Use the slider bar at the bottom of the palette to choose one of the Pattern strokes from the series of small boxes above it (**Figure 17**).

3. Use the large preview box on the left to edit the pattern by clicking on each of the pixels in the pattern. The large preview box on the right shows what your pattern will look like when applied to the object.

4. Use the Clear button to clear all the pixels from the large preview boxes so you can start on a fresh edit.

5. Use the Invert button to change the black pixels into white pixels and vice versa.

6. Use the color drop box to apply any color to the dark pixels of a pattern. (*See the Tips below for important information on how colored Pattern strokes will print.*)

7. The Pattern strokes appear the same way onscreen as they will print (**Figure 18**).

Tips

- ➦ To see all the default Pattern strokes, see Appendix C.

- ➦ All of the Pattern strokes have opaque backgrounds. Any objects behind these strokes will not be visible through the empty spaces of the strokes.

- ➦ Pattern strokes cannot be transformed with an object.

(*Continued on the following page*)

Pattern Stroke

- ❧ Pattern strokes are designed for use on low-resolution printers (including non-PostScript devices), not high-resolution imagesetters and film recorders.

- ❧ All of the Pattern strokes let you apply any color to the stroke. This color will be applied to the solid-color portion of the stroke. Any white area of the Pattern stroke will remain white.

- ❧ On PostScript Level 1 printers, Pattern strokes will print correctly only if the spot colors are not tints and the process colors use inks at 100%.

- ❧ On PostScript Level 2 printers, Pattern strokes print correctly using any spot or process colors.

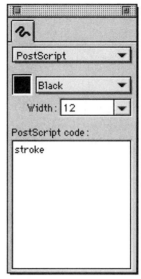

Figure 19. *The PostScript stroke settings in the Stroke Inspector.*

To apply a PostScript stroke:

When you choose a PostScript stroke from the Stroke Inspector pop-up menu, you will see a large box with the word "stroke" in it (**Figure 19**). The purpose of this box is to allow you to type in a specific PostScript code that will create a pattern. Learning and working with PostScript code is much too advanced to cover here. If you are interested in working with PostScript in FreeHand, consult *Real World FreeHand* by Olav Martin Kvern (Peachpit Press).

Pattern Stroke; PostScript Stroke

Figure 1a. *Blends give the effect of one object turning into another.* **Figure 1b.** *The same blend with only a few steps displayed to show the progression of the blend.*

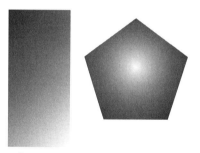

Figure 2a. *Two shapes with **a Linear Gradient fill** (left) and **Radial Gradient fill** (right).*

Figure 2b. *The same shapes with **Blends**.*

Blends are one of the most sophisticated features of FreeHand. With blends, you can create subtle shadings and contours, dramatic changes of shape, 3-D looks, and many other effects. In this chapter, you will learn some of the uses of blends and how blends differ from Gradient and Radial fills. You will learn how to create your own blends and how to set the number of steps in your blends. You will also learn how to use FreeHand's Live Blends feature to modify existing blends. The chapter will cover which objects can be blended and how to optimally view your blends onscreen. Finally, you will learn some of the proceedures to follow to ensure your blends will print correctly.

Blends give the effect of one object turning into another. When you see an object such as an oval that seems to turn into another object such as a star, what you are actually seeing is hundreds of intermediate steps in which the object has been reshaped ever so slightly in each step (**Figures 1a–b**).

If all you want to do is make an object change from one color to another, then all you need is a Linear Gradient fill or Radial Gradient fill (**Figure 2a**). (*For more information on Gradient fills, see Chapter 9, "Fills."*) But if you would like the object to transform into another shape during the color change, then you need to use blends (**Figure 2b**).

Blens

Blends don't have to be just for color or shape changes. They also can be used to create intermediate steps where both the stroke width and the stroke shape change (**Figure 3**).

To create a simple Blend:

1. Start with a simple shape such an oval or a rectangle. Fill this object with a dark color.

2. Create a second shape such as a star or a triangle. Fill this object with a lighter color or white (**Figure 4a**).

3. Select one point on the first object and another point on the second object (**Figure 4b**). (If you are blending between two open paths, these points must be endpoints on the paths.)

4. Choose Blend (Command-Shift-B) from the Combine submenu of the Modify menu (**Figure 4c**). (You can also create a blend by using the Blend command of the Operations Inspector.) You will see the blend from one object to another (**Figure 4d**).

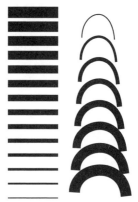

Figure 3. *Two different ways of using* **blends** *to change the shape and width of* **strokes**.

Figure 4a. *To create a simple Blend, start with two ungrouped objects.*

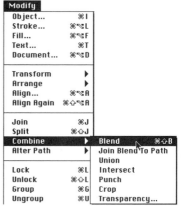

Figure 4c. *To blend an object, choose* **Blend** *from the* **Combine** *submenu of the* **Modify** *menu.*

Figure 4b. *Select one point on each object.*

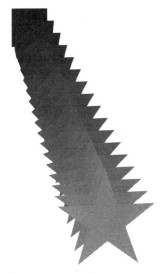

Figure 4d. *The results of blending the two shapes.*

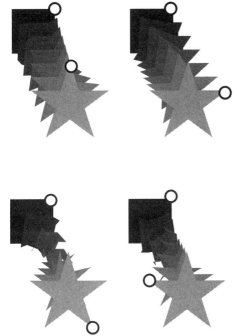

Figure 5. *These four blends were made by choosing different points (indicated by circles).*

Tips

•➤ You can also create blends between more than two objects.

•➤ If you want your blends to look as smooth as possible, try to pick points on each object that are in equivalent positions. Choosing nonequivalent points can result in unwanted blending (**Figure 5**).

Once you have a blend, you may want to change the number of steps. This may be to make the blend as smooth as possible or it may be to see each of the steps.

To change the number of steps in a Blend:

1. With the blend selected, open the Object Inspector (**Figure 6**).

2. Enter the number of steps you want in the Number of steps field.

3. Press the Return key or click anywhere on the Inspector palette. The blend will reform with the new number of steps.

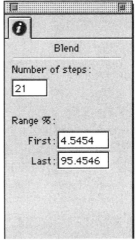

Figure 6. *In the Number of Steps field, type in the number of steps you want.*

To change the number of steps in your document:

FreeHand calculates the number of steps in a blend from the Printer resolution in the Document Inspector (*see page 9*). Higher resolutions give you greater number of steps. If you change the resolution, you will change the steps for new blends. Blends made before you changed the Printer resolution will not be changed.

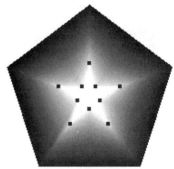

Figure 9a. *To make a **Live Blend**, hold down the **Option** key as you click on one of the original objects of the blend.*

Once you have created a blend, you can still make changes to any of the original objects of the blend. FreeHand calls this Live Blends.

To create a Live Blend:

1. Hold down the Option key and use the Selection tool to select one of the original objects of the blend (**Figure 9a**). (If you do not hold down the Option key, you will select the entire blend.)

2. Make any changes you want to the object, such as shape, fill color, or stroke width (**Figure 9b**).

3. The blend will automatically reform when you make the changes (**Figure 9c**).

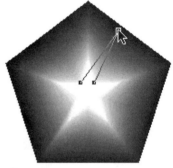

Figure 9b. *Make whatever changes you want to size, shape, color, etc. of the original object*

The rules of blends

There are limitations to which objects you can blend between.

1. You cannot blend an open path to a closed path.

2. You cannot blend a composite path.

3. You cannot blend between paths that have different stroke or fill types.

4. Blends between two spot colors must remain grouped in order to mix as spot colors.

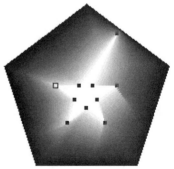

Figure 9c. *The blend will automatically be redrawn as you make changes to the original object.*

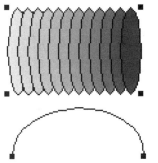

Figure 10a. *To **align a blend** to a path, select the blend and the path to which you want to align it.*

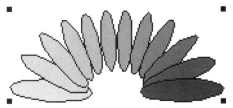

Figure 10b. *The results of aligning a blend to a path.*

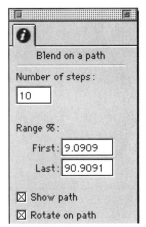

Figure 11. *The **Show path** and **Rotate on path** checkboxes affect how a blend is aligned to a path.*

Once you have created a blend, you can then align the blend to a path.

To align a blend to a path:

1. Create a blend and a path. Select both the blend and the path (**Figure 10a**).

2. Choose Join Blend to Path from the Combine submenu of the Modify menu.

3. The blend will automatically align to the shape of the path (**Figure 10b**).

4. To see the path, click on Show path in the Inspector palette (**Figure 11**).

5. To change the orientation of the objects in the blend, click on Rotate on path in the Inspector palette (**Figure 11**).

To release a blend from a path:

1. Select a blend that has been aligned to a path.

2. Choose Split (Command-Shift-J) from the Modify menu.

3. The blend will be released from the path.

Tip

➡ Blends that have been aligned on a path can still be modified using the same principles of Live Blends.

To view blends:

Once you have a blend, you may find that you do not like the way it looks onscreen. This is a function of the screen display. If you want to see your blend with a smoother display, you will need to change your Preferences settings (*see page 265*).

To print blends:

If you are printing to a low-resolution device such as a laser printer, you may not be satisfied with the printout of the blend. This is because those printers cannot reproduce all the tones necessary to create a smooth blend.

If you are printing on a high-resolution device such as an imagesetter, your blend should print smoothly. However, there are some situations where blends produce an effect called "banding" (**Figure 11**). The following is information for printing on PostScript devices. (*For more information on printing, see Chapter 21, "Printing."*)

1. Print at high resolutions. For most work, this is a minimum of 2400 dpi.

2. If you have banding, use a lower screen line count. This is especially helpful when printing to laser printers.

3. Avoid blends over 7 inches long. This is especially true if you are outputting to a PostScript Level 1 device. If you are sending to a PostScript Level 2 device, you may not need to limit the length of your blends.

4. Examine the difference between the tint values of colors. If you are getting banding, try increasing the difference between the tints.

5. If you are getting banding, try increasing the number of steps of the blend. However, if you are outputting to a PostScript Level 1 device, you do not need any more than 256 steps.

Figure 11. *A blend with* **banding** *(top). Notice that instead of looking smooth, there are lines between the changes in color. The same blend with more steps used to decrease the banding (bottom). Notice how it looks smoother.*

BASIC TEXT

Most people think of FreeHand as a program to create illustrations—graphics, drawings, and artwork. FreeHand also provides a wealth of features to create different text effects. In this chapter, you will learn how to: create text in text blocks; change the size of text blocks; apply borders to text blocks; inset text from the borders of text blocks; and place text blocks precisely where you want them. You will learn how to import text from word processing programs and format text characters and paragraphs. You will also learn how to use indents, tabs, text rulers, columns, and rows to create different paragraph effects. You will learn how to turn on and control hyphenation. Finally, you will learn how to link text so that it flows from one column, page or object to another.

Figure 1. *To create a text block, choose the* **Text** *tool in the toolbox.*

To create a text block by dragging:

1. Select the Text tool (**Figure 1**) from the toolbox and drag it on your work page. The size of your drag determines the size of the text block you create.

2. As soon as you let go, you will see the text block and the text block ruler (**Figure 2**).

3. Start typing. Your text will fill the text block. You do not have to hit the Return key at the end of a line. The text will automatically wrap within the text block.

Tip

- If you do not see the text ruler, choose Text Rulers from the View menu.

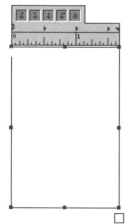

Figure 2. *A* **text block** *with a* **text ruler.**

To create a text block by clicking:

1. Select the Text tool from the toolbox and click anywhere on your page. You will see a blinking insertion point and a text ruler.

2. Start typing and you will see your text. Your text will not automatically wrap within the text block. If you want the text to shift to the next line, you will need to hit Return or Shift-Return. If your text does wrap within the box, check your Preferences settings (*see page 262*).

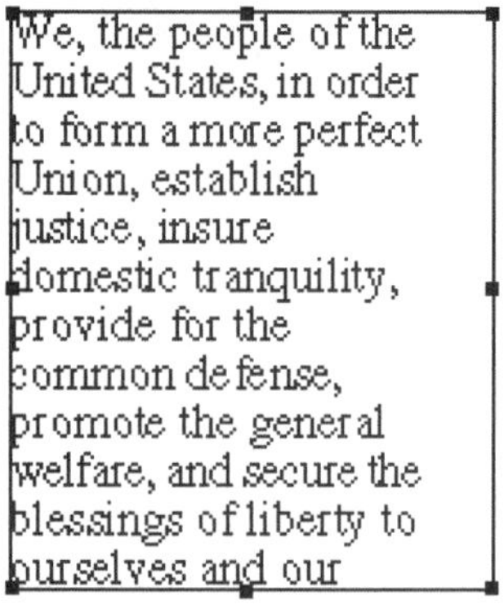

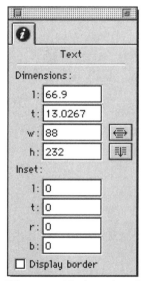

Figure 3. *To change the size of a text block, drag on one of the corner points of the block.*

Once you have created a text block, you may want to change its size. There are different techniques for doing this depending, on how you created the text block.

To change the size of a dragged text block:

Use the Selection tool and drag on one of the corner points of the text block (**Figure 3**).

or

With the text block selected, click on the Object Inspector. Under Dimensions, change the measurements in the w (width) or h (height) fields (**Figure 4**).

Figure 4. *When a text block is selected, the* **Object Inspector** *allows you to change the dimensions of that text block.*

Text Block by Clicking, Change Size of Text Block

Figure 5a. *When the icons next to the width and height fields are dark or when the side handles are white, it means that the field is **unlocked** and is set for **auto-expansion**.*

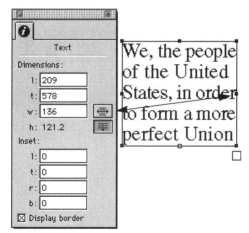

Figure 5b. *When the icons next to the width and height fields are light or when the side handles are dark, it means that the field is **locked** and auto-expansion is off.*

If you created the text block by clicking, the width and height fields will be set to auto-expansion. This means that the text block will automatically change its size as you type. However, you cannot drag to change the size of the text block nor can you enter new measurements in the fields (**Figure 5**).

To change the auto-expansion settings:

1. With the text block selected, click on the Object Inspector.

2. Click to change the icons next to the w and h fields. If the icon is dark, the field is set for auto-expansion as new text is entered (**Figure 5a**). If the icon is light, the field is not set for auto-expansion (**Figure 5b**).

3. When auto-expansion is off, you can drag to resize the text block or you can enter new measurements in the width and height fields.

Tips

➡ You can change the auto-expansion of a text block by double-clicking on the bottom handle or either of the side handles.

➡ Set the height of a text block for auto-expansion but keep auto-expansion turned off for the width. This is very useful for creating a column of text.

➡ If you hold the Control key as you drag horizontally to create a text block, the text block width will be fixed, but the height will change.

➡ If you hold the Control key as you drag vertically to create a text block, the text block height will be fixed, but the width will change.

Auto-Expansion Settings

Another way to resize a text block is to automatically shrink the block to fit the size of the text.

To automatically shrink a text block:

1. Select a text block that has extra space not filled by text.

2. Using the Selection tool, double-click on the Link box of the block (**Figure 6**). The text block will automatically shrink to fit the text.

Tip

➡ If there is no text in a text block, double-clicking on the Link box will delete the text block.

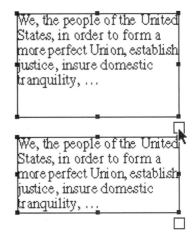

Figure 6. *Double-clicking on the **Link box** will shrink a text box with extra space (top) to the exact size of the text (bottom).*

To apply a border to a text block:

1. Select the text block around which you want to have a border.

2. Click on the Object Inspector.

3. Click on the Display border checkbox (**Figure 7a**). This allows you to see the border; however, it does not create the border.

4. Open the Stroke Inspector.

5. Apply a stroke using any of the stroke styles (**Figure 7b**).

Figure 7a. *The **Display border** checkbox of the Object Inspector will allow you to set a stroke or border around a text block.*

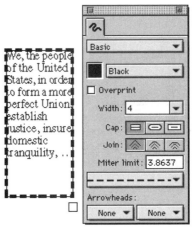

Figure 7b. *The **Stroke Inspector** lets you set the attributes of the text block border.*

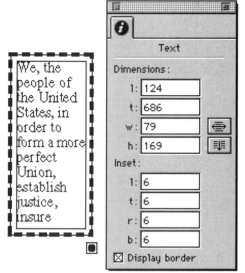

Figure 8. *Under **Inset**, the **l** (left), **t** (top), **r** (right), and **b** (bottom) fields let you move text away from the edges of a text block.*

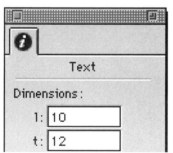

Figure 9. *Under **Dimensions**, the **l** (left) and **t** (top) fields let you move a text block to a specific position.*

Once you have given your text block a border, you will probably want to move your text away from the sides of the text block.

To inset text:

1. Select the text block.

2. Choose the Object Inspector.

3. Under Inset, enter the amounts you would like to move the text in the l (left), t (top), r (right), and b (bottom) fields. Press Return or Enter to set the amounts (**Figure 8**).

Tip

•◆ Negative amounts will position the text outside the border of the text block.

You can move a text block by dragging. Or, you can move it numerically to a precise position.

To position a text block numerically:

1. Select the text block.

2. Choose the Object Inspector.

3. Under Dimensions, enter the coordinate you want for the left edge of the text block in the l field.

4. Under Dimensions, enter the coordinate you want for the top edge of the text block in the t field. Press the Return or Enter key (**Figure 9**).

Tip

•◆ Unless you have changed the zero point of the rulers, your page starts at the bottom-left corner.

Once you have a text block on your page, you can type directly into it. However, if you are working on a document in a word processing program, you may want to import that text into FreeHand. To do so you will need to save your work in one of two different formats.

RTF Text (Rich Text Format): This is the preferred format. RTF text will allow you to import the text with its formatting intact. This includes font, size, style, margins, tabs, indents, alignment, baseline shift, letterspacing, and color (**Figure 10**).

ASCII (pronounced "as-kee"): Use this format only if you cannot get RTF text. ASCII text does not allow you to import with the formatting intact. Only the keystrokes (characters) are imported. If you import ASCII text, you will need to reformat it (**Figure 10**).

To import text:

1. Choose Place from the File menu and choose the text file you wish to import. Your cursor will change into a corner symbol.

2. Position the corner symbol where you would like your text to start.

3. If you want your text block to be a certain size on the page, drag the corner symbol to create a rectangle the size you want the text block to be.

4. If you just want the text on the page, click. You will now have a text block filled with text.

Figure 10. *RTF text (top) imports with all its formatting and styling. ASCII text imports its characters only (bottom).*

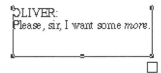

Figure 11a. *A white Link box indicates that all the text is visible within the text block.*

Figure 11b. *A circle in the Link box indicates an overflow—additional text is not visible in the text block.*

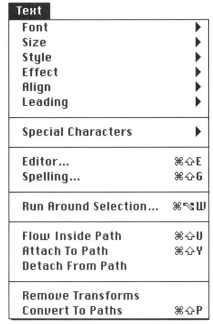

Figure 12a. *The various choices for changing text via the Text menu.*

There is a little square at the bottom of the text block. This is the Link box. There are several different ways this box appears.

To work with the Link box:

1. If the Link box is white, then all the text in the block is visible (**Figure 11a**).

2. If there is a black circle inside the Link box, it means there is more text than can fit inside the text block (**Figure 11b**). This is called an overflow.

3. If there are left and right arrows inside the Link box, it means the text block has been linked to another object (*see page 166*).

FreeHand gives you several places to change character attributes. Two are the Text menu and the Text toolbar.

Change text using Text menu or Text toolbar:

1. Select the text by dragging across it. Or, you can format without selecting any text; any text you type afterwards will be styled accordingly.

2. To change the Font, Size, or Style, choose those items from the Text menu (**Figure 12a**).

or

Press on the various pop-up menus of the Text toolbar (**Figure 12b**).

Tip

•• Type size will always be measured in points, regardless of which unit of measurement you have selected.

Figure 12b. *The various choices for styling text via the Text toolbar.*

The third place to change text attributes is the Text Inspector. This panel is divided into five areas that control character attributes as well as paragraph attributes; spacing; rows and columns; and copyfitting. These five areas will be discussed throughout the rest of this chapter.

To see the Text Inspector:

To see the Text Inspector, choose Text from the Modify menu, or choose Text from the Inspectors submenu of the Window menu. Or, press Command-T (**Figure 13**).

To change character attributes:

1. To change the typeface, press on the font, style, and point size pop-up menus (**Figure 14**).

or

Drag across the field and type in the name or point size desired.

2. Choose the alignment you want from the four Alignment icons (**Figure 15**).

3. Enter the amount of Leading in the field and press on the pop-up menu to choose one of the options: +, = or %. (**Figure 16**). The + sign adds space between the lines in addition to the space used by the characters. The = sign sets an amount of space that does not change if the text size changes. The % sign adds an amount of space that is a percentage of the point size of the text.

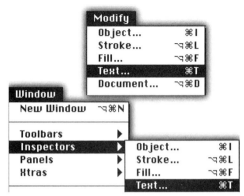

Figure 13. *Two ways to display the Text Inspector.*

Figure 14. *The pop-up menus control the typeface, style and point size.*

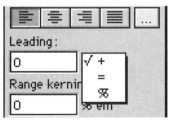

Figure 16. *The pop-up menu shows the three choices for Leading: Extra (+), Fixed (=), and Percentage (%).*

Figure 15. *The four alignment icons are (from left to right) Left, Centered, Right, and Justified.*

Figure 17. **Kerning** *adjusts the space between two letters. Here, a Kerning of -16 has been applied to the letters "T" and "r" in the bottom word.*

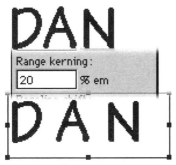

Figure 18. **Range kerning** *changes the letterspacing over a range of letters. Here, a Range kerning of 20 has been applied to the bottom text.*

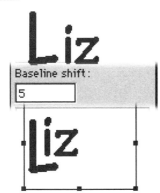

Figure 19. **Baseline shift** *raises or lowers text from its baseline. Here, the letters "iz" have been shifted up 5 points.*

4. If your insertion point is blinking between two letters, you can enter a value in the Kerning field. Positive values increase the space between the letters. Negative values decrease the space (**Figure 17**).

5. If you select more than two characters, you can enter a value in the Range kerning field. Positive values increase the space between the letters. Negative values decrease the space (**Figure 18**).

6. Enter an amount in the Baseline shift field. Positive values raise the text. Negative values lower the text (**Figure 19**).

Tips

- Use the following keystrokes to set the alignment of text in a selected paragraph:

  Command-Option-Shift-L for Left alignment.

  Command-Option-Shift-M for Centered alignment.

  Command-Option-Shift-R for Right alignment.

  Command-Option-Shift-J for Justified alignment.

- Drag the top or bottom middle handles of a text block to increase or decrease the leading of an entire text block.

- Drag the left or right middle handles to increase or decrease the Range kerning of an entire text block.

- Hold down the Option key as you drag the left or right middle handles of a text block to increase the Range kerning between words.

Once your text is inside a text block, you will want to format its paragraph attributes.

To change paragraph attributes:

1. Select the paragraph or paragraphs that you want to change. Choose the Text Inspector and then click on the Paragraph icon (**Figure 20**).

2. To add space above or below the paragraph, enter the amounts you want under Paragraph spacing in the Above or Below fields (**Figure 21**).

3. To change the margin indents, enter the amount in the Left, Right, or First fields. (**Figure 22**).

Tips

➤ Use the Paragraph spacing fields, rather than extra paragraph returns, to add space between paragraphs.

➤ FreeHand will not add space above a paragraph that starts at the top of a column or text block.

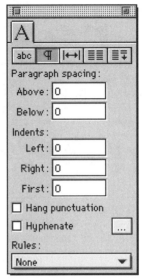

Figure 20. *Clicking on the **Paragraph** icon of the **Text Inspector** allows you to set various paragraph attributes.*

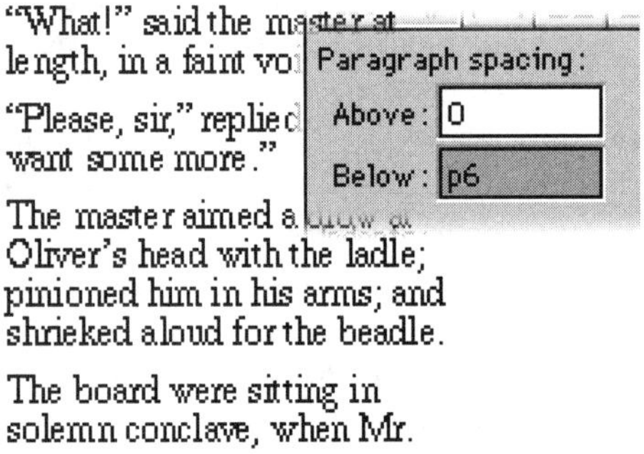

Figure 21. *Paragraph spacing of 6 points is added between the paragraphs by entering the amount p6 in the **Below** field.*

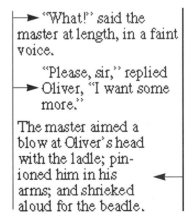

Figure 22. *Three different margin indents: The top paragraph has a **First line indent**. The middle paragraph has a **Left margin indent**. The bottom paragraph has a **Right margin indent**.*

Paragraph Attributes

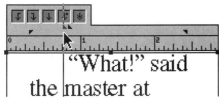

Figure 23. *Dragging the **indent triangles** of the Text Ruler allows you to change margin indents.*

"What!" said the master at length, in a faint voice.

"Please, sir," replied Oliver, "I want some more."

The master aimed a blow at Oliver's head with the ladle; pinioned him in

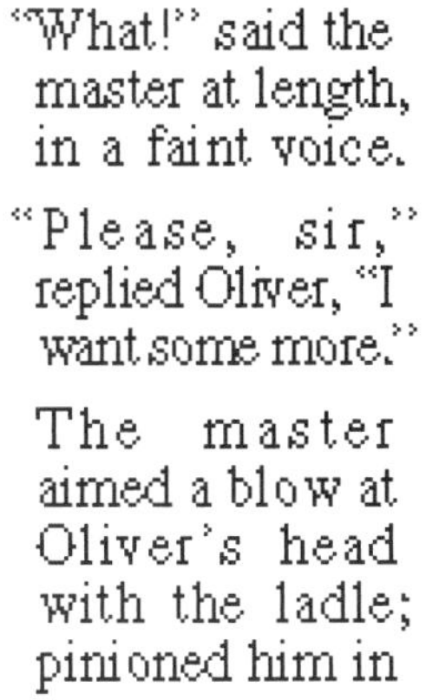

Figure 24. *An example of **hanging punctuation**. Notice how the quotation and punctuation marks hang outside the margins of the paragraphs.*

FreeHand also lets you use the text ruler to set the margin indents.

To change margin indents by using the text ruler:

1. Choose the Text Inspector and then click on the Paragraph icon. Select the paragraphs whose indents you would like to change.

2. If the text ruler is not visible, choose Text Rulers from the View menu.

3. Drag the bottom part of the left indent triangle to the spot on the ruler where you would like the left margin to be (**Figure 23**).

4. Drag the right indent triangle to the spot on the ruler where you would like the right margin to be (**Figure 23**).

5. Drag the top part of the left indent triangle to the spot on the ruler where you would like the first line of the paragraph to be (**Figure 23**).

To create hanging punctuation:

If you want your punctuation to "hang" outside the margins, click on Hanging punctuation in the paragraph attributes of the Text Inspector. This keeps paragraphs from looking ragged (**Figure 24**).

To use automatic hyphenation:

1. With the text block or paragraphs selected, choose the Paragraph icon of the Text Inspector.

2. To turn hyphenation on, click so that an "X" appears in the Hyphenation checkbox. To turn hyphenation off, click so that the "X" disappears in the Hyphenation checkbox (**Figure 25**).

To edit the hyphenation:

1. To further control hyphenation, click the Ellipse (…) button. The Edit Hyphenation dialog box will appear (**Figure 26**).

2. If you have foreign language dictionaries installed, press on the pop-up menu to choose the correct language.

3. To limit the number of hyphens at the end of consecutive lines, enter the number in the Consecutive hyphens field.

4. To prevent capitalized words from being hyphenated, click on Skip capitalized words.

5. To prevent a specific word (such as a company name) from being hyphenated, select the text and click on Inhibit hyphens in selection.

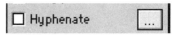

Figure 25. *The **Hyphenate** checkbox allows you to turn on or off the automatic hyphenation for individual words. Click on the **Ellipse icon** to see the hyphenation controls.*

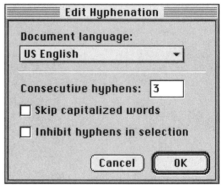

Figure 26. *The **Edit Hyphenation** dialog box allows you to control hyphenation.*

Automatic Hyphenation; Edit Hyphenation

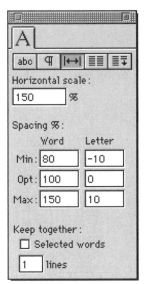

Figure 27. *The Horizontal scale stretches the width of the characters.*

FreeHand lets you control the scale and spacing of the paragraph.

To change the horizontal scaling of the typeface:

1. Select the text that you want to change selected, choose the Text Inspector and then click on the Spacing icon (**Figure 27**).

2. Enter the amount you want to horizontally scale the text in the Horizontal scale field.

Tips

➠ Hold the down Option key and drag a corner handle to change the Horizontal scale of all the text in a text block.

➠ Extreme amounts of horizontal scaling are unacceptable to professional typographers. Do not set large amounts of horizontal scaling unless you are trying to distort your type.

"What!" said the master at length, in a faint voice.	shrieked aloud for the beadle.
"Please, sir," replied Oliver, "I want some more."	The board were sitting in solemn conclave, when Mr. Bumble rushed into the room in great excitement, and addressing the gentle-
The master aimed a blow at Oliver's head with the ladle; pinioned him in his arms; and	man in the high chair, said,
	'Mr. Limbkins, I beg

Figure 28. *An example of **Keep together lines**. Notice that although there is room for one more line of text at the bottom of the left column, the lines together setting of 2 has forced the last two lines of the paragraph in the left column over to the top of the right column.*

To keep words and lines together:

1. To keep one word with another (such as a title with a last name), select the text and click on Keep Together: Selected words.

2. To keep paragraphs from breaking with fewer than a certain number of lines across columns, enter that number in Keep Together: Lines (**Figure 28**).

Tip

➠ The Spacing attributes also let you control the Minimum, Optimum, and Maximum amounts for wordspacing and letterspacing.

FreeHand also offers the ability to align text using tabs. There are five different types of tabs. Each one aligns the text in a specific way (**Figure 29**).

To align text by using tabs:

1. Begin typing the text you want to align.

2. As you are typing, press the Tab key on the keyboard to insert a tab character into the text.

3. The tabbed text will automatically be spaced at a .5″ interval from the rest of the text. The default tab settings are at .5″ intervals.

To set the tabs by dragging:

1. Select the paragraphs whose tabs you want to change.

2. If the text block does not have a text ruler visible, choose Text Rulers from the View menu.

3. Drag the left-aligned tab arrow from the top of the text ruler down to the area just above the numbers (**Figure 30a**).

4. Let go when the tab arrow is where you want it. The text will be realigned (**Figure 30b**).

English → German → Swedish
one   → eins   → en, ett

→English→ German   → Swedish
→ two →   zwei   →   två

→ English→ German →Swedish
→ three → drei →   tre

Terry →12.3 →3.45→23.67
Bonnie→ 5.67 →1.09→ 4.7

Age   → 37
Schooling → Great Nect South Senior High
Work   → Television & Print Advertising, Direct Marketing
Hobbies   → Guitar, Broadway Musicals

Figure 29. *Examples of the different types of* **tabs** *(from top to bottom):* **Left**, **Right**, **Centered**, **Decimal**, *and* **Wrapping**. *The gray arrows indicate where the tabs were entered.*

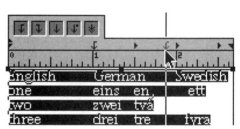

Figure 30a. *To set a tab position, drag a* **tab arrow** *directly to the* **text ruler**.

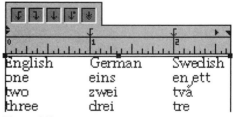

Figure 30b. *Text aligns itself along the tab arrow.*

Tabs

Figure 31. *To open the **Edit Tab** dialog box, double-click on any of the tab icons or the tab arrows on the text ruler (circled). open the dialog box. This allows you to set your tabs numerically and to add tab leaders.*

To set the tabs numerically:

1. Double-click on any of the tab icons at the top of the ruler. You should see the Edit Tab dialog box (**Figure 31**).

2. Choose the type of tab you want from the Alignment pop-up menu.

3. Enter a number for where you want the tab to be in the Position field. This number is in relation to the left side of the text block.

Tips

•❖ Use the Leader field or Leader pop-up menu to choose a repeating character that will automatically fill the space between the words that are aligned.

•❖ To change the repeating characters of a tab leader, double-click on the characters as they appear in the text and change their size, font, color, etc.

To change existing tabs:

1. To delete a tab from the text ruler, drag the tab arrow down off the ruler and then release.

2. To move a tab to a new position, drag the tab arrow along the ruler to the position you want.

Tabs

FreeHand gives you the ability to divide text blocks into columns and rows. (**Figure 32**).

To create columns and rows:

1. With the text block selected, choose the Text Inspector and then the Column-and-Row icon (**Figure 33**).

2. Enter the number of columns you want in the Columns field (**Figure 33**).

3. To change the Height of the columns, or the Spacing between each column, enter those amounts in their fields (**Figure 33**).

4. Enter the number of rows you want in the Rows field (**Figure 33**).

5. To change the Width of the rows, or the Spacing between each row, enter those amounts in their fields (**Figure 33**).

6. Click on the Flow icon to direct the text flow first down or first across the columns and rows (**Figure 33**).

1 tsp. Butter 35 calories	**1 stick Gum** 10 calories
1 tsp. Cream 25 calories	**1/2 cup Sorbet** 125 calories
2 tsp. Ketchup 10 calories	**1 oz. Chocolate** 150 calories

Figure 32. *Special effect created with columns and rows.*

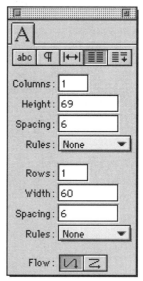

Figure 33. *The Column and Row settings of the Text Inspector.*

Group A	Group B	Group A	Group B
Group C	Group D	Group C	Group D

Figure 34. *Two examples of the* **rules** *between columns or rows. The rules on the left were set to* **Full height** *and* **Full width**. *The rules on the right were set to* **Inset**.

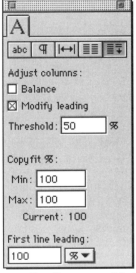

Figure 35. *The Copyfit settings of the* **Text Inspector**.

FreeHand also lets you create rules that fit in the spaces between columns or rows (**Figure 34**).

To add rules to columns and rows:

1. Select the text block to which you want to add rules. Choose the Text Inspector and then click on the Column-and-Row icon.

2. Select a rule style from the Rules pop-up menu under Column or Row. Inset will break in the space between the columns or rows. Full width or Full height will cross over the space between the columns or rows.

3. With the text block still selected, choose the Stroke Inspector to change the appearance of the rules.

You may need to use the copyfit commands to balance your columns.

To copyfit text:

1. Select the text block you want to adjust. Choose the Text Inspector and then click on the copyfit icon (**Figure 35**).

2. To adjust the columns by changing the number of lines, click on Balance.

3. To adjust the columns by changing the space between the columns, click on Modify leading.

4. To adjust the columns by changing the point size of the text, enter values in the Minimum and Maximum fields. Values below 100 will reduce the point size. Values above 100 will increase it.

5. To move the first line down from the top of a column, change the amount in First line leading field.

While it is very easy to create columns within a text block, you may want to have text flow from one text block to another. Or, you may want your text to flow onto an open path or into a closed path. You can link the text in these ways by using the Link box of the text block.

To link text between objects:

1. Select a text block you would like to link to another object.
2. Using the Selection tool, drag from the Link box of the text block. You will see a wavy line extend out.
3. Drag this wavy line onto the object to which you want to link your text (**Figure 36a**). Let go of the mouse.
4. If you had an overflow of text, you will see arrows in the Link box and the text will flow into the new object (**Figure 36b**).
5. If you did not have an overflow, you will see arrows in the Link box. If you add text or decrease the size of the first text box, the text will appear inside the new object.

Tip

- You can link text within a page or across pages.

When in the course of
human events it becomes
necessary for one people
to dissolve the political
bands which have
connected them with
another, and to assume
among the Powers of the

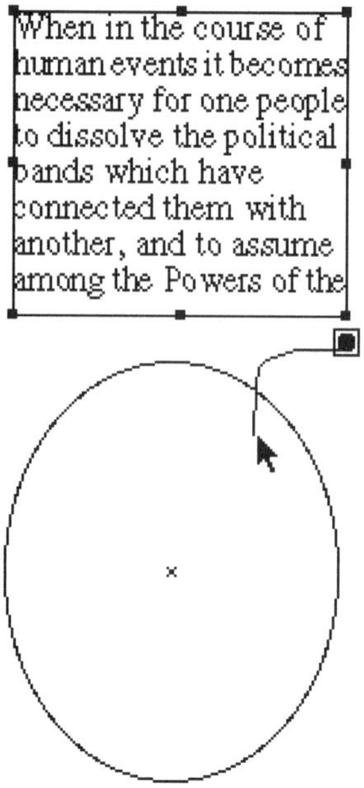

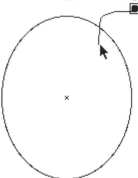

Figure 36a. *To link text, drag from the* ***Link box*** *to the text block or object to which you want the text to link.*

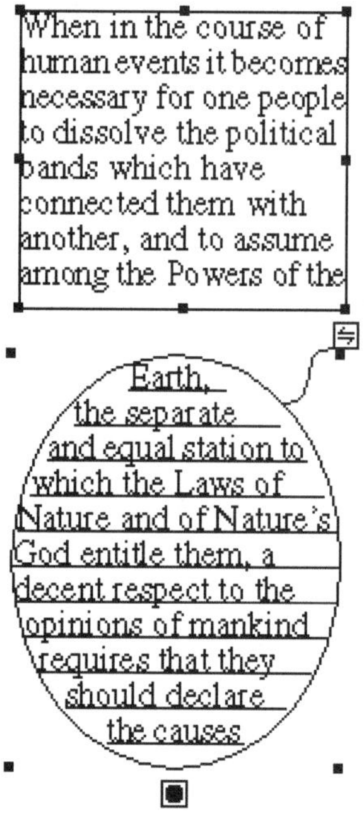

When in the course of
human events it becomes
necessary for one people
to dissolve the political
bands which have
connected them with
another, and to assume
among the Powers of the
Earth,
the separate
and equal station to
which the Laws of
Nature and of Nature's
God entitle them, a
decent respect to the
opinions of mankind
requires that they
should declare
the causes

Figure 36b. *After linking, the text will flow from one box to another.*

Link Text

Figure 1a. *With both a path and a text block selected, choose **Bind To Path** from the Type menu to align text to a path.*

Figure 1b. *The results of binding to a path.*

Figure 2. *As the text was typed a return was inserted after the word "PIXEL." The Bind To Path command was applied, and the text was aligned on each arc of the oval.*

With FreeHand, you can create looks for text that would be difficult, if not impossible, to create using an ordinary page layout program. In this chapter, you will learn how to align type to a path and how to adjust that alignment. You will also learn how to apply FreeHand's special text effects, including inline graphics. You will learn how to wrap text around a graphic element. Finally, you will learn how to convert text into artwork to create other effects.

One of the most popular effects in graphic design is to align text to a path. The path can be open or closed, with curve or corner points. The text can even be linked to other paths or text blocks.

To bind text to a path:

1. With the Selection tool, select both the text block you want to align to the path and the path to which you want the text aligned.

2. From the Type menu, choose Bind To Path (**Figures 1a–b**). The text will automatically align onto the selected path.

Tips

- If you are aligning text to a closed path, such as an oval, and you insert a paragraph return in the text, the text will align on both arcs of the path (**Figure 2**).

- If the path is not long enough to display all the text, the overflow box will be filled.

167

There are different ways to change how text is aligned to a path.

To change the direction in which the text flows:

1. Hold down the Option key and click with the Selection tool on the path. This selects just the path.

2. Choose Reverse Direction from the Path Operations submenu of the Arrange menu. The text will then flow in the opposite direction on the path (**Figure 3**).

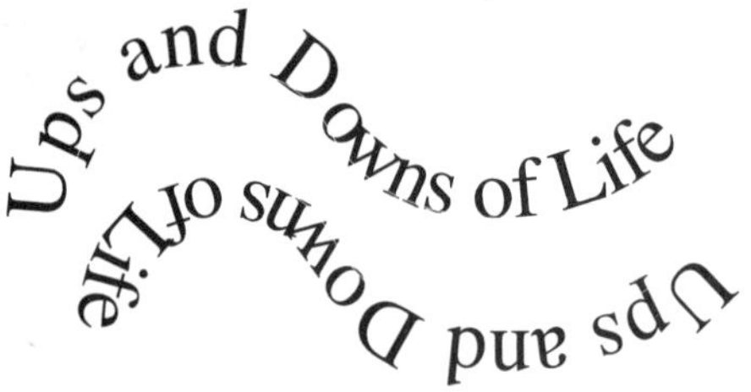

Figure 3. *The Reverse Direction command will cause the text (top) to change its direction (bottom).*

To move the text along the path:

1. With the Selection tool, click on the path. A small white triangle will appear at the left, center, or right of the text, depending on the text alignment.

2. Drag that triangle to move the text along the path (**Figure 4**).

Figure 4. *To move the text along the path, drag the white triangle next to the text on the path.*

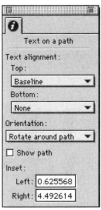

Figure 5. *The Object Inspector shows the Text on a path options.*

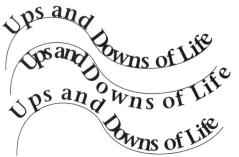

Figure 6. *The various ways text can be aligned to a path:* **Baseline** *(top),* **Ascent** *(middle), and* **Descent** *(bottom).*

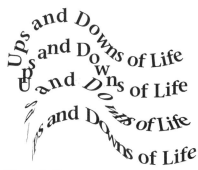

Figure 7. *The various ways text can be oriented to a path (from top to bottom):* **Rotate around path**, **Vertical**, **Skew horizontal**, *and* **Skew vertical**.

To work with text on a path:

1. Use the Selection tool to select the Text on a path.

2. Click the Object Inspector to show the Text on a path options (**Figure 5**).

3. To change how the text is aligned to the path, choose Baseline, Ascent, or Descent from the Text alignment pop-up menu (**Figure 6**). The Top pop-up menu controls any text before the paragraph return. The Bottom pop-up menu controls the text after the paragraph return.

4. To change how the the text is oriented to the path, choose Rotate around path, Vertical, Skew horizontal, or Skew vertical from the Orientation pop-up menu (**Figure 7**).

5. To move the text, you can drag the text using the white triangle or you can enter exact values in the Left and Right Inset fields. Once you enter the values, press the Return key to apply them to your path.

6. To see the fill and stroke attributes of the path to which the text is aligned, check Show path.

Tips

- An alignment setting of "None" will cause the text to disappear.

- To remove the text from the path, select the path and choose Remove From Path from the Type menu.

- Highlight text on the path by using the Text tool. Once it's highlighted, this text can be modified by using any of the functions of the Type menu or the Type palette.

One of FreeHand's most popular features is the automatic special effects that can be applied to text. These effects can be applied to entire blocks of text or to individual characters or words within a text block:

Highlight creates a color or tint that is applied as a block around the text (**Figure 8**).

Inline creates outlines of strokes and colors that surround the text (**Figure 9**).

Shadow creates an automatic drop shadow behind the text (**Figure 10**).

Strikethrough creates a line that runs across the text (**Figure 11**).

Underline creates a line that runs underneath the text (**Figure 12**).

Zoom creates a 3D effect where the text starts as one color and turns into another (**Figure 13**).

We, the people of the United States, in order to form a more perfect Union, establish justice,

Figure 8. *The Highlight effect on text.*

UNITED STATES

Figure 9. *The Inline effect on text.*

We the People...

Figure 10. *The single look for the Shadow effect on text.*

We, the ~~folks~~ people of the ~~Federated~~ United States, in order to form a more perfect ~~Club~~

Figure 11. *The Strikethrough effect on text.*

perfect Union, establish <u>justice</u>, insure <u>domestic</u> tranquility, … do <u>ordain</u> and <u>establish</u> this

Figure 12. *The Underline effect on text.*

July 4 1776

Figure 13. *The Zoom effect on text.*

Special Effects

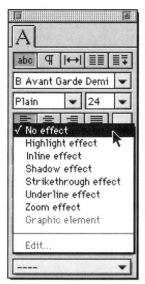

Figure 14. *Use the* **Effects** *pop-up menu of the* **Text Inspector** *to apply the special text effects.*

To apply any of the special text effects:

1. After using one of the methods described in the previous chapter to create text (*see page 149*), select the text to which you want to apply a special effect. You can select this text by highlighting it or by selecting the text block with the Selection tool.

2. Click on the Character icon of the Text Inspector. Unless you have previously applied a special effect to your text, "No effect" will be checked in the pop-up menu.

3. Choose one of the special effects from the pop-up menu: Highlight, Inline, Shadow, Strikethrough, Underline, or Zoom (**Figure 14**).

Tips

➻ You can turn the visual display of the text effects on or off by changing your Preferences settings (*see page 265*).

➻ Text effects may slow your screen redraw. Apply them after you have finished most of your work, or else work in the Keyline mode.

Apply Special Effect

Once you have applied a special effect to the text, you may find that you want to modify the effect. This is done by using the Edit button.

To edit the Inline effect:

1. Select the text that has the Inline effect and choose Edit from the pop-up menu. The Inline Effect dialog box will appear (**Figure 15**).

2. In the Count field, enter the number of sets of outlines you want to surround the text.

3. In the Stroke Width field, enter the width of the stroke.

4. To change the color of the stroke, press on the color pop-up menu.

5. In the Background Width field, enter the width of the background color that will be between the stroke and the text.

6. To change the background color, press on the color pop-up menu.

To edit the Zoom effect:

1. Select the text that has the Zoom effect applied to it and and choose Edit from the pop-up menu. The Zoom Effect dialog box will appear (**Figure 16**).

2. In the Zoom To field, enter the percentage that you want the final object to be.

3. In the x and y Offset fields, enter the distance you want to move the final object from the original text.

4. To change the color of the final object, press on the pop-up menu for the "From" color.

5. To change the color of the original text, press on the pop-up menu for the "To" color.

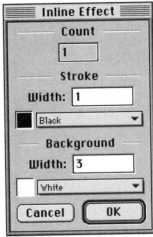

Figure 15. *The Inline Effect dialog box allows you to alter the look of the Inline effect.*

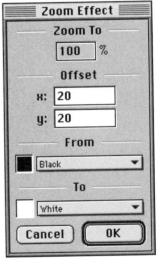

Figure 16. *The Zoom Effect dialog box allows you to alter the look of the Zoom effect.*

Inline Effect; Zoom Effect

Figure 17. *The three dialog boxes to edit the* **Highlight, Underline,** *and* **Strikethrough** *effects all have the same settings. The differences between the effects are created by changing the settings.*

Once you open the dialog boxes to edit the Highlight, Underline, and Strikethrough effects, you will notice that all three dialog boxes are really just variations on the same effect.

To edit the Highlight, Underline, and Strikethrough effects:

1. Select the text that has the effect applied to it and choose Edit from the pop-up menu. The dialog box will appear (**Figure 17**).

2. In the Position field, enter the distance from the baseline for effect.

3. In the Stroke Width field, enter the value of the thickness for effect.

4. To change the color of the effect, press on the color pop-up menu.

5. To apply a dash pattern, choose a pattern from the Dash pop-up menu.

6. To allow the effect to overprint the original text, click on Overprint.

To use the Shadow effect:

Choose Shadow effect from the Effects pop-up menu of the Text Inspector. There is no dialog box for editing the Shadow effect. The values of the Shadow effect are fixed. The shadow is always 50% gray. Its position is always down and to the right of the original text.

Highlight, Underline, and Strikethrough Effects; Shadow Effect

FreeHand lets you position graphics so that the text automatically flows around the graphic. This is called text wrap.

To wrap text around a graphic element:

1. Select the graphic element you want the text to wrap around. Do not group.

2. Move the graphic so that it is in the proper position in relation to the text.

3. Make sure the graphic is in front of the text block.

4. With the graphic still selected, choose Text Wrap (Command-Shift-W) from the Arrange menu. This will display the Text Wrap dialog box (**Figure 18**).

5. Click on the top right icon to display the Standoff Distances fields.

6. The Standoff Distances are the spaces that will be kept between the text and the edges of the graphic. Enter the amount for each side of the graphic.

7. If the object already has a text wrap applied to it, you can edit the Standoff Distances by changing the amounts in the fields. Or, you can turn off the Text Wrap by clicking on the top left icon of the dialog box.

8. Click OK when you are finished and the text will automatically flow around the graphic (**Figure 19**).

Tip

➻ If you want more control over the text wrap, draw a simple outline around the object. Do not give this outline a fill or a stroke. Choose this invisible outline as the object around to wrap the text. You can then add or delete points and manipulate the outline to create a more precise text wrap.

Figure 18. *The* **Text Wrap** *dialog box. Choosing the top right icon lets you enter the* **Standoff Distances** *for the four sides of the object.*

Figure 19. *An example of text wrapping around a graphic element. In this case, only Ben's outline was selected as the graphic to be wrapped.*

Wrap Text

do ordain and establish
this of the United States
of America

Figure 20a. *To create an inline graphic, select
the graphic and choose* **Copy** *or* **Cut***.*

do ordain and establish

this  of
the United States of
America

Figure 20b. *The inline graphic as it appears
within the text.*

You can also add inline graphics to text.
This lets you create elements, such as
ornate letters or logos, that are part of the
text. So if the text reflows, the inline
graphic flows along with the text.

To create an inline graphic:

1. Create the graphic you would like to
place inline. Examples of these
graphics may be FreeHand objects,
text on a path, text blocks, or placed
TIFF or EPS images.

2. Use the Selection tool to select the
graphic, and choose Copy or Cut from
the Edit menu (**Figure 20a**).

3. Use the Text tool to place an insertion
point where you would like the inline
graphic to appear.

4. Choose Paste from the Edit menu. The
inline graphic will appear
(**Figure 20b**).

Tips

➡ To remove an inline graphic from text,
use the Text tool to drag across the
graphic as you would a text character.
Choose Cut or Clear from the Edit
menu.

➡ To move the inline graphic up or down
on the baseline, drag across the graphic
as you would a text character. Change
the Baseline shift.

➡ If you select an inline graphic, the
Effects pop-up menu will display the
word "Graphic." Click on Edit and use
the Text Wrap dialog box to add more
space around the inline graphic.

➡ If you select all the text in a text block,
including the inline graphic, and then
change the point size of the text, the
inline graphic will scale up or down
along with the text.

Inline Graphics

175

So far, all the effects we have created with text have kept the text as text. This means that you can still edit the text. However, there may be times when you will want to convert the text to paths that can be edited as artwork.

To convert text into paths:

1. Use the Selection tool to select the text block or the text on a path you want to convert.

2. Choose Convert To Paths from the Type menu, or click on the Convert to Paths icon on the Text toolbar. If you convert the text aligned to a path, the path will be deleted, leaving only the text.

3. To manipulate the individual paths of the characters, choose Ungroup from the Arrange menu or hold down the Option key as you click on each individual path (**Figure 21**).

Tips

● Text that has been converted to paths does not require fonts installed for it to print.

● You cannot change the font, spelling, or characters of text that has been converted to paths.

● The fill of text converted to paths will automatically be set to overprint, indicated onscreen by little "O's."

● Any text characters that have holes in them, such as the letters "A," "O," or "B," will automatically be joined as a composite path (*see pages 193–194*).

● Text must be converted to paths in order to use that text as a mask (*see page 195*).

● You will need to convert text to paths in order to apply most of the FreeHand and third-party Xtras that create special effects (*see pages 207–212*).

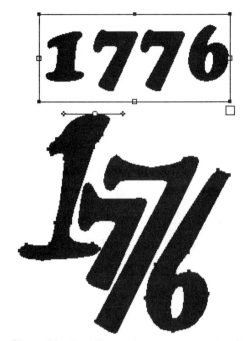

Figure 21. *The difference between **text** (top) and **text that has been converted to paths** (bottom). The converted text can be manipulated as artwork.*

EDITING TEXT 14

Anyone who has worked with a word processing program will recognize the usefulness of the features in this chapter—especially for lengthy text. In this chapter, you will learn how to use the Text Editor, to use the Spelling checker, to insert special typographic characters and formatting commands, and to use the Find Text feature to automate text editing.

Whenever you select text—either in a text block or on a path—you have the ability either to work with that text directly in the block or path or to work within the Text Editor. The Text Editor allows you to view the text all in one place or without formatting that might make the text difficult to see onscreen. The Text Editor is especially useful for reading type on a path.

To use the Text Editor:

1. Use the Selection tool to select the text block or path, or click with the Text tool to place an insertion point inside the text.

2. Choose Editor from the Text menu, or press Command-Shift-E to open the Text Editor dialog box. The Text Editor will open (**Figure 1**).

3. To change the viewing size of the text in the Text Editor dialog box, click on 12 Point Black. This will change the type to 12 points. It will also change any colored type to black.

(Continued on the following page)

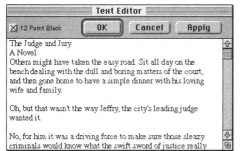

Figure 1. *The Text Editor allows you to see text that might be difficult to read. The scroll bar lets you scroll through the text.*

4. To change any attributes of the text, highlight the text in the Text Editor and make whatever changes you want via the Text menu or the Text Inspector.

5. To see how the text changes you are making will affect the actual text block or path, click on Apply. When you are satisfied with your changes, click OK.

Tips

➥ If you hold down the Option key as you click in a text block, you will open the Text Editor for that block and be positioned at the point in the text where you clicked.

➥ If you hold down the Option key as you click or drag to create a text block, you will open the Text Editor. You can then type your text directly into the Text Editor.

You may want to make sure the text in your document is spelled correctly. To do so, you can use the Spelling checker.

To use the Spelling checker:

1. Use the Selection tool to select the text block or path.

or

Place your insertion point at the point in the text where you would like the Spelling checker to start.

or

Deselected the text blocks to check the spelling of the entire document.

2. Choose Spelling from the Text menu or press Command-Shift-G. The Spelling checker will appear (**Figure 2**).

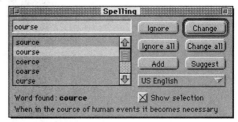

Figure 2. *The Spelling checker will check for unknown words, capitalization mistakes, and duplicate words.*

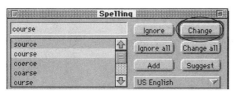

Figure 3a. *The Change button changes the word to one of the suggested alternates.*

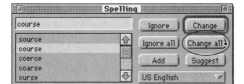

Figure 3b. *The Change All button changes all instances of the word.*

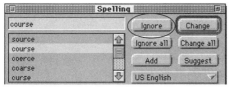

Figure 3c. *The Ignore button skips the word.*

Figure 3d. *The Ignore all button skips all instances of the word.*

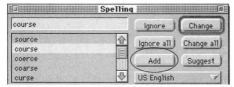

Figure 3e. *The Add button adds the word to the dictionary that FreeHand uses during a spelling check.*

3. To start checking the spelling of your text, click on Start. The Spelling checker will look through the text and stop when it finds an error. (After you click the Start button it changes to Ignore.)

4. If the Spelling checker finds a word it does not know, it will display the word in the top field. If it can, it will show a list of suggested alternates.

5. If the original word is incorrect, choose one of the alternates suggested or type in the correct word and then click on Change (**Figure 3a**). The incorrect word will be deleted and the correct word inserted.

or

If the original word is incorrect, choose one of the alternates suggested or type in the correct word and then click on Change all (**Figure 3b**). This will change all instances of the word in the text.

6. If the original word is correct, click on Ignore (**Figure 3c**). FreeHand will skip over that instance of the word, but will stop at it again if it is elsewhere in the text chain.

or

If the original word is correct, click on Ignore All (**Figure 3d**). The Spelling checker will ignore all instances of that word until you quit FreeHand.

or

If the original word is correct, click on Add (**Figure 3e**). This will add the word to the Spelling dictionary.

(Continued on the following page)

Spelling Checker

Tips

•• To check the spelling of just a portion of a lengthy text block, use the Text tool to select just that portion and then run the Spelling checker.

•• To check the spelling of an individual word without checking the entire text, type in the word at the top of the Spelling checker and then click on Suggest. FreeHand will give you a list of suggested spellings for that word (**Figure 3**).

•• To change how the Spelling checker finds words and how words are added to the dictionary, change the Spelling preferences (*see page 268*).

•• To see the section of text currently being checked by the Spelling checker, click on Show selection.

•• The Spelling checker is not a grammar checker. It will not find typos such as "He was reel good," since the word "reel" is a known word.

Figure 3. *Click on the **Suggest** button to see the list of suggested alternates.*

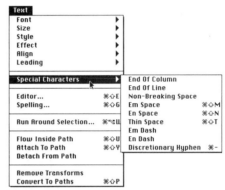

Figure 4. *To insert the special typographic characters, choose **Special Characters** from the **Type** menu.*

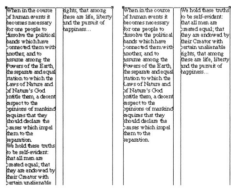

Figure 5. *Text before (left) and after (right) inserting the **End Of Column** character.*

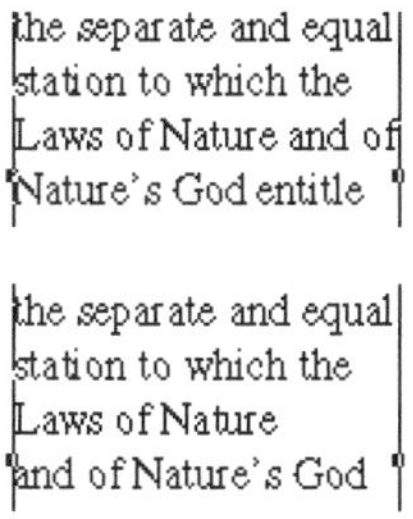

the separate and equal
station to which the
Laws of Nature and of
Nature's God entitle

the separate and equal
station to which the
Laws of Nature
and of Nature's God

Figure 6. *Text before (top) and after (bottom) inserting the* **End Of Line** *character.*

We congratulate Dr.
DuPrât on her recent
promotion. We expect
that this will be an
important advancement
for all the members of

We congratulate
Dr. DuPrât on her
recent promotion. We
expect that this will be
an important
advancement for all the

Figure 7. *Text before (top) and after (bottom) inserting a* **Non-Breaking Space** *character.*

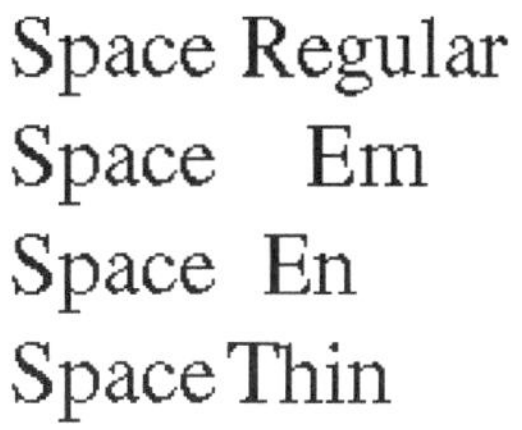

Space Regular

Space   Em

Space En

Space Thin

Figure 8. *The differences between (from top to bottom): a* **regular space**, **Em space**, **En space**, *and* **Thin space**.

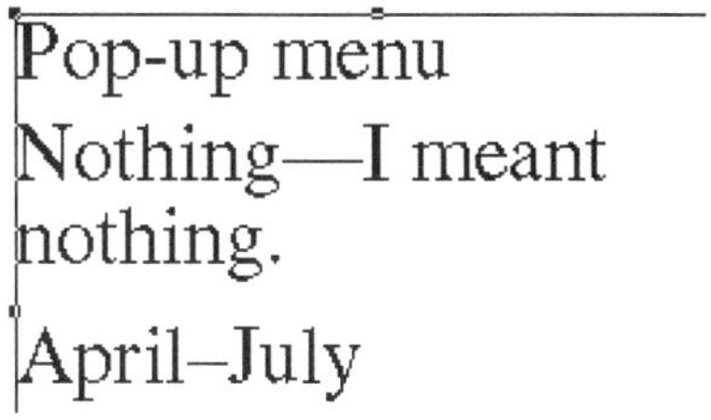

Pop-up menu

Nothing—I meant
nothing.

April–July

Figure 9. *The differences between a* **regular hyphen** *(top), an* **Em dash** *(middle), and an* **En dash** *(bottom).*

FreeHand allows you to insert special typographic characters that will improve the look of the text or control the flow of the text.

To use the Special Characters:

1. Place your insertion point where you would like the special character.

2. In the Text menu, choose one of the characters in the Special Characters submenu (**Figure 4**) or type the following keyboard commands:

End Of Column (Shift-Enter) inserts an invisible character that forces the text to the next column or next text block (**Figure 5**).

End Of Line (Shift-Return) inserts an invisible character that forces the text to the next line (**Figure 6**).

Non-Breaking Space (Option-Space) inserts a space that will not break across lines. This can be used to keep titles with the names they modify (**Figure 7**).

Em space (Command-Shift-M) inserts a space that is fixed as one em in width (**Figure 8**).

En space (Command-Shift-N) inserts a space that is fixed as one-half of an em in width (**Figure 8**).

Thin space (Command-Shift-T) inserts a space that is fixed as 10% of an em in width (**Figure 8**).

Em dash (Option-Shift-Hyphen) inserts an em dash, that is the length of one em (**Figure 9**).

En dash (Option-Hyphen) inserts an en dash, that is the length of one-half em (**Figure 9**).

Special Characters

If you are dealing with long amounts of text, you will need to use FreeHand's Find Text dialog box.

To use the Find Text dialog box:

1. Place your insertion point in the text block, or select the text block or path.

2. Choose Text Find from the Type menu or press Command-Shift-F. The Find Text dialog box will appear (**Figure 10**).

3. In the Find field, type the text string you want to search for. In the Change to field, type the text string you want as a replacement.

4. To search for only the word listed, click the Whole word checkbox. If you want to search for the text exactly as typed in uppercase and lowercase, click on Match case.

5. Use the Special pop-up menus to insert the codes for the Special Characters into the Find and Change fields or type the codes in the fields (**Figure 11**).

6. Click the Find First button to find the first instance of the text string.

7. To change the text, click on Change. Click the Find Next button to find the next instance of the text string.

8. To change all occurrences of the text strings, click on Change all.

Tips

•◆ Use the Special pop-up menu (**Figure 11**) to insert the codes to search for any single character, any single letter, any single number, white space.

•◆ To see the text currently being searched by the Find Text dialog box, click Show selection.

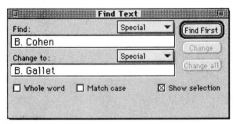

Figure 10. *The Find Text dialog box allows you to search and replace text strings or invisible characters.*

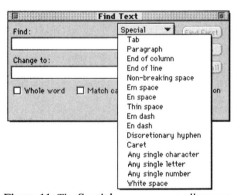

Figure 11. *The Special pop-up menus allow you to insert special characters into the Find and Change to fields.*

If you are working on a complicated document, there are two features that will help you edit and revise your work more efficiently: Styles and Find & Replace Graphics. In this chapter, you will learn how to open the Styles palette and work with the two default styles. You will learn how to define and edit styles, to base one style on another, and to duplicate styles. You will learn how to use the powerful Find & Replace Graphics dialog box to select objects and to find and change many attributes. You will also learn how to copy attributes from one object and paste them into another.

In order to see the styles in your document, you will need to open the Styles palette.

To view the default styles:

1. Choose Styles (Command-3) from the Panels submenu of the Window menu. If there is a checkmark next to the word "Styles," then the palette is already open.

2. If you have not added any styles to your document, you will see the two default styles (**Figure 1**).

3. The Normal style has an Object icon next to it. This is the default style for objects.

4. The Normal Text style has a letter "A" next to it. This is the default style for text.

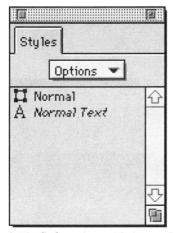

Figure 1. *The Styles palette with the two default styles. The Object icon next to Normal indicates it is an object style. The letter "A" next to Normal Text indicates it is a text style.*

The easiest way to define a style is by example. This means you can create the object or text and then use it as the example of the style.

To define a style by example:

1. Draw an object. In this case, draw a circle or type some text.

2. Choose the fill and the stroke or font attributes you want for your object or text (**Figure 2a**).

3. With the object or text selected, press on the Options pop-up menu of the Styles palette and choose New (**Figure 2b**).

4. A new style named "Style-1" will appear (**Figure 2c**).

To rename a style:

1. Double-click on the name of the style in the Styles palette. The name will be highlighted.

2. Type the new name of the style (**Figure 3**).

3. Press the Return or Enter key to apply the new name.

Figure 2a. *To define a style by example, create either the object or text and style it the way you want it to be.*

Figure 2b. *To define a style by example, select an object or text that already has the attributes you want for your style and then choose **New** from the **Options** pop-up menu.*

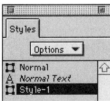

Figure 2c. *A new style is created with the name "Style-1."*

Figure 3. *Double-click on a style name to highlight it and rename it.*

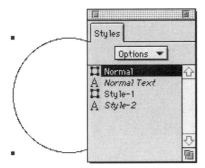

Figure 4a. *To apply a style, select an object or text that does not have the same attributes as the style you want to apply.*

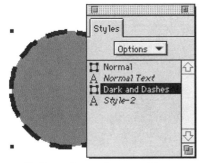

Figure 4b. *To apply a style to an object or text, select the object or text and then click on the name of the style in the Styles palette.*

Figure 5. *Styles can also be applied by dragging the icon for the style onto the object or text.*

Once you have defined a Style, you can then use it to change the attributes of any objects or text.

To apply a style:

1. Select an object or text that does not have the same attributes as the style you have already defined (**Figure 4a**).

2. Click on the previously created style. The selected object or text will automatically take on all the attributes of the style you want to apply (**Figure 4b**).

Tips

•➔ Styles are applied to text on a paragraph basis. You can, therefore, apply a style to a paragraph simply by placing your insertion point anywhere in the paragraph. Any style you select will be applied to the entire paragraph.

•➔ You can also apply styles by dragging the Object icon or paragraph symbol onto an object or paragraph (**Figure 5**).

You can also define a style by selecting all its attributes in the various Inspector panels and then defining the style according to those attributes.

To define a style by attributes:

1. Press the Tab key to deselect all objects and text blocks.

2. Make sure that one of the object or text styles is selected in the Styles palette.

3. Use the various Inspectors panels to choose the object or text attributes you would like for your style.

4. When you are satisfied with the attributes, choose New from the Options pop-up menu of the Styles palette. The new Style will appear with the name "Style-1."

Apply Styles; Define by Attributes

To redefine a style:

1. Make sure no objects or text blocks are selected, and select the style you want to change.

2. Use the Inspector palette or Type menu to change the style's attributes. You will notice that a plus sign (+) appears in front of the name of the style. This indicates that the current attributes differ from the original style definition.

3. When you are satisfied with the new attributes, choose Redefine from the Options pop-up menu of the Styles palette. The Redefine Style dialog box will appear, asking you which style you want to redefine. Click on the name of the style you want to redefine and then click OK (**Figure 6**).

4. You will see a dialog box listing the object or text styles in your document. Choose the style you want to change and then click on OK. The style definition will change and all objects or text with that style will be updated (**Figures 7a–b**).

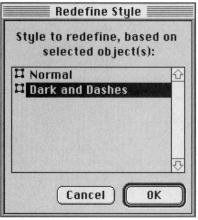

Figure 6. *The **Redefine Style** dialog box allows you to change a style definition to the attributes of the currently selected object or text.*

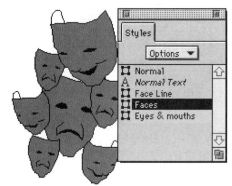

Figure 7a. *The style Faces was originally defined with a 50% black fill.*

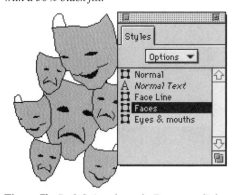

Figure 7b. *Redefining the style Faces to a lighter fill changed the shading inside all the artwork without selecting any object.*

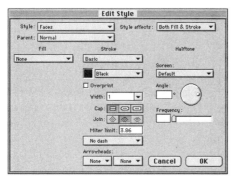

Figure 8. *The Edit Style dialog box for objects lets you change all the object attributes at once.*

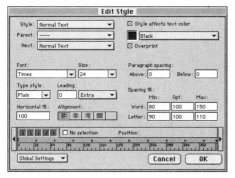

Figure 9. *The Edit Style dialog box for text lets you change all the text attributes at once.*

You can use the Edit Style dialog box to make changes to many styles at once.

To use the Edit Style dialog box:

1. Choose Edit Style from the Options pop-up menu of the Styles palette. The Edit Style dialog box will appear. If you had selected an object style, the dialog box will reflect object attributes (**Figure 8**). If you had selected a text style, the Edit Style dialog box will reflect text attributes (**Figure 9**).

2. Press on the Style pop-up menu to choose the name of the style you want to change.

3. Use any of the settings to change any of the style attributes.

4. If you want to make changes to another style, choose the name of that style from the pop-up menu.

5. When you have finished changing the styles, click on OK and all your updated styles will be applied.

Tip

•◆ You can use the Edit Style dialog box to define the attributes of a new style.

Edit Styles

FreeHand also offers the ability to base one style on another. FreeHand calls this the "Parent" and "Child" relationship.

To base one style on another:

1. Define a style. If it is an object style, give it a certain fill color but no stroke. If it is a text style, give it a certain typeface and a large point size.

2. Create a second style. If it is an object style, give it the same fill as in Step 1, but a different stroke. If it is a text style, give it the same typeface but a different point size.

3. Select the style created in Step 2 and choose Set parent from the Options pop-up menu of the Edit Style dialog box.

4. In the Set Parent dialog box, choose the style created in Step 1 as the parent. Click on OK (**Figure 10**).

To work with Parent and Child styles:

1. Use the previous exercise to create a style based on another style. Make sure the two styles are applied to two or more different objects or paragraphs.

2. Select the Parent style and choose Edit style from the Options pop-up menu.

3. Make whatever changes you want to the Parent style attributes. Click OK.

4. Notice how the changes have been applied to the objects or paragraphs. Only those attributes that are shared by both the Parent and Child styles will change when you edit the Parent style (**Figure 11**).

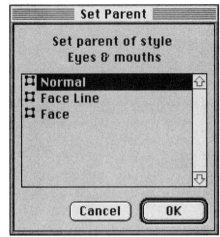

Figure 10. *The Set Parent dialog box allows you to base one style on another.*

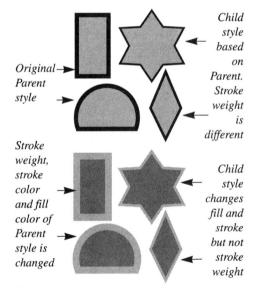

Figure 11. *An example of what happens when one style is based on another in a **Parent** and **Child** relationship.*

Figure 12. *Choose **Duplicate** from the **Options** pop-up menu of the **Styles** palette to make a copy of a style.*

Figure 13. *The **Remove** command deletes a Style from the Styles palette.*

To duplicate styles:

1. Choose the object or text style you want to copy.

2. Choose Duplicate from the Options pop-up menu of the Styles palette (**Figure 12**). A new style with the preface "Copy of" will appear.

3. Make any changes you want to this copy.

To remove a style:

1. Click on the name of the style you wish to delete.

2. Choose Remove from the Options pop-up menu of the Styles palette. The style will be deleted from the palette (**Figure 13**).

Tips

●◆ If you copy an object or text with a style and paste it into a new document, the object or text styles will appear in the Styles palette of the second document.

●◆ If you delete a style that has been applied to objects or paragraphs, those objects or paragraphs will maintain their attributes. But the name of the style applied to them will change to "Normal" with a plus sign (+) next to it, indicating that other attributes have been applied.

●◆ The Normal object style and Normal Text styles cannot be removed from a document. You can change the defaults for both of these Normal styles by changing how those styles are defined in the FreeHand Defaults file (*see page 272*).

Duplicate Styles; Remove Styles

As you have seen, styles let you make changes to many objects at once. However, FreeHand has another way to make changes to objects: the Find & Replace Graphics dialog box. The Select feature allows you to select an object based on certain attributes.

To use the Select feature:

1. Make sure your document has various objects with different fills, strokes, colors, shapes, fonts, text effects, attributes, etc.

2. Choose Graphics (Command-Option-E) from the Find & Replace submenu of the Edit menu. The Find & Replace Graphics dialog box will appear (**Figure 14**).

3. Click on the Select tab to bring up that part of the dialog box.

4. Use the Attribute pop-up menu (**Figure 15**) to select those features you would like to search.

5. Use the Search pop-up menu to choose, by searching within a selection, the active page or the entire document.

6. Click on Find. The objects meeting the search criteria will be selected. The number of objects found in that search will be listed at the bottom of the Find & Replace Graphics dialog box.

Tips

➡ Click on Add to selection to add the results of the search to the objects currently selected. This allows you to perform multiple searches for various features.

➡ To search for one stroke weight or for one type point size, enter a number in the Minimum field.

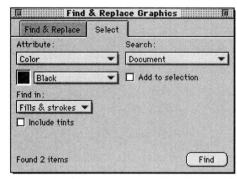

Figure 14. *The Select palette of the Find & Replace Graphics dialog box.*

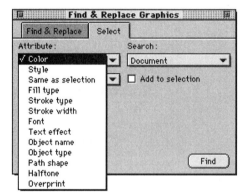

Figure 15. *The Attribute choices of the Find & Replace Graphics dialog box.*

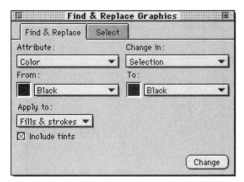

Figure 16. *The* **Find & Replace** *palette of the Find & Replace Graphics dialog box.*

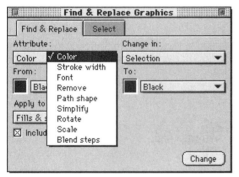

Figure 17. *The* **Attribute** *choices of the Find & Replace Graphics dialog box.*

The Find & Replace feature allows you to select an object based on certain attributes.

To use the Find & Replace feature:

1. Make sure your document has various objects with different attributes.

2. Choose Graphics (Command-Option-E) from the Find & Replace submenu of the Edit menu. The Find & Replace Graphics dialog box will appear (**Figure 16**).

3. Click on the Find & Replace tab to bring up that part of the dialog box.

4. Use the Attribute pop-up menu (**Figure 17**) to select those features you would like to search.

5. Use the Change in pop-up menu to choose, by searching within a selection, the active page or the entire document.

6. Click on Change. The number of objects that were changed will be listed at the bottom of the Find & Replace Graphics dialog box.

Tips

◆◆ Use the > or < symbol before a number to find amounts greater or less than that number.

◆◆ Use the + sign before a number in the To field to increase all the stroke weights or point sizes by that amount.

Find & Replace Feature

191

While not as powerful as the Styles or the Find & Replace Graphics dialog box, FreeHand offers another way to transfer the look of one object to another.

To use Copy and Paste Attributes:

1. Select an object with a set of attributes that you would like to apply to another object.

2. Choose Copy Attributes (Command-Option-Shift-C) from the Edit menu (**Figure 18**).

3. Select an object that you want to change, and choose Paste Attributes (Command-Option-Shift-V) from the Edit menu. The second object will not change shape but will change its attributes, such as fill and stroke, to match the first (**Figure 19**).

Edit	
Undo Transform	⌘Z
Redo	⌘Y
Cut	⌘H
Copy	⌘C
Paste	⌘V
Paste Behind	
Clear	
Cut Contents	⇧⌘H
Paste Inside	⇧⌘V
Copy Attributes	⇧⌥⌘C
Paste Attributes	⇧⌥⌘V

Figure 18. *The Copy Attributes command allows you to apply the attributes of one object to another without changing the shape.*

Figure 19. *The attributes of the hat in the left image were copied. The pants and shoes of the right image were then selected and **Paste Attributes** was applied.*

PATH OPERATIONS

O nce you have created paths, there are a wide variety of ways to modify them. These are called Path Operations and there are many places where you can make those modifications (**Figure 1**). In this chapter, you will learn how to Join Objects into composite paths and Paste Inside to create clipping paths. You will learn how to open and close paths, and to use the Knife tool to modify paths. You will also learn about some of the Path Operations commands from the Operations palette: Reverse Direction; Remove Overlap; Simplify; Add Point; Intersect; Punch; Union; Transparency; Expand Stroke; Inset Path; Crop; Envelope; Fractalize; and Set Note. And finally, you will learn how to use the Command-Shift-Plus sign command to apply Path Operations commands quickly.

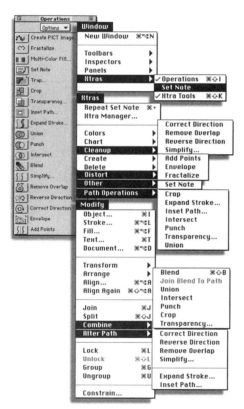

Figure 1. *The various menus and palettes where you can find **Path Operations**.*

Imagine you have created an illustration of a doughnut with a hole in the center. A composite path lets you see through the hole. In FreeHand, you join objects to create composite paths.

To join objects:

1. Use the Rectangle tool to create a closed object and fill it with one of the pattern fills. This will be used to show the composite path.

2. Draw another closed object and fill it with a solid color. This will be used as the outside of the composite path.

3. Draw a third closed object and position it inside the object created in Step 2.

(Continued on the following page)

4. Select the objects created in Steps 2 and 3 (**Figure 2a**).

5. Choose Join Objects from the Modify menu (Command-J) (**Figure 2b**). You will now be able to see the pattern through the hole created (**Figure 2c**).

Tips

➡ If the second object is not completely contained inside the first, the hole will appear where both objects overlap.

➡ To select and move individual parts of a composite path, hold down the Option key and click on one of the paths.

➡ If you change the fill or stroke attributes of one of the paths, that change will apply to all the paths of the composite.

To Split Objects:

1. Select the entire composite object.

2. Choose Split Object from the Modify menu. The paths comprising the composite will be released and will be separate paths again.

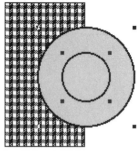

Figure 2a. *Two objects selected before they are joined to make a composite path.*

Arrange	
Bring To Front	⌘F
Bring Forward	⌘[
Send Backward	⌘]
Send To Back	⌘B
Lock	⌘L
Unlock	⌘⇧L
Group	⌘G
Ungroup	⌘U
Join Objects	**⌘J**
Split Object	⌘⇧J
Path Operations	▶
Stroke Widths	▶
Text Wrap...	⌘⇧W
Transform Again	⌘,

Figure 2b. *To make a composite path, choose* **Join Objects** *from the* **Arrange** *menu.*

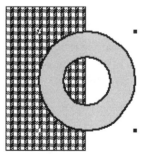

Figure 2c. *Two objects after they have been joined to make a* **composite path***.*

Figure 3a. *A clipping path is needed here so that the rectangles are not visible outside the edges of the star.*

Figure 3b. *When the rectangles are pasted inside the star, the star acts as a clipping path.*

Pasting an object inside another allows you to fill objects so that anything outside the objects will not be seen. The object that is filled is called a clipping path or mask.

To use Paste Inside:

1. Draw several objects that overlap one backmost object (**Figure 3a**).

2. Use the Selection tool to select just the rectangles, and choose Cut from the Edit menu.

3. Select the backmost object and choose Paste Inside from the Edit menu. The objects pasted will be visible only inside the backmost object (**Figure 3b**).

4. Hold the Option key as you click to select objects pasted inside.

5. To move the objects pasted inside, select the clipping path and drag the diamond-shaped handle for the pasted objects.

Tips

➥ To release the pasted objects, select the clipping path and choose Cut Contents from the Edit menu.

➥ If you want to transform just the clipping path without affecting any of the objects inside it, make sure the Contents checkbox in the Transform palette is not checked.

Paste Inside

To close an open path:

1. Select the open path.

2. Click on the Object Inspector.

3. Click on the Closed checkbox. The object will be closed with a straight line from one end point to the other (**Figure 4**).

or

Drag one of the endpoints of the path onto the other endpoint. This will close the path (**Figure 5**).

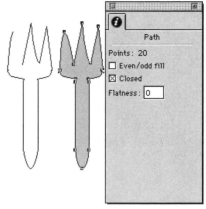

Figure 4. *To close an object with a line between its endpoints, check the* **Closed** *checkbox in the* **Object Inspector** *palette.*

To open a closed path:

1. Select the closed path that you want to open.

2. Click on the Object Inspector.

3. Click on the Open checkbox. The object will be opened by deleting the segment between the first and last points created on the path.

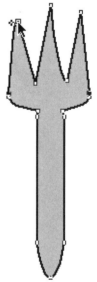

Figure 5. *You can drag one endpoint onto another to close an object.*

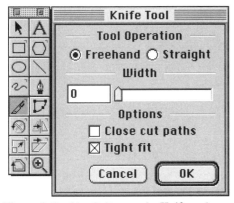

Figure 6. *Double-clicking on the* **Knife** *tool displays its dialog box.*

Figure 7. *The* **Freehand** *setting in the* **Knife** *tool dialog box lets you create wavy line cuts (top). The* **Straight** *setting allows you to cut straight segments (middle). Setting a* **large width** *lets the Knife be used as an eraser or hole puncher (bottom).*

With the Knife tool, you can open paths, slice objects into parts, punch holes in objects, and even erase parts of objects.

To use the Knife tool:

1. Double-click on the Knife tool in the toolbox. The Knife Tool dialog box will appear (**Figure 6**).

2. Click on the Freehand radio button to make a curved or wavy line cut. Click on the Straight radio button to make a straight line cut.

3. If you set the Width for greater than 0, you will create a space between the cuts you make.

4. Click on Close cut paths so that the two objects you create are closed paths.

5. Click Tight fit so that the Knife tool follows the movements of your mouse precisely. Click on OK.

6. Drag with the Knife across an object or objects (**Figure 7**).

Tips

- ➡ The Knife tool will only cut selected objects. If the Knife does not cut an object, it is most likely because that object is not selected.

- ➡ Hold down the Option key to temporarily set the Knife to the Straight setting.

- ➡ As you draw at the Straight setting, hold down the Shift key to constrain your cuts to 45° angles.

- ➡ Set the Width of the Knife to very large point sizes. This will allow you to take large chunks out of the rectangle.

Knife Tool

Ordinarily, you will not be concerned with the direction of a path. But you may want to reverse the direction of a path if text is aligned with it (*see page 168*) or when the path is used in a blend.

To use the Reverse Direction command with blends:

1. Create a blend between two open, stroked paths. Make the number of steps a low number so that you can see the objects in the blend (**Figure 8a**).

2. Hold down the Option key and use the Selection tool to select one of the original paths at the end of the blend.

3. Choose Reverse Direction from the Operations palette or from the Alter Path submenu of the Modify menu.

4. You will notice that the blend seems to "cross over" itself. That is because the two paths have different directions (**Figure 8b**).

To use the Remove Overlap command:

1. To see what the Remove Overlap command does, use the Freehand tool (*see page 53*) to create an object that overlaps itself. Make sure that Auto Remove Overlap is not checked.

2. Choose Remove Overlap from the Operations palette or from the Alter Path submenu of the Modify menu. Notice that the overlapping areas are eliminated (**Figure 9**).

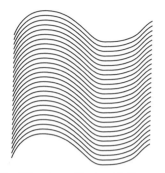

Figure 8a. *When two objects with the same direction are blended, the blend follows a smooth look.*

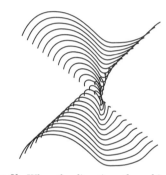

Figure 8b. *When the direction of an object in a blend is changed, the shape of the blend changes.*

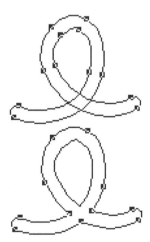

Figure 9. *The difference between an object before (top) and after the Remove Overlap command is applied (bottom).*

Reverse Direction; Remove Overlap

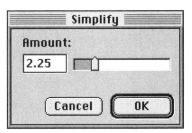

Figure 10. *The Simplify dialog box.*

Too many points on a path can cause problems when you print. The Simplify command lets you remove excess points.

To use the Simplify command:

1. Use the Freehand tool to create an intricate path with a number of points.

2. Choose Simplify from the Operations palette or from the Alter Path submenu of the Modify menu. The Simplify dialog box will appear (**Figure 10**).

3. Use the triangle slider to change the amount in the Allowable Change field. The greater the number, the more points will be eliminated. This may change the shape of the original object (**Figure 11**).

Tip

➡ Hold the Command key as you click on the icon in the Operations palette to apply the previous settings in the Simplify dialog box. This also applies to all of the commands in the Operations palette with a dialog box setting.

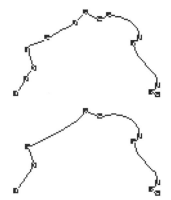

Figure 11. *The difference in the number of points between an object before (top) and after (bottom) the Simplify command has been applied to it.*

Certain effects need additional points on the path to look good. The Add Points command lets you easily add extra points to a path.

To use the Add Points command:

1. Select an object.

2. Choose Add Points from the Operations palette or from the Distort submenu of the Xtras menu.

3. Each time you choose the command, a new point will be added between each existing pair of points (**Figure 12**).

Figure 12. *The difference between an object before (left) and after (right) the Add Points command has been applied to it.*

The Intersect command lets you create a new object from the shape where two objects overlap.

To use the Intersect command:

1. Use the Polygon tool to draw a star.

2. Use the Oval tool to draw a circle that is slightly smaller than the star.

3. Position the circle on top of the star so that the points of the star extend beyond the circle.

4. Choose Intersect from the Operations palette or from the Combine submenu of the Modify menu.

5. The star will be converted to a star with rounded points (**Figure 13**).

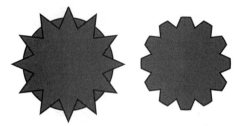

Figure 13. *The difference between an illustration before (left) and after (right) the* **Intersect** *command has been applied.*

The Punch command allows you to use one object to punch holes in another.

To use the Punch command:

1. Draw two objects so that one overlaps the other.

2. Choose Punch from the Operations palette or from the Combine submenu of the Modify menu.

3. The top object will punch holes in the bottom object (**Figure 14**).

Tips

➺ The Intersect command will delete the objects that do not overlap.

➺ If you do not want the Intersect and Punch commands to delete the original objects, you will need to change the Preferences setting (*see page 261*).

or

Hold down the Shift key as you apply the Intersect or Punch commands.

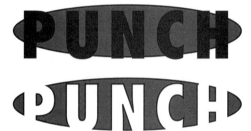

Figure 14. *The difference between an illustration before (top) and after (bottom) the* **Punch** *command has been applied.*

Intersect; Punch

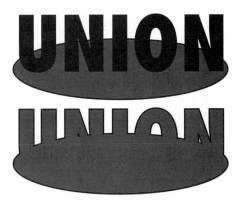

Figure 15. *The difference between an object before (top) and after (bottom) the* **Union** *command has been applied.*

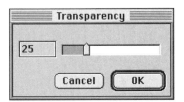

Figure 16. *In the* **Transparency** *dialog box, moving the triangle slider changes the mix of the foreground and background colors.*

Figure 17. *The difference an illustration before (top left) and after (top right) the* **Transparency** *command was applied. One object (bottom) was then moved to show how the effect was created.*

The Interset command allows you to take all of your selected objects and turn them into one path.

To use the Union command:

1. Draw two objects so that one overlaps the other.

2. Choose Union from the Operations palette or from the Combine submenu of the Modify menu.

3. The two paths will join into one (**Figure 15**).

Tip

→ If the selected objects for the Union, Intersect, or Punch commands have different attributes, the final object takes on the attributes of the backmost object.

The Transparency command lets you simulate a see-through effect.

To use the Transparency command:

1. Create two overlapping objects filled with different colors.

2. Select both objects and choose Transparency from the Operations palette or from the Combine submenu of the Modify menu. The Transparency dialog box will appear (**Figure 16**).

3. Set the amount of the transparency. If the transparency amount is less than 50%, the front color will be more obvious. If it is set to more than 50%, the back color will be more obvious.

4. Click OK. You will see the transparency effect (**Figure 17**).

FreeHand offers you a way to convert strokes or open paths to closed paths by using the Expand Stroke command.

To use the Expand Stroke command:

1. Select the path you wish to convert. Choose Expand Stroke from the Operations palette or from the Alter Path submenu of the Modify menu. The Expand Stroke dialog box will appear (**Figure 18**).

2. Enter the Width you want for the final object.

3. Set the Cap, Join, and Miter limit settings. Note that while these settings are the same as the settings for a stroke, the final object will actually be a filled path.

4. Click on OK. This will create a new filled path that has the stroke settings you chose (**Figure 19**). This new path can be used for other effects, such as the Transparency command or a Tiled fill.

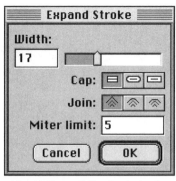

Figure 18. *The* **Expand Stroke** *dialog box.*

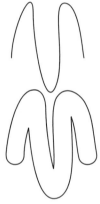

Figure 19. *The difference between an object before (top) and after (bottom) the* **Expand Stroke** *command has been applied.*

Expand Stroke

Figure 20. *The Inset Path dialog box.*

Figure 21. *How the Inset Path command affects an object: The original object (top left) had four steps applied at a 4-point inset. The settings were **Uniform** (top right), **Farther** (bottom left), and **Nearer** (bottom right).*

To use the Inset Path command:

1. Create a closed path.

2. With the path still selected, choose Inset Path from the Operations palette or from the Alter Path submenu of the Modfy menu. The Inset Path dialog box will appear (**Figure 20**).

3. In the Steps field, enter the number of copies you want to create.

4. Use the triangle slider or type in the amount in the Inset field to make an exact copy of the original that is smaller or larger by the amount set. Positive numbers place the new object inside the original. Negative numbers place the new object outside the original.

5. If you enter a number greater than 1, you should then choose Uniform, Farther, or Nearer from the pop-up menu to control the distances of the inset objects (**Figure 21**).

6. When you are satisfied with your choices, click the OK button. You will have multiple copies of the original object inset from the original.

Tips

➡ The Inset Path command will delete the original object when it creates the new one unless the Preferences settings are changed for Object Editing (*see page 261*).

➡ Hold the Shift key as you apply the Inset Path command. This will leave the original object and create a new object based on the command.

➡ Multiple copies of objects created with the Inset Path command will be created as grouped objects.

Inset Path

203

The Crop command allows you to use the top object as a "cookie cutter."

To use the Crop command:

1. Select various objects with one object on top.

2. Choose Crop from the Operations palette or from the Combine submenu of the Modify menu.

3. All the objects at the bottom will be trimmed so that only those portions that were under the topmost object will remain (**Figure 22**).

Tips

•◆ To crop text that has been converted to paths, ungroup and then choose Join.

•◆ The Crop command will delete the original object unless the Preferences settings are changed for Object Editing (*see page 261*).

> *or*

Hold down the Shift key as you apply the Crop command.

Figure 22. *The difference between an illustration before (top) and after (bottom) the Crop command has been applied.*

The Fractalize command allows you to distort an object for dramatic effects.

To use the Fractalize command:

1. Select the object you wish to distort.

2. Make sure the Even/odd fill box is checked in the Object Inspector.

3. Choose Fractalize from the Operations palette or the Distort submenu of the Xtras menu.

4. Repeat the command until you are satisfied with the effect (**Figure 23**).

Tip

•◆ Use the Join Objects command from the Arrange menu to create holes in the final object.

Figure 23. *The original object before (left) and after (right) the Fractalize command was applied three times.*

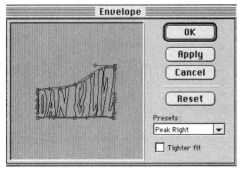

Figure 24. *The Envelope dialog box allows you to manipulate the bounding box that will distort the shape of your objects.*

Figure 25. *The difference between an object before (top) and after (bottom) the Envelope command has been applied.*

The Envelope dialog box allows you to distort objects into other shapes.

To use the Envelope command:

1. Select one or more objects.

2. Choose Envelope from the Operations palette or from the Combine submenu of the Modify menu. The Envelope dialog box will appear (**Figure 24**).

3. Use the Bézier handles to manipulate the bounding box that shapes the object in the preview box.

4. Press on the Presets pop-up menu to apply any preset shape to the envelope.

5. Press Apply to apply the changes to the object.

6. Click OK when you are satisfied. The envelope will be applied to your object (**Figure 25**).

The Set Note command allows you to add a name to an object and write notes or information about that object.

To use the Set Note command:

1. Select one or more objects.

2. Choose Set Note from the Operations palette. The Set Note dialog box will appear (**Figure 26**).

3. Give your selection a name and whatever notes you would like to have associated with the object.

4. To see a previously made note, select the object and choose Set Note from the Operations palette.

Figure 26. *The Set Note dialog box allows you to name an object and insert any information about that object.*

Tip

✏ If an object has already been given a name using the Set Note command, then your can search for that name in the Graphic Search & Replace (*see page 190*).

To use Repeat Command:

Once you have chosen any of the commands from the Xtras menu or the Operations palette, the next time you go to the Xtras menu, the last command will be listed at the top of the menu (**Figure 27**).

The keystroke for this is Command-Plus sign. This allows you to apply the command quickly to a series of objects.

Figure 27. *The very last command you have applied from the Xtras menu or the Operations palette appears at the top of the Xtras menu with the keyboard shortcut **Command-Plus**.*

Tip

✏ You must hold down the Shift key as you press Command-Plus sign. If you do not hold down the Shift key, you will be creating a clone (Command-=).

X tras are features that are added to the basic FreeHand program. Because Xtras can perform many different functions—change paths, create objects, convert vectors, etc.—some of them are covered in other chapters. In this chapter, you will learn about the majority of FreeHand Xtras, including the Xtra tools: 3D Rotation, Fisheye Lens, Smudge, Roughen, Eyedropper, and Bend. You will learn about the Colors Xtras that allow you to manipulate the colors in objects and in the Color List. You will also learn about the Trap, Create Blend, Empty Text Blocks, and Unused Named Colors Xtras. Finally, you will learn about how you can add even more Xtras to FreeHand by obtaining filters from Adobe Illustrator and from other software programs and companies.

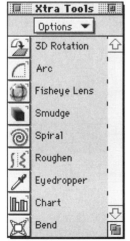

Figure 1. *To view the Xtra Tools palette, choose* **Xtra Tools** *from the* **Other** *submenu of the* **Window** *menu.*

Figure 2. *The* **Xtra Tools** *palette.*

The first set of Xtras are found in the Xtra Tools palette. To view this palette, choose Xtra Tools (Command-Shift-K) from the Other submenu of the Window menu (**Figure 1**). The complete Xtra Tools palette (**Figure 2**) contains the 3D Rotation, Arc, Fisheye Lens, Smudge, Spiral, Roughen, Eyedropper, Chart, and Bend tools. (*For more information on the Arc and Spiral Xtras, see Chapter 4, "Creation Tools." For more information on the Chart Xtra, see Chapter 18, "Charts & Graphs."*)

With the 3D Rotation tool, you can simulate the effect of what would happen to the perspective of an object if it were rotated in space.

To use the 3D Rotation tool:

1. Select the object or objects you wish to modify with the 3D Rotation tool.

2. Double-click on the 3D Rotation tool in the Xtra Tools palette. The 3D Rotation palette will appear (**Figure 3**).

3. With the Easy setting selected, press on the Rotate from pop-up menu to select the point from which the rotation should occur. There are several different choices: Mouse click is the point you press with your mouse. Center of Selection is the physical center of the object. Center of Gravity is the center of the object when adjusted for uneven shapes. Origin is the bottom-left corner of the bounding box surrounding the selection.

4. The Distance setting controls how much distortion will happen during the rotation. For the greatest distortion effect, choose the smaller numbers.

5. Position your cursor over the spot on the object from which you would like the object to rotate.

6. Drag your cursor away from this spot. A line will extend out. The farther along the line you drag, the greater the 3D rotation (**Figure 4**).

7. As you press, a triangle sign indicates the point of rotation.

8. When you are satisfied with your rotation, release the mouse and the object will be modified (**Figure 5**).

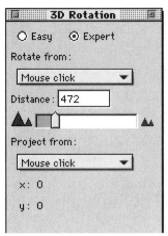

Figure 3. *The 3D Rotation palette controls how the 3D Rotation tool distorts objects.*

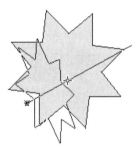

Figure 4. *As you use the 3D Rotation tool, a line extends from the point where you clicked. The farther you drag along this line, the greater the rotation will be.*

Figure 5. *An object before (left) and after (right) applying a 3D rotation.*

Fisheye Lens
Perspective
75
Concave
Convex
Cancel
OK

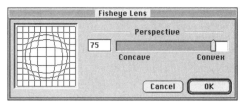

Figure 6. *The **Fisheye Lens** dialog box.*

GAINING WEIGHT?

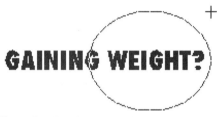

Figure 7. *When dragging with the Fisheye Lens tool, the oval indicates the area that will be distorted. The distortion will occur after the mouse is released.*

GAINING WEIGHT?
GAINING WEIGHT?

Figure 8. *The results of taking an object (top) and distorting it with the **Fisheye Lens** tool (bottom).*

Tips

- If you want to change the look of the rotation, use the 3D Rotation tool again on a different point in the object.
- In the Easy setting, the point of projection will be the point where the mouse is clicked.
- The Expert setting allows you to choose from which point the projection of the rotation will occur: Mouse click, Center of Selection, Center of Gravity, Origin, and x, y coordinates (which can be entered in the x and y fields).
- In the Expert mode, a plus sign (+) indicates the point from which the rotation is being projected.

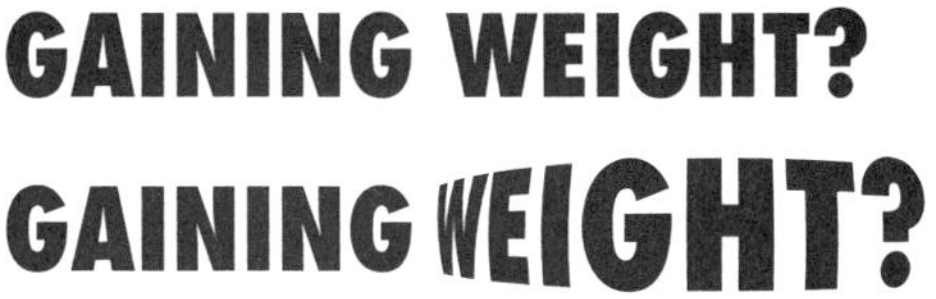

To use the Fisheye Lens tool:

1. Select the object you want to modify.
2. Double-click on the Fisheye Lens tool in the Xtra Tools palette. The Fisheye Lens dialog box will appear (**Figure 6**).
3. Drag the triangle slider or enter the amount you want in the Perspective field. Convex or positive numbers will cause the object to bulge. Concave or negative numbers will cause the object to be pinched. Click OK.
4. Drag your cursor to create an oval over the area you want to distort. (**Figure 7**).
5. Let go of the mouse and your selection will be distorted (**Figure 8**).

Tips

- Hold down the Option key to create a fisheye lens that goes from the center outward.
- Hold the Shift key to constrain the fisheye lens into a circular shape.

The Smudge tool provides you with a quick and simple way to create either a fuzzy or a soft edge on an object.

To use the Smudge tool:

1. Select the object or objects you want to modify.

2. Choose the Smudge tool from the Xtra Tools palette. Your cursor will turn into little Smudge "fingers."

3. Drag the fingers along the direction you would like the smudge to take. You will see a line extend from your object. This is the length of the smudge (**Figure 9**).

4. When you release the mouse, the smudge will be created (**Figure 10**).

Tips

•• Hold down the Option key to create a smudge that goes from the center outward.

•• Double-click on the Smudge tool in the Xtra Tools palette to display the Smudge dialog box (**Figure 11**). You can drop colors from the Color Mixer or Color List into both the Fill and the Stroke boxes. This allows you to have the smudge fade to a specific color rather than remain the default white.

•• The number of steps in a smudge is governed by the printer resolution as set in the Document Inspector. If your smudges look jagged, increase the printer resolution.

Tips

•• Hold down the option key to create a smudge that goes from the center outward.

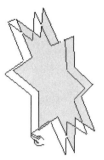

Figure 9. *Dragging with the **Smudge** fingers controls the length of the effect.*

Figure 10. *An object before (left) and after (right) the **Smudge** tool has been applied.*

Figure 11. *The **Smudge** dialog box lets you set the colors to which your fill and stroke will fade.*

Smudge

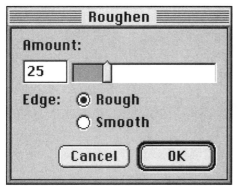

Figure 12. *The Roughen dialog box lets you control the amount of the roughness and whether the points should be **Rough** (corner) or **Smooth** (curved).*

Figure 13. *The results of applying the Roughen tool to an object. The top letters were roughed at the amount of 20. The bottom letters were roughed at the amount of 50.*

The Roughen tool take clean, smooth paths and makes them irregular and ragged. This can be very useful in making artwork look hand-drawn, or less "perfect."

To use the Roughen tool:

1. Select the object or objects you want to modify.

2. Double-click on the Roughen tool in the Xtra Tools palette. The Roughen dialog box will appear (**Figure 12**).

3. Use the Amount field or slider to increase the amount of segments that are added using the tool

4. Click on Rough radio button to create corner points. Click on Smooth radio button to create curved points.

5. Click on OK. With the Roughen tool still selected, press on the object and drag. The further you drag, the greater the distortion will be (**Figure 13**).

Roughen

The Eyedropper tool lets you copy colors between objects.

To use the Eyedropper tool:

1. Choose the Eyedropper tool from the Xtra Tools palette. The cursor will change to a little eyedropper.

2. Position the eyedropper over the color you want to copy.

3. Press down with the eyedropper. Do not let go of the mouse. Your cursor will turn into a little square of that color.

4. Drag that square onto the fill or stroke of another object. The color will be applied (**Figure 14**).

Figure 14. *To pick up the color from one object and apply it to another, press the **Eyedropper** on the first object and then drag the color swatch onto the second.*

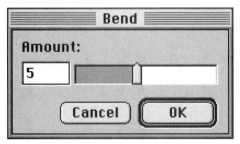

Figure 15. *The Bend dialog box allows you to control how much distortion a drag with the Bend tool will apply to an object.*

The Bend tool applies a distortion to objects to warp the path segments in or out.

To use the Bend tool:

1. Double-click on the Bend tool from the Xtra Tools palette. The Bend dialog box will appear (**Figure 15**).

2. Adjust the slider, or enter an amount in the field to increase or decrease the amount of the distortion. Click on OK.

3. With the object selected, press and drag down to create a rounded bend.

4. Press and drag up to create a spiked bend (**Figure 16**).

Tip

➡ The point you drag from will be the center of the distortion.

Figure 16. *The results of applying the Bend tool: original object (top), a Bend with a drag down (bottom left), and a Bend with a drag up (bottom right). The arrows indicate the point where the drag started and ended.*

Eyedropper; Bend

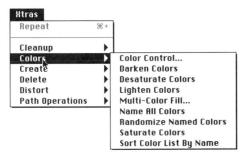

Figure 17. *The Colors Xtras are found in the* **Colors** *submenu of the* **Xtras** *menu.*

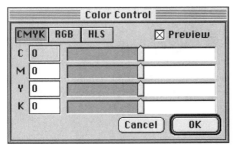

Figure 18. *The* **Color Control** *dialog box.*

FreeHand also offers Colors Xtras, located under the Xtras menu (**Figure 17**). The first of these, Color Control, allows you to adjust the colors in objects.

To use the Color Control dialog box:

1. Select the objects you want to adjust.

2. Choose Color Control from the Colors submenu of the Xtras menu. The Color Control dialog box will appear (**Figure 18**).

3. Choose from CMYK, RGB, or HLS color.

4. Use the triangle sliders or the fields to add or subtract color from the objects you have chosen. Positive numbers add color. Negative numbers subtract color.

5. Checking the Preview box lets you see how your adjustments are affecting the selected objects.

6. When you are satisfied with the color changes, click on OK. Your changes will be applied to the objects.

Tip

➥ The Color Control dialog box only works on objects that have been colored with process colors, not spot colors.

FreeHand also offers additional Xtras for working with colors: Darken Colors, Lighten Colors, Saturate Colors, and Desaturate Colors.

To use the Darken or Lighten Colors commands:

1. Select the object or objects you want to change.

2. Choose Darken Colors or Lighten Colors from the Colors submenu of the Xtras menu (**Figure 19a**).

3. Darken Colors decreases the Lightness value of the color in 5% increments.

4. Lighten Colors increases the Lightness value of the color in 5% increments.

5. To continue to darken or lighten the colors, press Command-Shift-+, which will repeat the command.

Figure 19a. *The flower pot at top was altered using the **Darken Colors** (lower left), and **Lighten Colors** (lower right) commands.*

To use the Saturate or Desaturate Colors commands:

1. Select the object or objects you want to change.

2. Choose Saturate Colors or Desaturate Colors from the Colors submenu of the Xtras menu (**Figure 19b**).

3. Saturate Colors increases the Saturation value of the color in 5% increments. This has the effect of making muted colors more vibrant.

4. Desaturate Colors decreases the Saturation value of the color in 5% increments. This has the effect of making colors less vibrant.

5. To continue to saturate or desaturate the colors, press Command-Shift-+, which will repeat the command.

Figure 19b. *The flower pot at top was altered using the **Saturate Colors** (lower left), and **Desaturate Colors** (lower right) commands.*

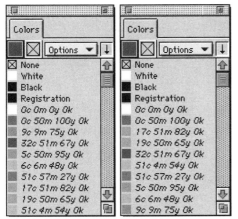

Figure 20. *An unsorted Color List (left) and the same list after applying the Sort Color List by Name command (right).*

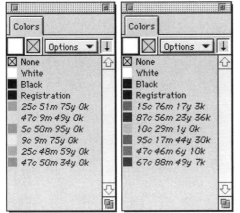

Figure 21. *The CMYK values of a named Color List before (left) and after (right) the Randomize Named Colors command has been applied.*

FreeHand offers you several Xtras that help you manage colors in the Color List and in your document.

To use the Name All Colors:

Choose Name All Colors from the Colors submenu of the Xtras menu. All colors used by objects in your document that are not named will be put on the Color List, and their CMYK percentages will be their names.

To use the Sort Color List By Name:

Choose Sort Color List By Name from the Colors submenu of the Xtras menu. This rearranges the Color List. The default colors appear first, followed by the colors named by their percentages, and then named colors (**Figure 20**).

To use the Delete Unused Named Colors:

Choose Unused Named Colors from the Delete submenu of the Xtras menu. Colors that are not applied to an object or a style will be deleted. The default colors will not be deleted even if they are not being used.

Tip

- Delete unused colors before exporting your artwork to layout programs such as Adobe PageMaker or QuarkXPress.

To use the Randomize Named Colors:

This command changes the values of the named colors in the Color List. All objects that have named colors applied to them will then be changed (**Figure 21**).

Trapping is a technique printers use to compensate for misregistration of colors when multiple color plates are used in the printing process. FreeHand lets you create traps with the Trap Xtra. While the Trap Xtra is very easy to apply, setting the proper values takes years of experience. If you do not understand trapping, and you want to set traps, consult the print shop that will print your work. Also consult the *Commercial Printing Guide* that came with FreeHand.

To use the Trap command:

1. Select two or more objects in your illustration that you want to trap.

2. Choose Trap from the Create submenu of the Xtras menu. The Trap dialog box will appear (**Figure 19**).

3. Use the sliders or type in the Trap width suggested by your print shop.

4. If your print shop agrees, choose Use maximum value to make the trap color the strongest available.

   or

   Choose the Use tint reduction setting and enter the reduction amount suggested by your print shop.

5. If you check the Reverse traps box, any traps that would have been spreads will be chokes and any chokes will be spreads. Consult your print shop as to when you should do this.

6. Click OK. The traps will be created.

Tip

•◊ When you create traps, you are creating new objects that overprint between the two original objects. If you move or delete objects later, be careful that you do not leave the trap objects behind.

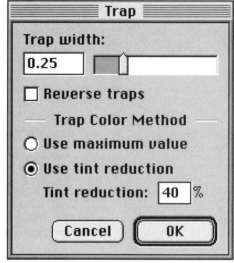

Figure 22. *The* Trap *dialog box.*

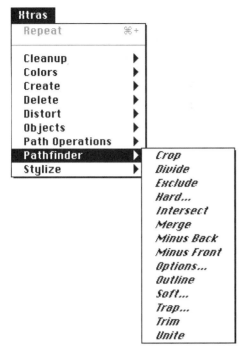

Figure 20. *The Adobe Illustrator Pathfinder filters as displayed in the FreeHand Xtras menu.*

To use the Create Blend command:

This command is identical to the Blend command in the Combine submenu of the Modify menu (*see page 144*).

To use Delete Empty Text Blocks:

If you drag with the Text tool, you will create a text block. If you then decide not to type anything, and deselect the block, you will have an empty text block on your page. Choose Empty Text Blocks from the Delete submenu of the Xtras menu to delete all such empty text blocks.

To add Xtras from other companies:

In addition to the Xtras that come with the program, there are other Xtras that you can use within FreeHand. These include the plug-ins that come with Adobe Illustrator.

You can also get plug-ins or Xtras from other software companies. Some of these Xtras are KPT Vector Effects from MetaTools, Infinite FX from BeInfinite, DrawTools from Extensis, and Letraset Envelopes from Letraset.

To use Xtras from other companies:

After you install them, Xtras from other companies will be listed either in their own menu or in one of the FreeHand Xtras categories. These third-party Xtras will be listed in an italic typeface (**Figure 20**). They can be used just like any of the original FreeHand Xtras.

Create Blend; Delete Empty Text Blocks; Add Xtras

If you install many Xtras from third party software companies, you may find that the Xtras conflict with each other. For instance, you may find that the Xtras from one company conflict with Xtras from another.

However, rather than going into the Xtras folder and taking the Xtras in and out, FreeHand comes with a built-in Xtras Manager. This allows you to turn the Xtras on or off right from within the program and will help you avoid conflicts.

To use the Xtras Manager:

1. Choose Xtras Manager from the Xtras menu (**Figure 21**).

2. The Xtras Manager dialog box will appear (**Figure 22**).

3. Click next to each Xtra to make it active or inactive. Use the Options pop-up menu to turn all the Xtras on or off.

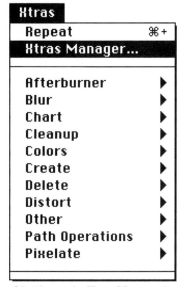

Figure 21. *Choose the **Xtras Manager** from the **Xtras menu** to access the Xtras Manager dialog box.*

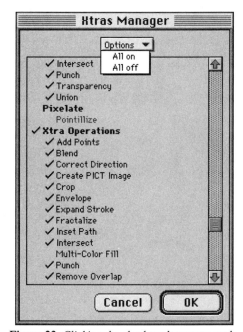

Figure 22. *Clicking the checkmarks next to each Xtra in the Xtras Manager will make the Xtras active or inactive.*

Xtras Manager

CHARTS & GRAPHS 18

Here's where FreeHand really gets down to business—creating mathematically correct charts and graphs. In this chapter, you will learn the basics of entering data into the FreeHand spreadsheet. You will then learn how to take that data and style it in different charts and graphs. Finally, you will learn how to create special graphic elements to use in your graphs.

Before you create a chart or graph, you will need to open the spreadsheet to enter the data.

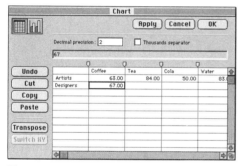

Figure 1. *The Chart spreadsheet is where you can enter the data for your chart or graph.*

To open the spreadsheet:

1. Click on the Chart tool in the Xtra Tools palette.

2. Drag the + sign cursor to create a rectangle on your work page. (The size of the rectangle will be the size of your chart or graph.) The Chart spreadsheet data window will appear (**Figure 1**).

To enter data:

1. Type the data in the top entry area.

2. Use the Return or Enter keys to apply the data and to jump to the cell below.

3. Use the Tab key to apply the data and to jump to the cell to the right.

4. Use the up, down, left, or right arrow keys, or click with the mouse, to jump to a specific cell.

Tip

⦁ If you import tab delimited ASCII or RTF text into your document, you can then copy and paste it into your spreadsheet.

Once you have entered the data, you need to choose the type of graph or chart you will create.

To style your graph or chart:

1. Click on the Chart style icon at the top of the Chart window. The spreadsheet will disappear and the styling selections will appear (**Figure 2**).

2. Click on one of the six Chart type icons: grouped column, Stacked column, Line, Pie, Area, and Scatter (**Figure 3**).

Tip

➡ To see the effects of changing the style and features of your graph, click on Apply at the top of the Chart window. This applies the changes but does not leave the dialog box. (This tip also applies to the rest of the exercises in this chapter.)

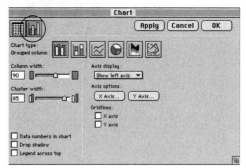

Figure 2. *Clicking on the Style icon (circled) switches from the spreadsheet to the controls for styling charts and graphs.*

Figure 3. *From left to right: the icons for* **Grouped column, Stacked column, Line, Pie, Area, and Scatter** *graphs.*

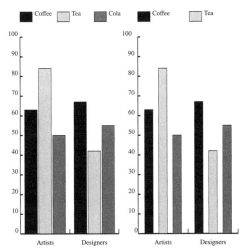

Figure 4. *The difference between a* **Column width** *of 90 (left) and a column width of 50 (right).*

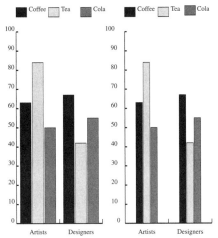

Figure 5. *The difference between a* **Cluster width** *of 85 (left) and a cluster width of 50 (right).*

While there are six different types of graphs you can create, the two most popular are the Grouped column (bar graph) and the Pie chart. The next exercises will show how to create each of these types of graphs. In each case, you should have entered data into the spreadsheet according to the exercise on page 219.

To modify a Grouped column graph:

1. Click on the icon for Grouped Column.

2. To change the width that each column takes up within its cluster (**Figure 4**), drag the slider or enter the amount in the Column width field.

3. To change the width of the cluster of the columns (**Figure 5**), drag the slider or enter the amount in the Cluster width field.

4. To see the data values, click on Data numbers in chart.

5. To Add a drop shadow behind each of the columns, click on Drop shadow.

6. To change the legend from the side of the chart, click on Legend across top.

Modify Grouped Column Graph

The most powerful part of modifying a column graph is in working with the X (horizontal) axis and the Y (vertical) axis. The Y axis usually contains the numerical data for a graph. It, therefore, has more choices than the X axis.

To modify the axis values of the Y axis:

1. With a chart selected and the Chart window open, click on the Y Axis button. The Y Axis Options dialog box will appear (**Figure 6**).

2. Under Axis values, click on Calculate from data radio button if you want the numbers along the Y axis to be calculated from the data entered in the spreadsheet.

3. Under Axis values, click on Manual to enter your own values for the Y axis.

4. Choose from the Major Tick marks pop-up menu to change how the tick marks sit along the Y axis.

5. Choose from the Minor Tick marks pop-up menu to show those added tick marks and how they sit along the Y axis.

6. Enter the number of minor tick marks in the Count field.

7. Use the Prefix and Suffix Axis value labels to add a prefix (such as a $) in front of the data or a suffix (such as /hour) after the data in the Y axis.

8. When you are satisfied with your choices, click on OK to see the finished chart.

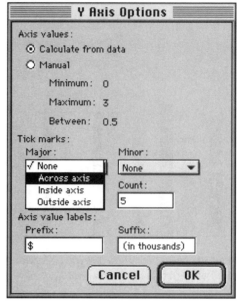

Figure 6. *The Y axis options.*

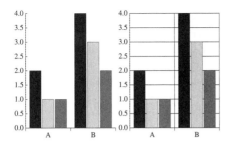

Figure 7. *The difference between* **Gridlines** *turned off (left) and gridlines* **turned on** *(right).*

To modify the X axis of a column graph:

1. With a chart selected and the Chart window open, click on the X Axis button. The X Axis Options dialog box will appear.

2. Choose from the Major Tick marks pop-up menu to change how the ticks marks sit along the X axis.

To create gridlines along both axes:

1. To turn the tick marks on the Y axis into gridlines, check the Gridlines X axis checkbox.

2. To turn the tick marks on the X axis into gridlines, check the Gridlines Y axis checkbox (**Figure 7**).

Once you have created a chart, you can make changes later.

To modify an existing chart:

1. Select the chart you want to modify.

2. Double-click on the Chart tool in the Xtra Tools palette

or

Choose Edit from the Chart submenu of the Xtras menu.

Another popular type of chart is a Pie chart. FreeHand lets you create this type of chart with ease.

To create a Pie chart:

1. With the data entered in the spreadsheet, click on the Pie chart icon in the Chart type area. The Pie chart choices will appear (**Figure 8**).

2. To have the legend on the side of the chart, press on the Legend pop-up menu and choose Standard.

3. To have the legend next to each piece of the pie, press on the Legend pop-up menu and choose In chart.

4. To move the first segment of the chart away from the other segments, drag the slider or enter an amount in the Separation field.

5. To see the data values, click Data numbers in chart.

6. To add a drop shadow behind each of the segments, click Drop shadow.

7. To change the legend from the side of the chart, click Legend across top.

8. When you are satisfied with your choices, click OK to see the finished Pie chart (**Figure 9**).

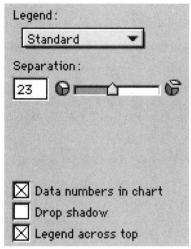

Figure 8. *The options for a Pie chart.*

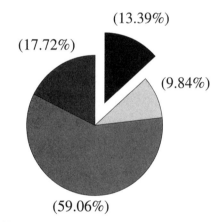

Figure 9. *A Pie chart with a separation of 23 for the first segment.*

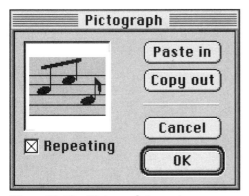

Figure 10. *The Pictograph box, where you can paste in the pictograph for a selected series.*

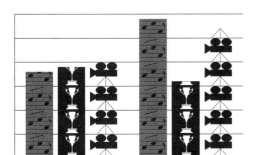

Figure 11. *A chart that uses pictographs for the columns.*

FreeHand also lets you put graphics into the columns of your charts. These graphics, called pictographs, give visual representations of the type of data being shown.

To insert a pictograph in a chart:

1. Find the graphic that you would like to have in the chart. (This may be any FreeHand graphic or imported PICT, TIFF, or EPS file.)

2. Select the graphic and copy it.

3. Select one column of the series to which you want to apply the Pictograph.

4. Choose Pictograph from the Chart submenu of the Xtras menu. The Pictograph dialog box will appear.

5. Click on Paste in. The copied graphic will appear in the preview window (**Figure 10**).

6. To repeat the graphic within the column, click the Repeating checkbox. To stretch the graphic within the column, leave the box unchecked.

7. Click on OK. The Pictograph will have been inserted (**Figure 11**).

Insert a Pictograph in a Chart

Tips

➥ Do not ungroup a chart or graph, as you will lose the link to the spreadsheet information. If you must ungroup, make sure you have a backup file with the link.

➥ Because all charts and graphs are grouped items, you need to use an Option-click to select individual elements.

➥ Once you have selected an individual element, use the tilde (~) key to select the other members of any subgroups in the graph.

➥ To enter numbers as labels, not graph data, insert quotation marks around the numbers. For example, the year 1997 would be entered as "1997".

OTHER APPLICATIONS 19

N o one program can do it all, so on occasion you may need to work with other applications along with FreeHand. In this chapter, you will learn how to place, resize, transform, and modify artwork, such as TIFF, PICT, and EPS files in FreeHand. You will also learn how to modify the size, position, and colors of pixel-based artwork and how to apply Photoshop plug-ins. You will learn how to extract an embedded placed image from a file, how to export your files in different formats, how to use the Create PICT Xtra, and how to convert your FreeHand files into Adobe Acrobat PDF files. Finally, you will learn how to use FreeHand's Fetch Info dialog box for cataloging your files in the Extensis Fetch database.

You may find that you wish to add artwork, such as scans, to your FreeHand file. This means importing artwork.

To import artwork:

1. Choose Import from the File menu.

2. Use the dialog box to find the artwork you want to import. If you are going to print your final file, you should import either TIFF or EPS artwork.

3. After you open the file, your cursor will change into a corner symbol (**Figure 1**).

(Continued on the following page)

Figure 1. *The **corner symbol** indicates that you have a file ready for importing.*

4. Click on the corner symbol to import the file in its original size.

or

To specify a certain size for the image, drag the corner symbol to fill the size you want (**Figure** 2).

Tip

➻ Unless you have changed the Preferences settings for Expert Input/ Output (*see page 271*), your placed image is only linked to the FreeHand file. If you send the file somewhere else, you must include the original image along with the FreeHand file.

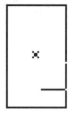

Figure 2. *Dragging the corner symbol sizes the placed image.*

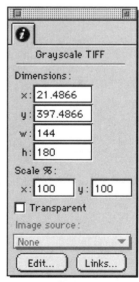

Figure 3. *Drag the corner handle to change the size of an imported image.*

Once you have imported an image, there are many ways to modify that image.

To resize imported images by dragging:

1. Place the Selection tool on one of the corner handles of the imported image.

2. Drag to change the size of the image (**Figure** 3).

Tip

➻ Press down on the Shift key to constrain the horizontal and vertical proportions of the image.

To resize imported images numerically:

1. With the imported image selected, open the Object Inspector (**Figure** 4).

2. Use the Scale % x and y fields to change the size of the image.

or

Enter the exact dimensions you want for the image in the w and h fields.

3. Press Return or Enter to apply the changes.

Figure 4. *Use the Object Inspector to resize imported images.*

Figure 5. *Any of the transformation tools, such as the Rotating tool shown here, may be used on imported images.*

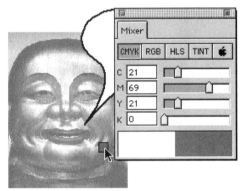

Figure 6. *Black-and-white or grayscale TIFF or PICT images may be colorized by dragging a color swatch onto the image.*

To transform an imported image:

1. Select the imported image.

2. You can modify the image using the transformation tools either by eye or by using the Transform palette (**Figure 5**).

FreeHand also offers you ways to modify the color and shade of grayscale or black-and-white TIFF and PICT images.

To colorize an imported image:

1. Select a black and white or grayscale image.

2. Drag a color swatch from the Color List or Color Mixer onto the image (**Figure 6**).

To change the shade of an imported image:

1. Select a black and white or grayscale image.

2. Open the Object Inspector and click on the Edit button. The Image dialog box will appear (**Figure 7**).

3. Click on the controls for Lightness or Contrast, or adjust the slider bars to change the image.

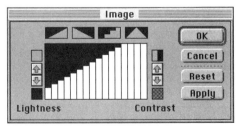

Figure 7. *The **Image** dialog box allows you to adjust the lightness or contrast of the image. Click the Apply button to view your changes before you click OK.*

Transform Images; Colorize Images; Change Shade

To make an image transparent:

1. Select a grayscale imported image.

2. Click on Transparent to turn the image from grayscale to a 1-bit image. This lets objects behind your image show through the white areas (**Figure 8**).

Tips

➽ Transforming, colorizing, or modifying the lightness or the contrast of an imported image in FreeHand may add to the printing time for the file. If possible, replicate the changes on the original image, and then reimport the image into the file.

➽ If you want to swap one imported image for another, click on the Links button in the Object Inspector. Then click on the Change button to select the new file.

FreeHand lets you use Photoshop filters to modify imported images.

To install Photoshop filters:

1. With FreeHand not running, open the Xtras folder in the Macromedia folder in the Macintosh System Folder.

2. In the Xtras folder, place a copy or alias of whichever Photoshop filters you want installed into FreeHand. Or put an alias of the Photoshop Plug-ins folder into the FreeHand Xtras folder.

3. Close the System Folder and launch FreeHand.

4. Any filters that are able to run in FreeHand will be found under the Xtras menu with the label *[TIFF]* preceding the name of the filter (**Figure 9**).

Figure 8. *The placed image before (top) and after (bottom) the **Transparent** option was applied.*

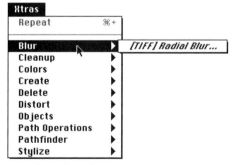

Figure 9. *A **Photoshop filter** as it appears in the FreeHand **Xtras** menu.*

Figure 10. *The **Radial Blur** filter as applied to a placed image.*

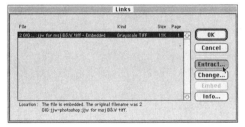

Figure 11. *The **Links** dialog box lets you extract an embedded image from the FreeHand file and then create a separate file that is linked to the FreeHand file.*

To apply a Photoshop filter to a TIFF image:

1. Select the placed TIFF image.

2. From the Xtras menu, choose the Photoshop filter you wish to apply to the image.

3. If a dialog box or a settings box appears, follow the steps necessary to adjust the settings for the filter.

4. The filter will automatically be applied to your image (**Figure 10**).

When you use any Photoshop filters on TIFF images in FreeHand, the result is an embedded TIFF image. This will make your FreeHand file larger than it was before the TIFF was embedded. To keep the file size low, use the Extract feature of the Links dialog box to create a copy of the modified image.

To extract an embedded image:

1. Select the image that is embedded in the FreeHand file.

2. Click on the Links button in the Object Inspector. The Links dialog box will appear (**Figure 11**).

3. The Extract button opens the Extract dialog box, which lets you choose a name and destination for the extracted image.

Photoshop Filters; Extract Embedded Images

FreeHand offers you many different ways to convert or export your FreeHand files into formats that can be read by other applications. Because some formats can change the contents of your file, you must pick your format according to your needs.

To export files:

1. With the file open, choose Export from the File menu. The Export document dialog box will appear (**Figure 12a**).

2. At the bottom of the box, you will see the field for the name of the file. The name will automatically be followed by a period and a suffix that reflects the nature of the exported file.

3. The Format pop-up menu lists all the formats supported by the FreeHand Export feature (**Figure 12b**).

4. Click on the Selected objects only to export only those objects that are currently selected.

5. Once you have selected a format, click on Options to choose those attributes that are applicable to the format you have chosen.

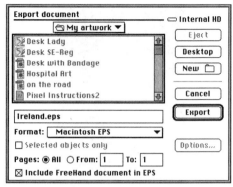

Figure 12a. *The* **Export** *document dialog box.*

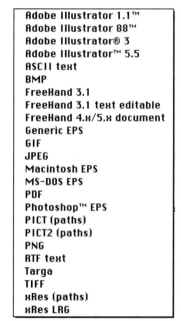

Figure 12b. *The* **Format** *pop-up menu gives you the options for exporting your file to different formats.*

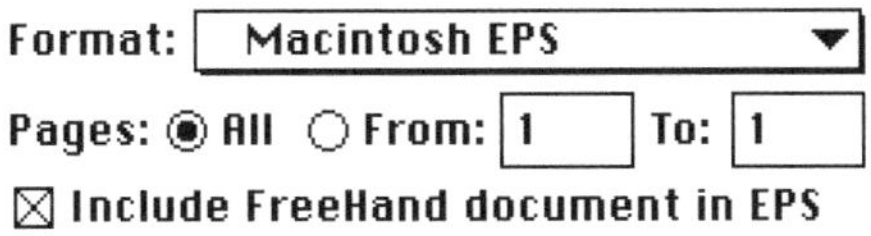

Format: | Macintosh EPS ▼ |

Pages: ⦿ All ○ From: | 1 | To: | 1 |

⊠ Include FreeHand document in EPS

Figure 13. *Setting controls for the Export document dialog box.*

Tips

➡ If you export as an EPS without including the FreeHand document, you will be able place that exported EPS in page layout programs but you will not be able to open the document in FreeHand to edit the artwork later on.

➡ If you export in a format that does not support multiple pages, you will need to select which pages of a multi-page document you want to export (**Figure 13**).

➡ If you export in the Photoshop EPS format, your file will be saved in the Illustrator format. This format can then be read by Photoshop and converted into a Photoshop file.

➡ If you export in the FreeHand 3.1 format, all artwork will be saved in a single file, regardless of which pages it was on.

➡ If you export in the FreeHand 3.1 format, the text blocks will be broken up to make the text look similar to the FreeHand 7 layout.

➡ If you export in the FreeHand 3.1 text editable format, the text blocks will stay unbroken.

➡ If you export in the PICT or PICT2 formats, you will be able to open your files in MacDraw or Canvas.

➡ If you export your file in the Rich Text format, you will keep the formatting of the text.

➡ If you export your file in the ASCII format, you will lose the formatting of the text.

Export

If you have chosen an export format, such as GIF or JPEG, that will convert your file to a bitmapped format, you will need to set the Options for the bitmapped format.

To set the Bitmap Options:

1. Once you have chosen a bitmapped format in the Export dialog box (*see page 232*), click on Options to open the Bitmap Export Defaults dialog box (**Figure 14**).

2. Press on the Resolution pop-up menu, or enter the amount in the field.

3. Press on the Anti-aliasing pop-up menu to choose the amount of smoothing, or softening, that will be applied to the image.

4. To create an alpha channel that can be used as a mask in programs such as Photoshop and Fractal Painter, click on Include alpha channel. To make the alpha channel include the background, click on Alpha includes background.

Tip

➺ To change the default settings for the Bitmap Export Defaults dialog box, change the settings in Import/Export Preferences (*see page 263*).

Once you have chosen the bitmap options, you will still need to set additional bitmap options depending on the type of format. (*If you have chosen the GIF, JPEG, or PNG formats, see Chapter 20, "Web Graphics" for more information on setting those export options.*)

To set the additional bitmap options:

Click on More to display the options for your specific format (**Figures 15a–d**).

Figure 14. *The **Bitmap Export Defaults** allows you to set the general attributes for any files to be exported in a bitmapped format.*

Figure 15a. *The options for a **BMP** file.*

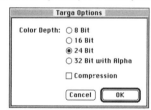

Figure 15b. *The options for a **Targa** file.*

Figure 15c. *The options for a **TIFF** file.*

Figure 15d. *The options for a **LRG** file.*

Bitmap Options

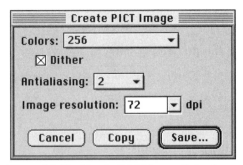

Figure 16. *The Create PICT Image dialog box lets you set how your artwork will be converted into a PICT image.*

Figure 17a. *A PICT image created using 256 colors, the dithering turned on, an anti-aliasing of none, and a 72-dpi resolution.*

Figure 17b. *A PICT image created using millions of colors, anti-aliasing of 4, and entering a 150-dpi resolution.*

FreeHand offers you another way to change the format of your artwork: the Create PICT Image Xtra. This command converts the items you have selected into pixel-based art.

To create a PICT image:

1. Select the objects you wish to convert.

2. Choose Create PICT Image from the Xtras menu or the Operations palette.

3. The Create PICT Image dialog box will appear (**Figure 16**).

4. Choose Copy to create a pixel-based copy of your image that will be stored on the Macintosh Clipboard. This copy can then be pasted into FreeHand, the Scrapbook, or other applications.

5. Choose Save to save your image as a separate PICT file. This file can be placed back into a FreeHand file or can be used by other applications.

Tips

- Hold down the Shift key while you select Create PICT Image to skip the dialog box and to copy the PICT image to the Clipboard using current settings.

- If you want your images to print looking their best, you may need a higher number of colors, anti-aliasing, and resolution (**Figures 17a–b**). These higher settings may require more RAM allotted to FreeHand.

PICT Image

FreeHand also lets you save documents as Adobe Acrobat PDF (portable document format) files.

To export an Acrobat PDF:

1. Choose Export from the File menu.

2. Choose PDF from the Format pop-up menu.

3. Click on the Options button. The PDF Export box will appear (**Figure 18**).

4. To choose the amount of compression applied to Color images, press on the Color Image Compression pop-up menu.

5. To choose the amount of compression press on the Grayscale Image Compression pop-up menu.

6. To export All the pages, choose the Pages: All radio button.

7. To choose a specific set of pages, click the Pages: From radio button and fill in the From and To fields.

8. Click OK and then click Export.

FreeHand also lets you add information you can use to catalog your files with the Extensis Fetch program.

To add Fetch Info:

1. With the file open, choose Fetch Info from the File menu. The Fetch Info dialog box will appear (**Figure 19**).

2. Type in the keywords and description information you want for your Fetch catalog.

3. Click OK. The Fetch information will be saved when you save the file.

4. To add a preview to your FreeHand file so it can be seen in the Fetch program, you need to check the Preferences settings for Importing/Exporting (*see page 263*).

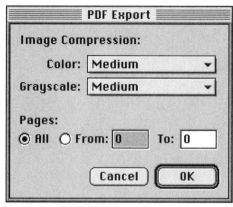

Figure 18. *The **PDF Export** dialog box allows you to set the compression attributes and the pages for your Acrobat file.*

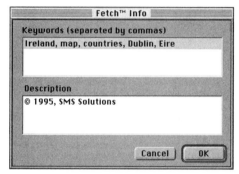

Figure 19. *The **Fetch Info** dialog box allows you to create keywords and descriptions that can help you search through an Extensis Fetch database.*

Acrobat PDF; Fetch Info

WEB GRAPHICS 20

O ne of the most exciting aspects of working with FreeHand is the ability to create graphics for the World Wide Web. This means that, in addition to creating graphics for print, you can use your FreeHand artwork as part of Web pages, or the pages that are accessed via the millions of computers connected to the Web. In this chapter you will learn how to create URL "links" for your FreeHand elements. You will also learn how to take FreeHand artwork and save it in a format that can be used as part of the Shockwave graphics technology. Finally, you will learn how to save your artwork in other formats that can be used for creating Web pages.

Tips

➻ The technology for Web pages is changing dramatically. Every month brings new features, techniques, and formats. If the Web browser you are working with has new information on creating Web graphics, follow that information.

➻ For more information on designing Web graphics, see *Elements of Web Design* by DiNucci et al published by Peachpit Press.

FreeHand lets you turn objects into a link for a Web URL. This means that when your graphic is viewed on the Web, clicking on the linked object will open a new Web page. Before you link objects to URLs, you will need to enter the Web address in FreeHand's URLs panel.

To add addresses to the URLs panel:

1. Open the artwork that will be used as part of your Web page.

2. Choose URLs from the Xtras submenu of the Window menu. The URLs panel will appear (**Figure 1**).

To create a new URL:

1. Choose New from the Options pop-up menu. The New URL dialog box will appear (**Figure 2**).

2. Type the address for the link in the URL field.

3. If you want to add more URLs, choose New from the Options pop-up menu, and type in the additional addresses.

Tips

➥ If you need a Web address with minor changes from one that is entered, use the Duplicate command in the Options pop-up menu. Then choose Edit to make the changes.

➥ Use the Remove command in the Options pop-up menu to delete URLs that are no longer needed.

Once your URLs are in the panel, you can then apply them to objects.

To apply a URL to an object:

1. Select the object or objects.

2. Click on the URL in the URLs panel. The object will be linked to that address.

or

Press on the address in the URLs panel. Drag from the address onto the object to which you want to apply it. A white square will appear as you drag. Let go when this white square is over the object (**Figure 3**). The object will be linked to that address.

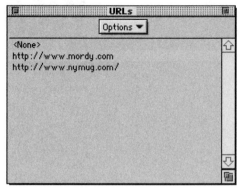

Figure 1. *The URLs panel holds the Web addresses for a document.*

Figure 2. *The New URL dialog box allows you to type in the URL address for whatever link you would like to have in your Web graphic.*

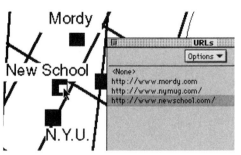

Figure 3. *To link an object to a URL, drag from the URLs panel and drop the white square onto the object you want to have linked.*

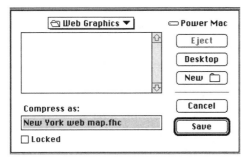

Figure 4. *The Afterburner Xtra opens a Save dialog box where you can save your FreeHand document in a special format that can be read by the Shockwave technology.*

Once you have a FreeHand file with Web links, you still need to save it in a format that can be read by the Shockwave technology. This means that you must save the file using the Afterburner compression format. This allows the Shockwave plug-in to open the file in a Web browser.

To save a file for use by Shockwave:

1. Choose Compress document from the Afterburner submenu of the Xtras menu. The Save dialog box will appear (**Figure 4**).

2. Make sure you follow the proper naming conventions for the type of server that will be displaying your file. For instance, while the Macintosh allows you to name your file with spaces and upper and lower-case letters, Unix systems require all lower case letters and no spaces.

3. Make sure the suffix ".fhc" is appended to the end of your file name. This ensures that the file will be read by the Shockwave plug-in.

Save for Shockwave

One of the benefits of saving your FreeHand files for use by the Shockwave plug-in is that they can be magnified while they are viewed on the Web. Also, clicking on linked objects allows you to jump to new Web addresses. However, if you do not want to use Shockwave, FreeHand lets you save your files in other Web formats. All of these formats are accessible once your document is exported as a bitmap.

To save a file as a bitmap:

1. Create the artwork you want to turn into a bitmapped graphic.

2. Choose Export from the File menu.

3. Choose GIF, JPEG, or PNG from the Format pop-up menu.

4. Click on the Options button in the Save dialog box (*For more information on exporting, see page 232–234*). The Bitmap Export Defaults will appear (**Figure 5**).

5. Press on the Resolution pop-up menu, or enter the proper resolution in the field. For most Web graphics, this amount does not have to be higher than 72 dpi.

6. Press on the Anti-aliasing pop-up menu to control how much softening of the image is applied. (*For more information on anti-aliasing, see page 235.*)

7. To create an alpha channel that can be used as a mask for your image, click on Include alpha channel.

8. To include the background area in the alpha channel, click Alpha includes background.

Figure 5. *To convert a file from vector to bitmapped format, you need to set the file attributes in the **Bitmap Export Defaults** dialog box.*

Save as a Bitmap

Figure 6. *GIF Options let you control how the image is displayed on the Web.*

Figure 7. *The difference between an image without a transparent background (left) and one with a transparent background (right).*

Once you have set the bitmapped attributes, you then need to set the options for the specific file format you have chosen. One of the most common formats for Web graphics is the GIF (pronounced as either "gif" or "jif") format.

To set the GIF attributes:

1. Choose Export from the File menu.

2. Make sure that GIF is selected in the Format pop-up menu of the Export dialog box.

3. Click on More in the Bitmap Export Defaults dialog box. The GIF Options box will appear (**Figure 6**). (If you do not see GIF Options it is because you did not set GIF in the Format pop-up menu.)

4. Click on Interlaced GIF to create an image that appears almost immediately and that slowly becomes clearer. This gives the viewer a rough idea of what the image looks like without waiting for a long download time.

5. Click on Transparent GIF to create an image where the background is transparent when viewed on the Web. This allows you to lay your image over a pattern or other design on the Web page (**Figure 7**).

GIF Attributes

Another format used on the Web is the JPEG (pronounced Jay-peg) format.

To set the JPEG attributes:

1. Choose Export from the File menu.

2. Make sure JPEG is selected in the Format pop-up menu of the Export dialog box.

3. Click on More of the Bitmap Export Defaults box. The JPEG Options dialog box will appear (**Figure 8**).

4. Enter a percentage for Image Quality.

5. Click on Progressive JPEG to create an effect similar to the Interlaced GIF. (*See previous page.*)

Tip

∞ The lower the image quality, the smaller your file.

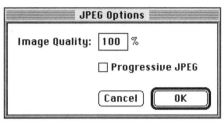

Figure 8. *JPEG Options let you control the quality of your image and how that image is displayed on the Web.*

The last format is the PNG (pronounced "Ping") format. This format has applications in both Web graphics and printing.

To set the PNG attributes:

1. Make sure that PNG is selected in the Format pop-up menu of the Export dialog box.

2. Click on More of the Bitmap Export Defaults box. The PNG Options box will appear (**Figure 9**).

3. Choose from the options for the color bit depth. For most Web graphics, you do not need anything greater than 24-bit. The higher bit depths are for high-end print work.

4. Click on Interlaced PNG to create an effect similar to the Interlaced GIF. (*See previous page.*)

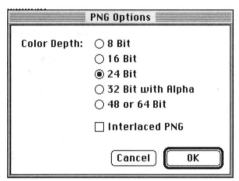

Figure 9. *PNG Options let you control the color quality of your image and how that image is displayed on the Web.*

PRINTING 21

Once you've finished your illustration on screen, you will probably want to print it. This chapter is divided into two parts. The first part, Basic Printing, covers the print options for printing to a simple desktop printer. Here, you will learn about the settings in the Printer dialog box: setting the number of copies; setting which pages to print; picking the paper source; setting the tiling options; scaling the illustration or making it automatically fit the size of the page; and choosing separations or composite proof.

The second part, Advanced Printing, covers the print options for printing to high-resolution imagesetters: adding crop marks and registration marks; adding the name of the file and adding separation-name labels; setting the imaging options; setting global trapping; selecting and setting the proper PostScript Printer Description file (PPD); setting halftone screens; setting the transfer function; setting the inks that need to knockout or overprint; and setting the screen angles. You will also learn about the Output Options: splitting complex paths; printing the objects on invisible layers; choosing the image data; converting RGB TIFF images to CMYK; setting the maximum number of color steps; and setting the flatness. You will learn how to create a report about your document. Finally, you will learn which files you need to include when you send your work to be printed at a service bureau.

BASIC PRINTING

Before you print your document, you should determine what kind of printer you will be using. If your printer is not a PostScript device, the Custom, Textured, and PostScript fills and strokes will not print. If you are in doubt as to the type of printer you have, check the specifications that came with the printer.

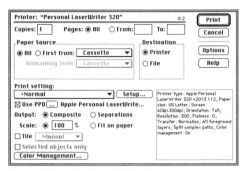

Figure 1. *The Printer dialog box.*

To open the Printer dialog box:

Choose Print from the File menu or press Command-P. The Printer dialog box will appear (**Figure 1**). Some of the options that appear may change depending on the type of printer you have and the LaserWriter software installed.

Figure 2. *The Pages choices in the Printer dialog box.*

To set up the Printer dialog box:

1. In the Copies field, enter the number of copies you want to print.

2. For the Pages choices (**Figure 2**), choose All if you want all the pages in your document to print.

   or

   Choose a range of pages by entering numbers in the From and To fields.

3. Choose the Paper Source you want your printer to use (**Figure 3**).

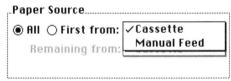

Figure 3. *The Paper Source choices in the Printer dialog box.*

4. If you wish to tile your illustration (*see page 246*), click on Tile and choose Manual or Automatic from the Tile options (**Figure 4**).

Figure 4. *The Tile choices in the Printer dialog box.*

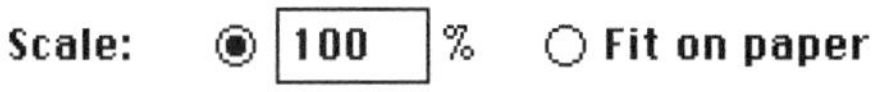

Scale: ⦿ | 100 | % ◯ **Fit on paper**

Figure 5. *The Scale choices in the **Printer** dialog box.*

Output: ⦿ **Composite** ◯ **Separations**

Figure 6. *The **Composite** or **Separations** choices in the **Printer** dialog box.*

☒ **Selected objects only**

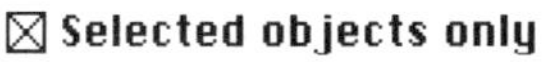

Figure 7. *The **Selected objects only** checkbox in the **Printer** dialog box.*

5. To change the size of your illustration, enter an amount in the Scale field (**Figure 5**).

or

If you want your illustration to fit on the paper you are printing on, choose Fit on paper (**Figure 5**).

6. If your illustration has color in it, you will need to choose Composite or Separations (**Figure 6**). If you are printing to an ordinary desktop printer, you will most likely want to print your job as a composite. If you are outputting to a high-resolution printer, you will want to make separations into individual prints or plates of film.

7. If you click Selected objects only (**Figure 7**), then only the objects that are currently selected will print.

Tip

➡ Unlike other programs that use the Macintosh Page Setup dialog box, FreeHand has put most of those options in its Print dialog box.

If your artwork is bigger than the paper in your printer, you will not be able to print the entire illustration at actual size on one page. FreeHand lets you "tile" your illustration onto multiple pieces of paper that can be assembled to form the larger illustration.

To tile an oversized illustration

1. In the Printer dialog box, choose Manual or Auto from the Tile options.

2. If you choose Auto, FreeHand will automatically divide your artwork into different pages.

3. If you choose Auto, you have the choice of how much overlap there will be between each page.

4. If you choose Manual, you will need to move the zero point from the ruler down onto the artwork to set the lower-left corner (**Figure 8**). FreeHand will print whatever is up and to the right of that zero point.

Tips

•◆ When you choose Manual tiling, you must set the zero point and then choose Print from the File menu. You will then need to repeat this process as many times as necessary to print all the sections of your document.

•◆ Manual tiling can be useful in printing just those elements of your artwork that you do not want to run across a cut line.

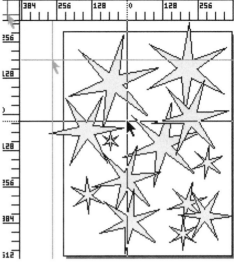

Figure 8. *Drag the zero point from the ruler to set the position of the page for **Manual** tiling.*

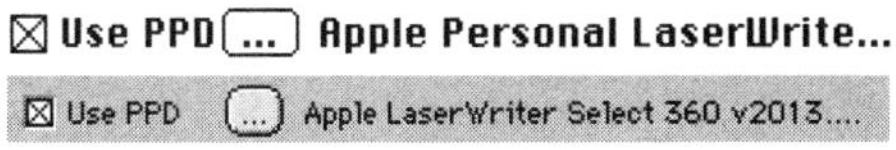

☒ **Use PPD** ⬚ **Apple Personal LaserWrite...**

☒ Use PPD ◯ Apple LaserWriter Select 360 v2013....

Figure 9. *The two ways to select the correct PPD: from the Printer dialog box (top) or within the Print Setup box (bottom).*

FreeHand uses the PPD (PostScript Printer Description) information for the page setup settings. To set choices such as paper size and orientation, you will need to select the correct PPD for your printer.

To select the PPD:

1. In either the Printer dialog box or the Print Setup dialog box, click on Use PPD (**Figure 9**).

2. Click on the ellipses (...) button to find the list of PPDs that are installed in the Printer Descriptions folder in the Extensions folder of your Macintosh System Folder.

3. Find the PPD for your printer and click Open. The information from that PPD will be shown in the Print Setup box.

Select the PPD

ADVANCED PRINTING

To change the print setup:

With the Printer dialog box open, click on Setup (**Figure 10**). This opens the Print Setup dialog box. Then, click on one of the three tabs at the top right of the box switches from Imaging, Separations, or Paper Setup (**Figure 11a–c**).

Figure 10. *The **Print** button under Options in the **Printer** dialog box gives you the **Print Options**.*

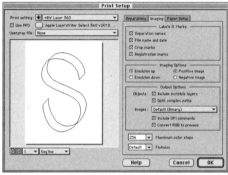

Figure 11a. *The **Imaging** Options in the **Print Setup** dialog box.*

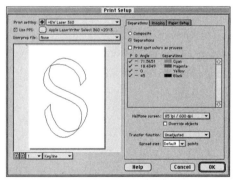

Figure 11b. *The **Separations** Options in the Print Setup dialog box.*

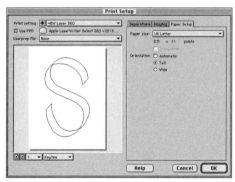

Figure 11c. *The **Paper Setup** Options in the Print Setup dialog box.*

Print Setup

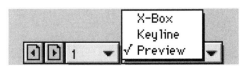

Figure 12. *The **Print** button under Options in the **Printer** dialog box gives you the **Print Options**.*

Figure 13a. *The **Print Preview** box in the Preview mode.*

Figure 13b. *The **Print Preview** box in the Keyline mode.*

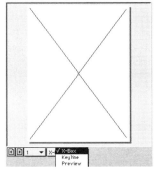

Figure 13c. *The **Print Preview** box in the X-Box mode.*

The left side of the Print Setup box shows the Print Preview. This image shows how your artwork will be printed.

To control the Print Preview:

1. Press on the page number pop-up menu (**Figure 12**) to control which pages will be visible.

2. Choose Preview from the pop-up menu to see the artwork with all the fills, colors, etc (**Figure 13a**).

3. Choose Keyline from the pop-up menu to see the paths that define each of the objects of your artwork without the fills, colors, etc (**Figure 13b**).

4. Choose X-Box to see fill the area of each page with an "X" (**Figure 13c**).

Tips

●◆ If your artwork is extremely detailed, you may find it faster to view the print preview in the Keyline or X-Box modes.

●◆ Drag to move the artwork to different positions in the Print Preview area.

●◆ If you have moved the artwork around the Print Preview area, click on the area just outside the print preview to restore it to the original position.

Print Preview

When you print a file, the print shop that will be printing the job may ask you to add certain labels and marks. Rather than create these marks manually, you can have FreeHand automatically add them.

To add labels and marks:

1. There are four options under Labels & Marks (**Figure 14**).

2. Click on Separation names to add a label with the name of the color plate that is being printed.

3. Click on File name and date to add the name of the file, page number, and date and time that the file is printed.

4. Click on Crop marks to add crop marks.

5. Click on Registration marks to add registration marks and color bars.

Tip

➨ You will not see the labels and marks you have chosen until you print the illustration (**Figure 15**).

The imaging options (**Figure 16**) are usually for high-resolution output.

To choose the imaging options:

1. Choose Emulsion up if you are outputting to paper. (Choose Emulsion down for paper prints to make a mirror image of your artwork.)

2. Choose Emulsion up or Emulsion down when outputting to film.

3. Choose Positive image for printing to paper.

4. Negative image is the usual choice when printing to film separations. Choose Negative image for paper when you want to invert the image.

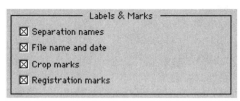

Figure 14. *Click the checkboxes for* **Crop marks** *and* **Registration marks** *to have these printer marks print outside your artwork.*

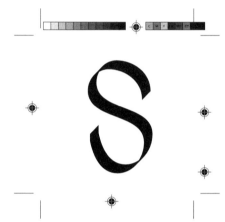

Figure 15. *Artwork printed with* **Crop marks** *and* **Registration marks.** **Color bars** *are also added when the Registration marks box is checked.*

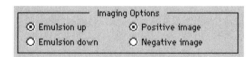

Figure 16. *The four* **Imaging Options.**

Labels & Marks; Imaging Options

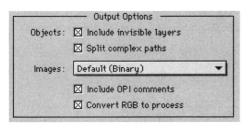

Figure 17. *The Output Options dialog box.*

Figure 18. *To change the **Maximum color steps** press on the pop-up menu*

Figure 19. *To change the **Flatness** setting, press on the pop-up menu.*

FreeHand offers you various output options for printing to a PostScript output device. These options are then contained inside the file when it is saved or exported as an EPS file (*see pages 16 or 232*).

To set the Output Options:

1. Open Output Options (**Figure 17**) by choosing Output Options from the File menu or under the Imaging settings of the Print Setup dialog box.

2. Check on Include invisible layers if you want to print objects that are on hidden layers.

3. Check on Split complex paths, so that FreeHand will, if necessary, split up paths that could cause printing errors.

4. Press on the Images pop-up menu to indicate how your placed images should be process. Choose Default (Binary) for most purposes. Choose ASCII (Windows) only if you are outputting to the Windows platform or are having trouble outputting on the Macintosh platform.

5. Click Include OPI comments if your TIFF images will be replaced by a high-resolution version at a color electronic prepress system.

6. Click on Convert RGB to process if you have RGB TIFF images that need to be converted to CMYK plates.

7. Enter a number from 8 to 255 in the Maximum color steps field (**Figure 18**) only if you are having trouble converting a file using an electronic prepress system.

8. Enter a number from 1 to 100 in the Flatness field (**Figure 19**) only if the Print Monitor reports a limitcheck error when printing your file.

The Separation options (**Figure 20**) control how your file will be separated when outputting color work to separate pieces of film.

To choose the Separations options:

1. If you want all the colors to print together, click on Composite.

2. To separate the colors to different plates, click on Separations.

3. Click on Print spot colors as process to override the settings for spot colors.

4. To prevent a color from printing, click in the "P" column to delete the checkmark for that color.

5. To set a color to overprint, click in the "O" column. The Overprint Ink dialog box will appear (**Figure 21**). Click On to make all instances of that color overprint. Click on Threshold and enter an amount in the field to control what tint of that color will overprint.

6. To set the screen angle for a color, click on the angle for that color. The Screen Angle dialog box will appear (**Figure 22**). Enter the angle you want for that color and click OK. Repeat for each color.

Tip

◆ Do not adjust the screen angles, screen frequency, or overprinting options unless you know what you are doing. Consult with the print shop that will be producing your job.

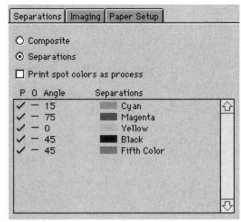

Figure 20. *The Separations box lets you select which colors will print (indicated by a check in the P column) and which colors will overprint (indicated by a check in the O column).*

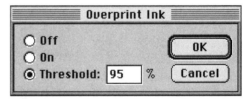

Figure 21. *The Overprint Ink dialog box lets you turn on overprinting for a color and lets you set the Threshold for what tint values of the color should overprint.*

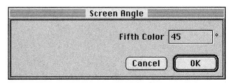

Figure 22. *The Screen Angle dialog box lets you set the angle that a color's screens will be printed.*

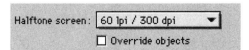

Figure 23. *The Halftone screen pop-up menu for a typical laser printer.*

If your artwork has any screened objects, you may want to set the Halftone screen.

To set the halftone screen:

1. If you have a PPD selected, there is a Halftone screen pop-up menu in the Separations options (**Figure 23**).

2. Choose from the list of common screens for your output device.

3. To override any halftone screens set for individual objects, click on Override objects.

Tip

➥ If you are printing to a laser printer and are getting banding in your blends, try lowering the screen frequency to something like 35 lpi (lines per inch) or 40 lpi. While the screened artwork may look a little "dotty," this should reduce the banding.

In addition to setting the halftone screen for the entire illustration, you can set the halftone screen for individual objects.

To set the Halftone screen for individual objects:

1. Select the object for which you want to set the halftone screen.

2. Choose Halftone from the Panels submenu of the Window menu or press Command-H. The Halftone panel will appear (**Figure 24**).

3. Choose the shape of the screen dot from the Screen pop-up menu.

4. Enter the angle of the screen in the Angle field or rotate the wheel to set the screen angle. If no value is set, the default is 45°.

5. Enter the frequency of the screen in the Frequency field or use the slider to set the number. If no value is set, the default of the output device is used.

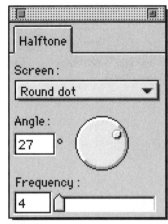

Figure 24. *The Halftone panel lets you change the halftone screen for individual objects.*

The Transfer function controls the dot gain for screened images.

To set the Transfer function:

1. With the Separations tab selected in the Print Setup dialog box, press on the pop-up menu for the Transfer function (**Figure 25**).

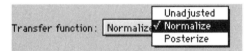

Figure 25. *The Transfer function choices.*

2. Choose Unadjusted if you are printing to an output device that has been specially calibrated.

3. Choose Normalize if you are printing to an ordinary laser printer.

4. Choose Posterize if you want to speed the printing and don't mind sacrificing quality. This will reduce the number of levels of screens that are printed.

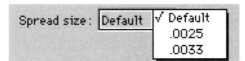

Figure 26. *The Spread size field allows you to have all artwork "spread" a certain amount to compensate for misregistrations in the final printing.*

In addition to the trapping created by the Trap Xtra (*see page 216*), FreeHand provides a trapping option called "spread."

To choose the spread size:

In the Spread size field (**Figure 26**), enter the amount that you want basic fills and strokes to expand. This compensates for misregistrations in the final printing. Trapping amounts vary depending on the type of printing press, paper, inks, etc. Do not enter any amount unless you have spoken to the print shop where your artwork will be printed.

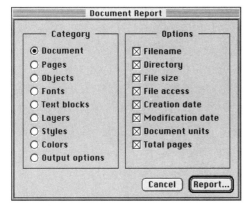

Figure 27. *The Document Report dialog box lets you select the information to be included in the document report.*

There may be times when you want a record or report of all the information about your FreeHand file. FreeHand provides you with a very sophisticated report for all your documents.

To create a document report:

1. With the document open, choose Report from the File menu. The Document Report dialog box will appear (**Figure 27**).

2. Click on the categories listed on the left side of the Document Report dialog box. Each one of these categories then displays a different set of Options.

3. Click on each of the Options for each category to indicate which information you want listed.

4. Click on Report to see the Document Report Viewer, where you can read the complete document report. Or, click on Save to create a permanent text file of your report.

Unless you have your own high-resolution imagesetter, you will want to transfer your work onto a floppy disk or some type of removable cartridge and then send this disk or cartridge to a service bureau that will output the file. There are certain files you will want to include, depending on your FreeHand settings.

To send out a file for imagesetting:

1. If the file has no placed images from other programs, such as PICT, TIFF, or EPS image , then all you have to do is copy the FreeHand file onto the disk or cartridge you are sending.

2. If your file does have placed images in it, then you need to check if the images have been embedded or are linked to your FreeHand file. This can be done by checking the option for External Files found in the Document Info category of the document report (*see previous page*).

3. If external files are listed in the document report, it means that those placed images are linked—not embedded—in your FreeHand file. This means that, in addition to the FreeHand file, you need to send the original files of the linked images to the service bureau (**Figure 28**).

4. If no external files are listed in the document report, it means that any placed images are embedded in the FreeHand document. You do not have to send the original files of these embedded images along with the FreeHand file. However, FreeHand files with embedded placed images can grow to very large sizes.

5. To turn the option to embed images on and off, change the Preferences settings for the Expert Input/Output (*see page 271*).

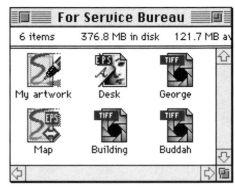

Figure 28. *When a FreeHand file is sent to a service bureau, the files of all placed images that are not embedded in the FreeHand document should also be included. In this case the FreeHand file "My artwork" has the other files placed in it.*

CUSTOMIZING 22

J ust because FreeHand comes with certain settings doesn't mean you have to keep those settings. FreeHand gives you a wealth of choices as to how your application will operate. In this chapter, you will learn how to set your preferences for a wide variety of features. You will also learn how you can change the default settings for new documents.

Preferences control the entire application. This means that any changes you make to the Preferences settings will be applied to all documents—past, present, and future.

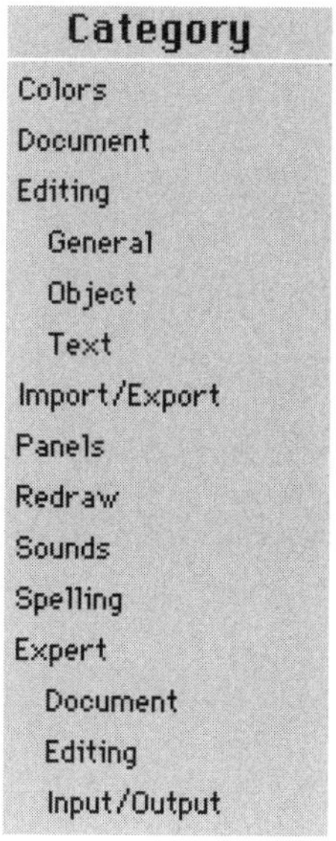

To change the preferences:

1. Open FreeHand.

2. Choose Preferences from the File menu.

3. The Preferences settings are divided into 15 different categories listed on the left side of the Preferences box (**Figure 1**). Click on the category you want to control.

Category

Colors
Document
Editing
  General
  Object
  Text
Import/Export
Panels
Redraw
Sounds
Spelling
Expert
  Document
  Editing
  Input/Output

Figure 1. *The categories for the **Preferences** settings.*

The Color category controls how colors are displayed both in the Color List and onscreen (**Figure 2**).

To set the Colors preferences:

1. Clicking on the boxes for Guide color or Grid color opens the Macintosh Color Picker where you can choose the colors FreeHand uses for guides and grid dots.

2. Choosing Container color option means that when a text block is selected, the Fill color will be the color of the text block.

3. Choosing Text color option means that when a text block is selected, the Fill color in the Color List shows the fill color of the text, not the block.

4. Choosing Auto-rename colors option means the names of colors will automatically change when their CMYK or RGB values change.

5. Choosing Color Mixer uses split color well allows you to compare any changes to a color in the Color Mixer with the original color.

6. Choosing Dither 8-bit colors will improve how colors are displayed onscreen if you are working on a monitor with only 256 colors.

7. Choosing Color management gives you the options of how colors are displayed onscreen. Consult with your print shop for the proper choices for these controls.

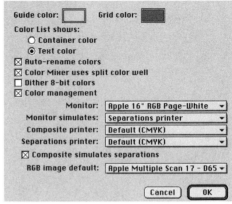

Figure 2. *The Preferences settings for the Color category.*

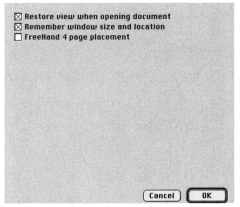

Figure 3. *The* **Preferences** *settings for the* **Document** *category.*

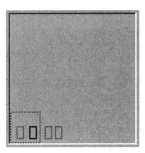

Figure 4. *The dotted line around two of the pages shows the area of the pasteboard that will be kept when the FreeHand 7 document is converted to FreeHand 4. In this case, two of the pages lie outside the area.*

The Document category controls how FreeHand opens documents. It also controls the size of the pasteboard of the documents (**Figure 3**).

To set the Document preferences:

1. Choosing Restore last view when opening document prompts FreeHand to remember the last view of a document before it was closed.

2. Choosing Remember window size and location prompts FreeHand to remember the size and position of the window that holds the file.

3. Choosing FreeHand 4 page placement allows you to see the area on the pasteboard that will be kept when a FreeHand 7 document is converted to FreeHand 4 (**Figure 4**).

Document Preferences

The Editor category is divided into three areas. Editing General controls the overall editing features (**Figure 5**).

To set the Editing General preferences:

1. The number in the Undo's field lets you enter the number of times you can undo your actions. The Pick distance field controls how close you have to come to manipulate a point or handle with the Selection tool. The Cursor distance field sets how far the up, down, left, or right arrow keys will move objects. The Snap distance field controls how close you have to come when snapping one object to another.

2. The Smoother editing changes how paths are displayed (**Figure 6**). Smaller handles changes how the control handles of points are displayed (**Figure 7**). "Smart cursors" changes how the cursors for the tools are displayed (**Figure 8**).

3. Choosing Dynamic scrollbar lets you see your illustration move as you drag on the scrollbars of the window.

4. Choosing Remember layer info means that if an object is copied and pasted from one document to another, it will be pasted into the new document onto the same layer it originally had.

5. Choosing Dragging a guide scrolls the window means that if you drag a guide into the ruler, you will scroll to a different section of your artwork.

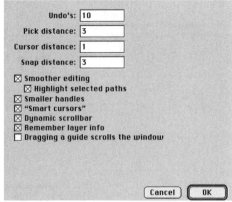

Figure 5. *The Preferences settings for the Editing General category.*

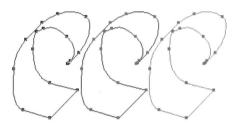

Figure 6. *Smoother Editing off (left) means that selected objects have points and paths highlighted in black.. Smoother Editing on (middle) means that selected objects have points highlighted in color. Highlight selected paths on (right) means that both the points and the paths will be highlighted in color.*

Figure 7. *The difference between Smaller handles turned off (top) and turned on (bottom).*

Figure 8. *The difference between Smart Cursors turned on (top) and turned off (bottom).*

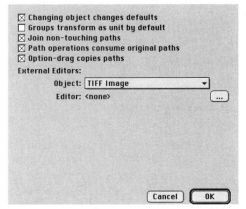

Figure 9. *The **Preferences** settings for the **Object Editing** category.*

The Object Editing category controls how your objects are modified (**Figure 9**).

To set the Object Editing preferences:

1. Choosing Changing object changes defaults means that if you change an object's fill or stroke, the next object will have those attributes.

2. Choosing Groups transform as unit by default means that all items in a group will automatically transform together, but may result in unwanted distortions.

3. Choosing Join non-touching paths means that when you choose Join for objects that do not touch, FreeHand will draw a line between the two nearest end points.

4. Choosing Path operations consume original paths means that when you apply commands such as Punch and Intersect, the original paths will be deleted.

5. Choosing Option-drag copies paths controls whether or not holding the Option key while dragging or transforming will create a copy.

6. The External Editor pop-up menu allows you to select the application that will automatically open when you double click on imported files.

Tip

➹ Hold the Shift key as you apply any of the Path Operations commands to override the Path operations consume original paths setting.

The Text Editing category controls how text and text blocks are modified (**Figure 10**).

To set the Text Editing preferences:

1. Choosing Always use Text Editor means that the Text Editor will appear when you click with the text tool.

2. Choosing Track tab movement with vertical line means a line will extend through the text when tab stops are placed on the ruler (**Figure 11**).

3. Choosing Show text handles when text ruler is off lets you see the text block handles and boundary when you are in a text block (**Figure 12**).

4. Choosing New default-sized text containers auto-expand means that if you click to create a text block, the text block will expand as you type.

5. Choosing "Smart quotes" and its pop-up menu allows you to have FreeHand substitute typographer quotes instead of plain tick marks (**Figure 13**).

6. Choosing Build paragraph styles based on controls if styles are defined by the first paragraph or the shared attributes of the text block.

7. Choosing Dragging a paragraph style changes controls if the whole paragraph or just the first paragraph changes when you drag a style icon.

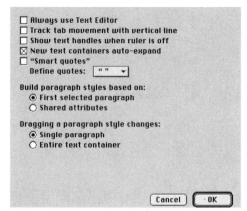

Figure 10. The Preferences settings for the Text Editing category.

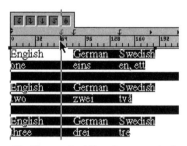

Figure 11. The vertical line that extends through the text when Track tab movement with vertical line is turned on.

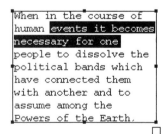

Figure 12. Working in a text block with the Show text handles when text ruler is off option turned on.

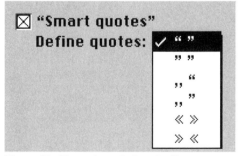

Figure 13. The various choices for Smart Quotes.

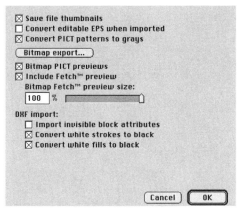

Figure 14. *The Preferences settings for the Import/ Export category.*

The Import/Export category controls how FreeHand imports and exports graphics (**Figure 14**).

To set the Import/Export preferences:

1. Choosing Save file thumbnails means that FreeHand creates a preview of the artwork, which will be visible in the File> Open dialog box.

2. Choosing Convert editable EPS when imported means that, when possible, placed EPS files are converted in order that they can be selected and modified.

3. Choosing Convert PICT patterns to grays means that when bitmapped patterns in MacDraw Pro and Canvas PICT files are imported, the patterns will be gray.

4. Clicking Bitmap export… lets you set the default attributes for exporting files in bitmapped format.

5. Choosing Bitmap PICT previews means that the preview will be bitmapped when you export your file to a program such as QuarkXPress or Adobe PageMaker. (This means faster screen redraw in the layout program.)

6. Choosing Include Fetch preview means that a preview of the image will be created which can be used in the program Extensis Fetch. The slider lets you control the size of this preview.

7. The DXF import options control how object are converted from the DXF format when they are imported into FreeHand.

Import/Export Preferences

The Panels category controls how the palettes are displayed (**Figure 15**).

To set the Panels preferences:

1. Choosing Hiding panels hides the Toolbox means that the toolbox will be hidden when Hide Palettes is selected.

2. Choosing Remember location of zipped panels means that FreeHand will remember the position of a panel when it is zipped. If you unzip the panel and move it around, the panel will move back to its original position when is rezipped.

3. Choosing Black and white interface means that the gray shading boxes and panels will be replaced by a black and white interface (**Figure 16**).

4. Choosing Show Tool Tips means that you will see explanations of what the icons in the toolbars mean when your cursor passes over them (**Figure 17**).

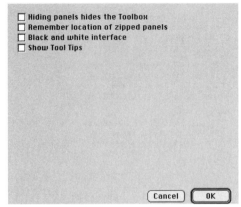

Figure 15. *The* **Preferences** *settings for the* **Palettes** *category.*

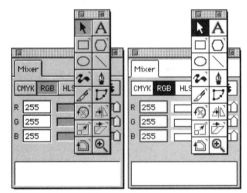

Figure 16. *The difference between the* **gray interface** *(left) and the* **black and white interface** *(right).*

Figure 17. *When* **Show Tool Tips** *is turned on, passing your arrow over an icon on the toolbars will show the label describing the function of the icon.*

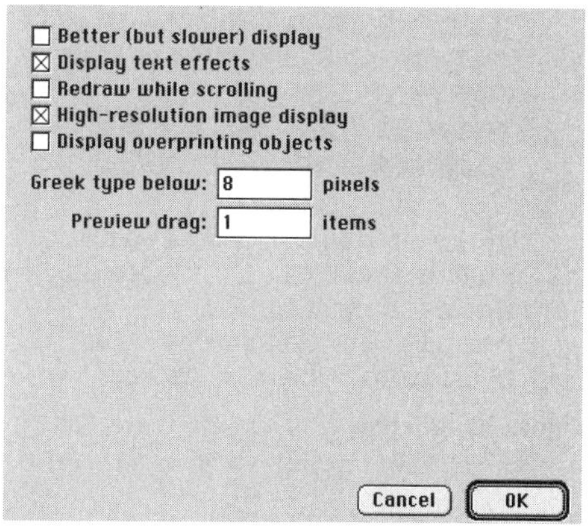

☐ Better (but slower) display
☒ Display text effects
☐ Redraw while scrolling
☒ High-resolution image display
☐ Display overprinting objects

Greek type below: 8   pixels

Preview drag: 1   items

(Cancel)   (OK)

Figure 18. *The Preferences settings for the Redraw category.*

The Redraw category controls how objects, placed art, and text are displayed (**Figure 18**). None of the Redraw features will affect final output.

To set the Redraw preferences:

1. Choosing Better (but slower) display means that Graduated and Radial fills are displayed in smoother blends rather than distinct steps (**Figure 19**).

2. Choosing Display text effects means that special effects such as Inline and Zoom will be visible.

3. Choosing Redraw while scrolling means that you will see your artwork as you scroll.

4. Choosing High-resolution image display means that TIFF images will have a better display (**Figure 20**).

5. Choosing Display overprinting objects means that "O's" will be displayed when an object is set to overprint (**Figure 21**).

(Continued on the following page)

Figure 19. *Better (but slower) display turned on (top) and turned off (bottom).*

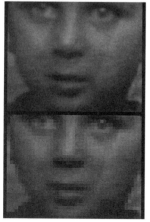

Figure 20. *The difference between a TIFF placed with a high-resolution display (top) and with a lower-resolution display (bottom).*

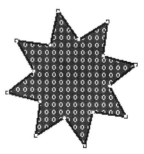

Figure 21. *The "O's" inside the fill indicate that the object is set to **overprint**.*

Redraw Preferences

6. Entering an amount in the Greek type below field controls which size of text will be "greeked" or turned from letters to a gray band (**Figure 22**).

7. Entering an amount in the Preview drag field changes how many items are seen as a preview when you move or transform items (**Figures 23a–b**).

Tips

•• If you start to drag several items and then wish to see a preview of what you've done, press and release the Option key as you drag. You will then preview all the items regardless of how the preferences are set.

•• If you are holding down the Option key to make a copy of the items, release the Option key and then hold it down again while you are still dragging. You will add a preview to your drag and copy the items.

Figure 22. *An example of text that is **greeked** (top) and the same text block with its text visible (bottom).*

Figure 23a. *Dragging **without a preview**.*

Figure 23b. *Dragging **with a preview**.*

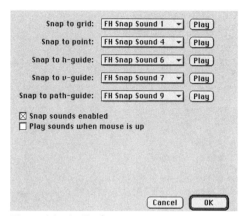

Figure 24. *The Preferences settings for the Sounds category.*

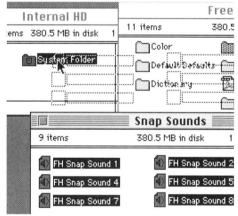

Figure 25. *To install the Snap sounds, drag the FreeHand Snap Sounds files onto your System Folder.*

The Sounds category controls the sounds that are heard when you snap to different objects such as grids, points, guides, etc. (**Figure 24**). In order to use the Snap sounds, they must be installed in your Macintosh operating system.

To install the Snap sounds:

1. Find the folder called Snap Sounds. This should be in the FreeHand folder.

2. Select all the Snap Sounds files and drag them onto the System Folder (**Figure 25**).

3. An alert box will appear, asking if you wish to store these files in the System file. Click OK. The sounds will now be available to apply to the snap-to functions.

To set the Snap sounds preferences:

1. Press on the pop-up menu next to each Snap Sounds choice. Choose whichever sound you want. Choose None to turn off the sound.

2. Click Play to hear each sound.

3. Choosing Snap sounds enabled will turn on the sounds for all the choices.

4. If you choose Play sounds when mouse is up, you will hear the sound whenever your mouse passes over the snap object, even if the mouse button is not pressed. (Very noisy!)

The Spelling category controls several choices about how the Spelling checker feature works (**Figure 26**).

To set the Spelling preferences:

1. Choosing Find duplicate words controls whether the Spelling checker finds duplicate words such as "the the."

2. Choosing Find captialization errors controls whether the Spelling checker finds capitalization errors such as "Really? how did that happen?"

3. Choose Add words to dictionary Exactly as typed if you wish to add case-sensitive words. This means words such as "FreeHand" or "QuickStart" are entered with capitalization intact.

4. Choose Add words to dictionary All lowercase if you do not wish to add the words as case-sensitive.

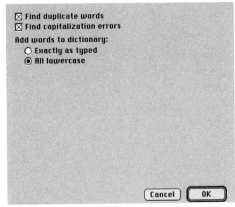

Figure 26. *The **Preferences** settings for the **Spelling** category.*

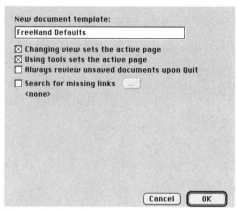

Figure 27. *The Preferences settings for the Expert Document category.*

There are three Expert categories: Document, Editing, and Input/Output. The Expert Document category controls sophisticated document features (**Figure 27**).

To set the Expert Document preferences:

1. Choosing the FreeHand Defaults template for new documents lets you change the file that FreeHand uses for the defaults file.

2. Choosing Changing the view sets the active page means that, as you are scrolling, the page that comes into view will be the active page.

3. Choosing Using tools sets the active page means that if you use a tool on a page, that page will be the active page.

4. Choosing Always review unsaved documents upon Quit means that you will be presented with a dialog box for each unsaved document when you quit.

5. Choosing Search for missing links and then clicking on the "…" lets you set which folder to search through for graphics that have lost their links to the original image.

Expert Document Preferences

The Expert Editing category controls stroke weights and the changes that you make to objects and text (**Figure 28**).

To set the Expert Editing preferences:

1. Entering numbers in the Default line weights (relaunch to apply) field controls the weights listed in the Stroke Widths submenu of the Arrange menu. Put spaces between the numbers. All sizes are listed in points.

2. Choosing Auto-apply style to selected objects does the following: If an object is modified and this modified object is used to define a new style, the new style will be applied to any selected objects.

3. Choosing Define style based on selection means that a style will take its attributes from the selected object.

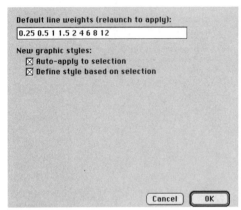

Figure 28. *The Preferences settings for the* **Expert Editing** *category.*

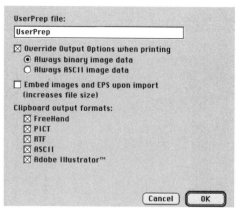

Figure 29. *The Preferences settings for the Expert Input/Output category.*

The Expert Input/Output category controls how files are printed, how images are placed, and how the clipboard is handled (**Figure 29**).

To set the Expert Input/Output preferences:

1. The UserPrep file field lets you choose the file FreeHand looks for when printing a document. For more information, see the ReadMe file in the UserPrep folder.

2. Choosing Override Output Options when printing lets you set the defaults for the Output Options. Your file will print faster if you choose Always binary image data.

3. Choosing Embed images and EPS upon import (increases file size) means that the information necessary to print those graphics is embedded in the FreeHand document—not linked.

4. Choosing Clipboard output formats controls the kind of information that is kept on the Clipboard when you switch from FreeHand to another application. The format choices are FreeHand, PICT, RTF, ASCII, and Adobe Illustrator format.

To save your Preferences settings:

While most changes you make to the Preferences settings will take effect in your document immediately, they are not saved onto your hard disk until you quit FreeHand.

FreeHand also lets you change the default settings for your documents. Defaults are the settings that you have when you open a new FreeHand document. Default settings include such things as how many and which colors will be listed in the Color List, if the rulers are visible, how many pages a new document should have, and if the document is in Preview or Keyline. To change the defaults, you need to work with the FreeHand Defaults file.

To set the FreeHand Defaults file:

1. With FreeHand open, choose Open from the File menu and find the FreeHand Defaults file in the application folder.

or

In the Macintosh Finder, double-click on the FreeHand Defaults file. This will launch FreeHand and open the FreeHand Defaults file (**Figure 30**).

2. Make whatever changes you would like in this file.

3. Save the file in the same folder where you found it under the same name. When asked to replace the existing file click Replace.

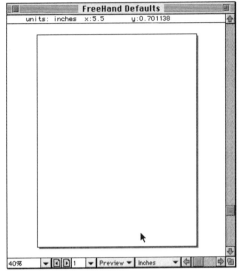

Figure 30. *Any changes you make to the* **FreeHand Defaults** *file will become the default settings for all new files.*

The following appendixes have been created to be used as references to the various features and functions in FreeHand. Some of this information appears in the FreeHand User Manual. Other information has been assembled especially for this book. All of the appendixes have been included together so you can refer to the information quickly.

Appendix A contains information about FreeHand's windows, toolbox, panels, and menus. There is also a sample dialog box that shows the different buttons, fields, controls, etc. that are used to enter and change information.

Appendix B contains lists of the commonly used keystrokes for various FreeHand commands. These lists have been arranged into three categories: menu commands, general commands, and text commands. As you progress in FreeHand, you will find that using keystrokes will help you work much faster. Many of the keystroke commands are listed in the menus. Others are found in these lists.

Appendix C shows the custom fills and strokes that you can apply to objects. These fills and strokes will not preview on your screen, so you will want to refer to this appendix to get an idea of how they will print.

FreeHand document window

The document window is the main window where your artwork is actually created.

Zoom or Zip box: Click to expand or contract a window or palette.

Close box: Click to close a window or palette.

Title bar: Displays the name of the file.

Zero point: Drag to reset the lower-left corner of the page to a new position.

Info bar: Displays measurements and information.

Horizontal ruler: Shows the horizontal measurements.

Document grid: Grid evenly spaced into squares along your page.

Vertical ruler: Shows the vertical measurements.

Ruler guides: Created by dragging from the horizontal or vertical rulers.

Scroll arrow: Press to move the page to a new position in the window.

Magnification pop-up menu: Press to change the magnification level.

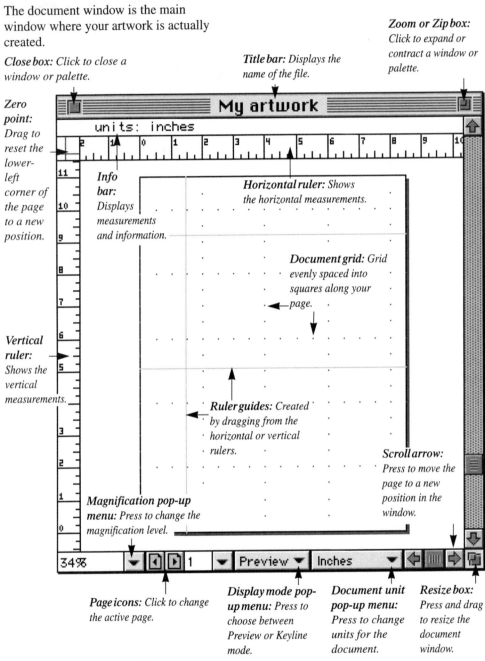

Page icons: Click to change the active page.

Display mode pop-up menu: Press to choose between Preview or Keyline mode.

Document unit pop-up menu: Press to change units for the document.

Resize box: Press and drag to resize the document window.

Figure 1. *The document window.*

Document Window

Toolbox

The toolbox contains 16 different tools that perform selection, creation, text, transformation, and magnification functions. Click with the mouse to select each tool, or use the keyboard commands to access the tools. Double-click on tools with a corner symbol to access their dialog box settings.

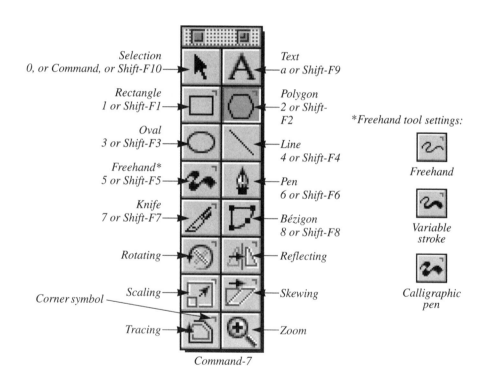

Figure 2. *The toolbox.*

Sample dialog box

Many of FreeHand's features are set using dialog boxes. Though each dialog box differs, they all use similar setting devices: pop-up menus, fields in which to enter numbers, sliders, wheels, color drop boxes, checkboxes, icons, radio buttons and buttons.

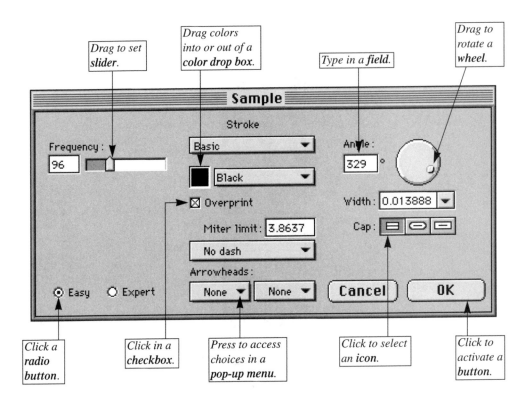

Drag to set slider.

Drag colors into or out of a color drop box.

Type in a field.

Drag to rotate a wheel.

Click a radio button.

Click in a checkbox.

Press to access choices in a pop-up menu.

Click to select an icon.

Click to activate a button.

Figure 3. *The setting devices of a typical dialog box.*

Menus

The FreeHand menus are used to access most of the commands. Keyboard shortcuts are shown to the right of some of the menu commands. Triangular pointers to the right of a command name indicate that there is a submenu.

File
New	⌘N
Open...	⌘O
Close	⌘W
Save	⌘S
Save As...	⌘⇧S
Revert	
Import...	⌘⇧D
Export...	⌘E
Report...	
Page Setup...	
Print...	⌘P
Preferences...	⌘⌥U
Output Options...	
My artwork	
Quit	⌘Q

Edit
Undo Add Path	⌘Z
Redo	⌘Y
Cut	⌘X
Copy	⌘C
Paste	⌘V
Paste Behind	
Clear	
Cut Contents	⌘⇧X
Paste Inside	⌘⇧V
Copy Attributes	⌘⇧⌥C
Paste Attributes	⌘⇧⌥V
Duplicate	⌘D
Clone	⌘=
Select	▶
Find & Replace	▶
Editions	▶
External Editor...	
Links...	

View
Fit Selection	⌘0
Fit To Page	⌘⇧W
Fit All	⌘⇧0
Magnification	▶
✓ Preview	⌘K
✓ Toolbars	
✓ Panels	⌘⇧H
✓ Info Bar	⌘⇧R
✓ Page Rulers	⌘R
✓ Text Rulers	⌘/
Grid	▶
Guides	▶
✓ Snap To Point	⌘'
✓ Snap To Guides	⌘\
Snap To Grid	⌘;
Fetch™ Info...	

Modify
Object...	⌘I
Stroke...	⌘⌥L
Fill...	⌘⌥F
Text...	⌘T
Document...	⌘⌥D
Transform	▶
Arrange	▶
Align...	⌘⌥A
Align Again	⌘⇧⌥A
Join	⌘J
Split	⌘⇧J
Combine	▶
Alter Path	▶
Lock	⌘L
Unlock	⌘⇧L
Group	⌘G
Ungroup	⌘U
Constrain...	

Text
Font	▶
Size	▶
Style	▶
Effect	▶
Align	▶
Leading	▶
Special Characters	▶
Editor...	⌘⇧E
Spelling...	⌘⇧G
Run Around Selection...	⌘⌥W
Flow Inside Path	⌘⇧U
Attach To Path	⌘⇧Y
Detach From Path	
Remove Transforms	
Convert To Paths	⌘⇧P

Xtras Window
Repeat	⌘+
Xtra Manager...	
Colors	▶
Chart	▶
Cleanup	▶
Create	▶
Delete	▶
Distort	▶
Other	▶
Path Operations	▶

Window
New Window	⌘⌥N
Toolbars	▶
Inspectors	▶
Panels	▶
Xtras	▶
✓ My artwork	

Menus

Figure 4. *The FreeHand menus.*

Inspector panels

There are five different Inspector panels. The panels may change depending on the icons that are selected and what type of object is select. The keyboard commands will both show and hide the panels.

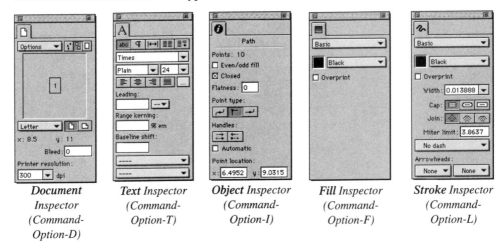

Document Inspector (Command-Option-D)	*Text* Inspector (Command-Option-T)	*Object* Inspector (Command-Option-I)	*Fill* Inspector (Command-Option-F)	*Stroke* Inspector (Command-Option-L)

Figure 5. *The five* **Inspector** *panels.*

The Other Panels

In addition to the Toolbox and Inspector panels, FreeHand has seven other panels. The keyboard commands will show or hide the panels.

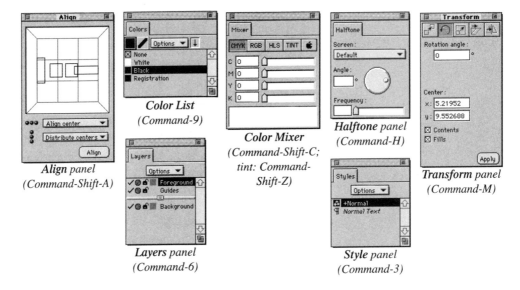

Align panel
(Command-Shift-A)

Color List
(Command-9)

Layers panel
(Command-6)

Color Mixer
(Command-Shift-C;
tint: Command-Shift-Z)

Halftone panel
(Command-H)

Style panel
(Command-3)

Transform panel
(Command-M)

Figure 6. *The seven* **Panels.**

Xtra Tools panel and Operations panel

The Xtra Tools panel contains additional drawing and modification tools. The Operations panel lets you apply operations to objects.

Xtra Tools panel (Command-Shift-K)

Operations panel (Command-Shift-I)

Figure 7. *The Xtra Tools and Operations panels.*

Menu bar Toolbars

FreeHand also has a Menu bar and two toolbars, which stretch across the screen.

Figure 8. *The Menu bar.*

Figure 9. *The Main toolbar.*

Stacking panels

All of the panels that have "tabs" at the top can be stacked together into any combination. To stack a panel, drag it into another panel's window. To separate the panels, drag one out from the others.

Figure 11. *Stacking panels.*

Docking panels

To dock a panel, hold the Control key as you move one panel next to another. A gray docking bar will appear. To release, click on the docking bar.

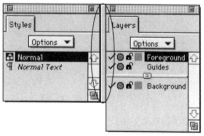

Figure 12. *Two Docked panels. The gray docking bar (circled) indicates they are docked.*

Times | Plain | 24 | ⬍ 0 | -- ▾

Figure 10. *The Text toolbar (Command-Option-T).*

Keyboard commands:

The following are lists of most of the keyboard shortcuts available. Try to use one or two of these commands each week until they are familiar to you.

Cmd.	=	Command key
Opt.	=	Option key
L arr.	=	Left arrow key
R arr.	=	Right arrow key
D arr.	=	Down arrow key
U arr.	=	Up arrow key
Space	=	Spacebar

Menu commands

Blend . . . . Cmd.-Shift-B
Bring Forward . . . . Cmd.-[
Bring To Front . . . . Cmd.-F
Clone . . . . Cmd.-=
Copy . . . . Cmd.-C or F3
Copy Attribute . . . . Cmd.-Opt.-Shift-C
Cut . . . . Cmd.-X or F2
Cut Contents . . . . Cmd.-Shift-X
Deselect All . . . . Tab
Duplicate . . . . Cmd.-D
Export . . . . Cmd.-Shift-R
Group . . . . Cmd.-G
Import . . . . Cmd.-Shift-R
Join . . . . Cmd.-J
Lock . . . . Cmd.-L
New . . . . Cmd.-N
Open . . . . Cmd.-O
Paste . . . . Cmd.-V or F4
Paste Attributes . . . . Cmd.-Opt.-Shift-V
Paste Inside . . . . Cmd.-Shift-V

Preview . . . . Cmd.-K
Print . . . . Cmd.-P
Quit . . . . Cmd.-Q
Redo . . . . Cmd.-Y
Repeat Last Xtra . . . . Cmd.-Shift-+
Rulers . . . . Cmd.-Opt.-M
Save . . . . Cmd.-S
Save As . . . . Cmd.-Shift-S
Select All . . . . Cmd.-A
Select All in Document . . . . . . Cmd.-Shift-A
Send Backward . . . . Cmd.-]
Send To Back . . . . Cmd.-B
Snap To Grid . . . . Cmd.-;
Snap To Guides . . . . Cmd.-\
Snap To Point . . . . Cmd.-'
Split Elements . . . . Cmd.-Shift-J
Text Ruler . . . . Cmd.-/
Transform Again . . . . Cmd.-,
Undo . . . . Cmd.-Z or F1
Ungroup . . . . Cmd.-U
Unlock . . . . Cmd.-Shift-L

General commands

50% magnification	Cmd.-5
100% magnification	Cmd.-1
200% magnification	Cmd.-2
400% magnification	Cmd.-4
800% magnification	Cmd.-8
Calligraphic pen size down	1 or [or L arr.
Calligraphic pen size up	2 or] or R arr.
Close document	Cmd.-W
Close knife path cut	Cmd.-Knife Tool
Close multiviews	Opt.-Click Close Box
Fit all	Cmd.-Opt.-0 (zero)
Fit selection	Cmd.-0 (zero)
Fit to page	Cmd.-Opt.-W
Grabber hand	Space Bar
Help cursor	Cmd.-Shift-? or Help key
Hide all palettes	Cmd.-Shift-H or F2
Info bar	Cmd.-Opt.-J
New window	Cmd.-Opt.-N
Next page	Cmd.-Page Down
Previous page	Cmd.-Page Up
Stop screen redraw	Cmd.-period
Thicker stroke	Cmd.-Opt.-Shift->
Thinner stroke	Cmd.-Opt.-Shift-<
Zoom in	Cmd.-Space Bar-Click or Drag
Zoom out	Cmd.-Opt.-Space Bar-Click

Text commands

Baseline Shift down (1 pt.)	Opt.-D arr.
Baseline Shift up (1 pt.)	Opt.-U arr.
Attach To Path	Cmd.-Shift-Y
Bold italic type	Cmd.-Opt.-Shift-O or F8
Bold type	Cmd.-Opt.-B or F6
Centered alignment	Cmd.-Opt.-Shift-M
Convert To Paths	Cmd.-Shift-P
Decrease point size (1 pt.)	Cmd.-Shift-<
Discretionary hyphen	Cmd.--
Em space	Cmd.-Shift-M
En space	Cmd.-Shift-N
Find Text palette	Cmd.-Shift-F
Flow Inside Path	Cmd.-Shift-U
Highlight effect	Cmd.-Opt.-Shift-H
Increase point size (1 pt.)	Cmd.-Shift->
Italic type	Cmd.-Opt.-Shift-I or F7
Justified alignment	Cmd.-Opt.-Shift-J
Kern/Track by –1% em	Opt.-L arr.
Kern/Track by –10% em	Opt.-Shift-L arr.
Kern/Track by +1% em	Opt.-R arr.
Kern/Track by +10% em	Opt.-Shift-R arr.
Left alignment	Cmd.-Opt.-Shift-L
No effect	Cmd.-Opt.-Shift-N
Non-Breaking Space	Opt.-Space
Plain type	Cmd.-Opt.-Shift-P or F5
Right alignment	Cmd.-Opt.-Shift-R
Spelling	Cmd.-Shift-G
Text Editor	Cmd.-Shift-E
Text Wrap	Cmd.-Shift-W
Thin space	Cmd.-Shift-T
Underlined type	Cmd.-Opt.-Shift-U

Custom fills

The ten Custom fills appear onscreen as a series of "C's" in the artwork. The examples below show how each Custom fills prints at its defaults settings. The gray circles show which of the Custom fills allow background objects to show through their transparent areas.

Black & white noise   *Bricks*   *Circles*   *Hatch*

Noise   *Random grass*   *Random leaves*   *Squares*

Tiger teeth   *Top noise*

Figure 1. *The ten **Custom fills** at their default settings.*

Textured fills

The nine Textured fills appear onscreen as a series of "C's" in the artwork. The examples below show how each Textured fill prints at its default settings. The final example shows how only the black area responds to a change in color.

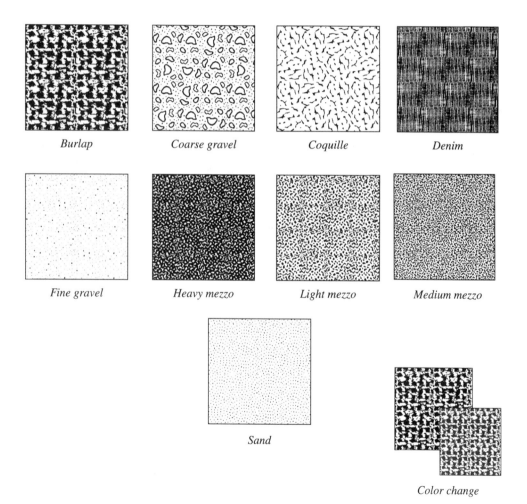

Burlap　　Coarse gravel　　Coquille　　Denim

Fine gravel　　Heavy mezzo　　Light mezzo　　Medium mezzo

Sand

Color change

Figure 2. *The nine **Textured fills** at their default settings. The two boxes on the bottom right show how the fills respond to a color change.*

Pattern fills and strokes

The Pattern fills and strokes are bitmapped patterns that appear onscreen and print as shown below. In addition to these default settings, each of the patterns either may be inverted or have its pixels edited one by one.

Pattern Fills and Strokes

Figure 3. *The 64 Pattern fills and strokes at their default settings.*

Custom strokes

The twenty-three Custom strokes appear onscreen as solid strokes (*see example in lower-right corner of this page*). The examples below show how each of the fills will print at its default settings. The gray circles show how the white areas react with backgrounds—either staying white or becoming transparent.

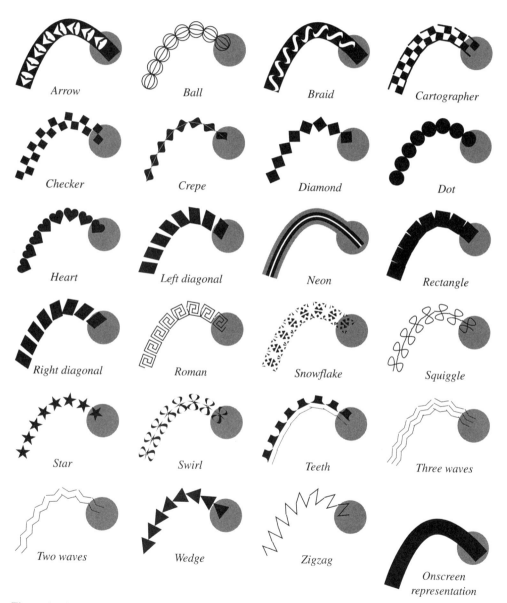

Arrow

Ball

Braid

Cartographer

Checker

Crepe

Diamond

Dot

Heart

Left diagonal

Neon

Rectangle

Right diagonal

Roman

Snowflake

Squiggle

Star

Swirl

Teeth

Three waves

Two waves

Wedge

Zigzag

Onscreen representation

Figure 4. *The twenty-three* **Custom strokes***. The twenty-fourth curve is a depiction of how they look onscreen.*

INDEX

Index

Designing Multimedia

Lisa Lopuck

If you're interested in being part of the booming field of multimedia, this beautifully illustrated volume shows you how. Its concept-to-product approach is highly visual, with stunning, full-color samples of actual multimedia projects. Title structure, user interface, software dynamics, and many other factors that affect design decisions are explained in detail. *$34.95 (144 pages)*

Director 5 Demystified

By Jason Roberts

Newly updated for version 5, this dual-platform book contains real-world projects that readers can put together using the assembled graphics, sounds, and text on the accompanying CD. The book offers a special chapter on advanced Lingo, Director's powerful scripting language, and addresses key multimedia design and organization principles, such as clarity, consistency, and user needs. Dubbed "a career in a box" by multimedia professionals. *$39.95 (856 pages, w/ CD-ROM)*

Electronic Highway Robbery: An Artist's Guide to Copyrights in the Digital Era

By Mary E. Carter

If you are an artist working in the digital world, you frequently face a key legal question: Who owns what? *Electronic Highway Robbery* tackles the thorny questions that arise around copyright law on the digital frontier. Artist and author Mary Carter interviewed top digital copyright lawyers for this clearly written, easy-to understand guide, which covers copyrighting original work, public domain, ownership of scanned images, and tips on protecting your rights while respecting those of others. *$18.95 (248 pages)*

Elements of Web Design

By Darcy DiNucci with Maria Giudice and Lynne Stiles

Elements of Web Design introduces traditional designers to the opportunities and pitfalls of Web design. Assuming readers understand traditional design issues but not the specific demands of the Web, this book includes chapters on every step of assembling pages—from pulling together a team with the appropriate skills, to choosing the right design formats, to creating contracts with clients to reflect the ever-changing nature of Web pages. The work and wisdom of successful pioneers of Web design is highlighted throughout the book. *$39.95 (208 pages)*

Illustrator 6 for Macintosh: Visual QuickStart Guide

Elaine Weinmann and Peter Lourekas

Illustrator 6 for Macintosh: Visual QuickStart Guide offers users easy-to-follow, step-by-step instructions for getting the most of Adobe Illustrator 6. This book is filled with hundreds of screen-shots and loads of tips. As with all the Visual QuickStart Guides, information is presented in a straightforward, graphic fashion, so you'll find what you need, understand it, and get right to work. *$19.95 (292 pages)*

The Illustrator 6 Wow! Book

Sharon Steuer

The Illustrator 6 Wow! Book includes eye-catching and time-saving techniques and tips for beginning through advanced users of Adobe Illustrator, using real-life "step-by-step" examples and full-page "gallery" samples from over 70 of the nation's leading Illustrator artists and designers. Covers the latest features, tools, and techniques in Illustrator 6. The accompanying CD-ROM is packed with demo versions of Illustrator and Photoshop, plug-in filters, tutorials, and many more specially created goodies. *$39.95 (224 pages w/ CD-ROM)*

The Macintosh Bible, 6th Edition

Edited by Jeremy Judson

This classic reference book is now completely updated. *The Macintosh Bible, 6th Edition* is crammed with tips, tricks, and shortcuts that will help you to get the most out of your Mac. Written by 13 editors and over 70 contributors, *The Macintosh Bible* tackles every subject area with a clear vision of what Macintosh users need to know in an engaging, no-nonsense style. Use it to find the right Mac, printer, monitor, and hard disk. Discover when and how to upgrade your system, how to protect your data, and what to do when disaster strikes. Get the latest on fonts, word processing, spreadsheets, graphics, desktop publishing, data bases, communications, utilities, multimedia, games, and more—and benefit from hundreds of practical tips. *$29.95 (992 pages)*

The Painter 4 Wow! Book

Cher Threinen-Pendarvis

Fractal Design Painter has so many features even power users don't know all the tricks. Whatever your skill level, you'll scurry to the computer to try out the examples in *The Painter 4 Wow! Book*. This full-color volume uses hundreds of stunning, original illustrations from dozens of artists and designers depicting Painter's full range of styles and effects. Step-by-step descriptions clearly explain how each piece was created by well-known artists, designers, and multimedia producers. *$44.95 (264 pages w/ CD-ROM)*

Shocking the Web, Macintosh Edition

By Cathy Clarke, Lee Swearingen, and David K. Anderson

This is the authoritative, hands-on guide to creating movies for the Internet using Macromedia's Shockwave. Includes detailed case studies of "shocked" Web sites, step-by-step design examples, Lingo tips and tricks, and techniques for integrating Shockwave with JavaScript. The CD-ROM contains case studies, tutorials, template files, setup software, and more. **A Macromedia Press book.** *$44.95 (464 pages w/ CD-ROM)*

Start With a Scan

By Janet Ashford and John Odam

Start with a Scan shows designers and illustrators how to transform raw scanned images into high-quality finished illustrations. While the opening section covers the technical basics of scanning, the bulk of the book uses gorgeous four-color illustrations and clear, step-by-step instructions to show you how to take a scan of almost anything—a lackluster photo, a piece of clip art, a household object—and turn it into beautiful artwork using programs such as Photoshop, FreeHand, and Illustrator. *$34.95 (144 pages)*

Real World QuarkImmedia

David Blatner

Quark expert and bestselling author David Blatner shows you how to use Quark's exciting new multimedia design tool, which enables you to create interactive presentations while working in the familiar XPress environment. Covers such topics as: making the transition from print to multimedia; using animations, sounds, and QuickTime movies; and exporting projects to CD-ROMs and the Web. The accompanying CD includes sample Immedia projects and many of the essential ingredients you'll need to create your own multimedia projects. *$39.95 (448 pages w/ CD-ROM)*

Order Form

USA 800-283-9444 • 510-548-4393 • FAX 510-548-5991
CANADA 800-387-8028 • 416-447-1779 • FAX 800-456-0536 OR 416-443-0948

Qty	Title	Price	Total
	SUBTOTAL		
	ADD APPLICABLE SALES TAX*		
	SHIPPING		
	TOTAL		

Shipping is by UPS ground: $4 for first item, $1 each add'l.

*We are required to pay sales tax in all states with the exceptions of AK, DE, HI, MT, NH, NV, OK, OR, SC and WY. Please include appropriate sales tax if you live in any state not mentioned above.

Customer Information

NAME

COMPANY

STREET ADDRESS

CITY   STATE   ZIP

PHONE (   )   FAX (   )
[REQUIRED FOR CREDIT CARD ORDERS]

Payment Method

❑ CHECK ENCLOSED   ❑ VISA   ❑ MASTERCARD   ❑ AMEX

CREDIT CARD #   EXP. DATE

Tell Us What You Think

PLEASE TELL US WHAT YOU THOUGHT OF THIS BOOK: TITLE: _____

WHAT OTHER BOOKS WOULD YOU LIKE US TO PUBLISH?

MAC   **PEACHPIT PRESS** • 2414 Sixth Street • Berkeley, CA 94710